NEW DIMENSIONS IN PAY MANAGEMENT

Michael Armstrong graduated from the London School of Economics and is a Fellow of the Chartered Institute of Personnel and Development and a Fellow of the Institute of Management Consultants. He has had over 25 years' experience in personnel management, including 12 as a personnel director. He has also practised as a management consultant for 16 years and is now chief examiner, employee reward, for the CIPD. His previous publications for the CIPD include: (with Angela Baron) *The Job Evaluation Handbook* (1995) and *Performance Management: The new realities* (1998); *Employee Reward* (1999); and *Rewarding Teams* (2000).

Duncan Brown has an MA from Cambridge University and an MBA from the London Business School, and is a Fellow of the Chartered Institute of Personnel and Development, whose compensation forum he also chairs. A principal consultant in the London office of Towers Perrin, the international remuneration and human resource consultancy, he has over 15 years' experience of managing remuneration issues. His clients include major energy, manufacturing and technology companies, government departments and agencies, banks, insurance companies and large charities.

Other titles in the series:

Appraisal (2nd edition)
Clive Fletcher

Benchmarking for People Managers
John Bramham

The Competencies Handbook
Sarah Hollyforde and Steve Whiddett

Counselling in the Workplace
Jenny Summerfield and Lyn van Oudtshoorn

Development and Assessment Centres (3rd edition)
Charles Woodruffe

Employee Attitude and Opinion Surveys
Mike Walters

Empowering Team Learning
Michael Pearn

Flexible Working Practices
John Stredwick and Steve Ellis

From Absence to Attendance
Alastair Evans and Steve Palmer

HR Know-How in Mergers and Acquisitions
Cary L. Cooper and Sue Cartwright

I.T. Answers to H.R. Questions
Peter Kingsbury

The Job Evaluation Handbook
Michael Armstrong and Angela Baron

Learning Alliances
David Clutterbuck

Managing Redundancy
Alan Fowler

Performance Management
Michael Armstrong and Angela Baron

Project Management
Roland and Frances Bee

Recruitment and Selection
Gareth Roberts

Stress and Employer Liability
Cary L. Cooper and Sue Cartwright

360-Degree Feedback
Peter Ward

The Chartered Institute of Personnel and Development is the leading publisher of books and reports for personnel and training professionals, students, and for all those concerned with the effective management and development of people at work. For details of all our titles, please contact the Publishing Department:
tel. 020-8263 3387
fax 020-8263 3850
e-mail publish@cipd.co.uk
The catalogue of all CIPD titles can be viewed on the CIPD website:
www.cipd.co.uk/publications

NEW DIMENSIONS IN PAY MANAGEMENT

Michael Armstrong and Duncan Brown

Chartered Institute of Personnel and Development

First published in 2001

Design by Paperweight
Typeset by Action Publishing Technology, Gloucester
Printed in Great Britain by
the Cromwell Press, Trowbridge, Wiltshire

British Library Cataloguing in Publication Data
A catalogue record for this book is available from the
British Library

ISBN 0-85292-883-1

The views expressed in this book are the authors' own and
may not necessarily reflect those of the CIPD.

Chartered Institute of Personnel and Development, CIPD House,
Camp Road, London SW19 4UX
Tel: 020-8971 9000   Fax: 020-8263 3333
E-mail: cipd@cipd.co.uk
Website: www.cipd.co.uk
Incorporated by Royal Charter. Registered charity no. 1079797.

CONTENTS

Foreword   viii

PART I: **THE BACKGROUND**

1   CHANGING TRENDS IN REWARD SYSTEMS   3
    Focus on total reward – Strategic pay – Business-
    driven pay – Flexible pay systems – Integrated pay
    and HR processes – Lateral/continuous development
    focus – Pay-for-contribution – Market-driven –
    People-centred – Best fit – Devolution to the line –
    Broadbanded and job family structures – Conclusion

2   PAY STRUCTURES: FEATURES AND CHOICE   17
    Definition – Rationale for pay structures – Types of
    pay structures – Selecting a structure – *Individual
    recognition and reward at Littlewoods Retail* – Moving
    to a business and market-driven employment package
    at Standard Life Investments – A flexible approach at
    Thistle Hotels*

3   PAY STRUCTURES IN ACTION   35
    The IPD 1999/2000 research – Institute of
    Personnel and Development 1996 research –
    Research by Duncan Brown – Towers Perrin 1997
    Survey – American Compensation Association –
    Conclusions

˙Headings in italics = names of case studies

Part II: BROADBANDED PAY STRUCTURES

4   FEATURES OF BROADBANDED PAY
    STRUCTURES   55

Definition of broadbanding – Why broadbanding? –
Characteristics of broadbanding – Designing
broadbanded structures – *The BBC – BP Amoco
Exploration – Bristol Myers Squibb – Halifax plc
– The RNLI: Bringing pay and reward
arrangements into the twenty-first century*

5   MANAGING BROADBANDING   87

Using job evaluation – Allocating roles to bands –
Positioning roles within bands – Progressing pay
within bands – Achieving equity and consistency
– Controlling costs – *Yorkshire Building Society*

6   INTRODUCING BROADBANDED PAY
    STRUCTURES   115

The development process – Analysis – Objectives
– Project planning – Designing broadbanded
structures – Developing processes – Implementation –
*Normalising the move into broad bands at an
international oil company – Introducing a harmonised
pay and grading structure at the Ministry of Defence –
Pay restructuring in a merger situation – Developing an
integrated approach to job valuation, performance
management, employee development and reward at
Southern Focus Trust – Introducing broad bands in
Zurich Financial Services UK Life*

Part III: JOB FAMILY PAY STRUCTURES

7   FEATURES OF JOB FAMILY PAY STRUCTURES   167
Definitions – Features – Career mapping – Managing
job family structures – Operating issues – Readiness
for job families

8   JOB FAMILY PAY STRUCTURES IN PRACTICE   185
Developing job family structures – *Coventry
Building Society – IMS Health – Nationwide
Building Society – The Prince's Trust: Pay
harmonisation through broadbanded job families –
Business-based pay at the Royal Bank of Scotland –
Xerox (GB)*

PART IV: CREATING NEW PAY STRUCTURES

9   DEVELOPING AND INTRODUCING NEW
PAY STRUCTURES   217
A phased approach – Phase 1: diagnosis and
architecture design – Phase 2: detailed design –
Phase 3: preparation and implementation – Phase
4: ongoing monitoring and review – A quick
but intensive work approach – Summary

References and further reading   255

Index   257

FOREWORD

This book focuses on what is happening to pay systems and the directions in which basic pay structures and processes for managing base pay are going. It is based on extensive research in the UK and USA into what organisations are doing about pay, why they are adopting new practices and how effective these practices are. It contains many illustrations in the form of case studies, and we should like to express our gratitude to those who spent time in talking to us about what they were doing and agreeing to the publication of details of their practices. We should also like to thank Dr Malcolm Walder of Norwich City College, who carried out extensive field work and whose case studies have made an important contribution to this book.

The idea for this book first arose in mid-1999, when we discussed what was happening in the world of pay structures and in particular the phenomenon of broadbanding. Both of us had conducted research before (Brown and Armstrong 1999). We are both management consultants specialising in the development of pay structures and their associated reward processes; but we were aware that there was much more to learn about new developments and how they function. Questions that seemed to us to have been inadequately covered in the current pay literature included the following:

- How widespread is the move towards broad pay bands?
- Are the features of broad bands referred to in US sources, such as the use of a very few wide bands and the removal of job evaluation, very evident?
- What are the effects of implementing and operating broad bands?
- Are job family structures being adopted instead of or in conjunction with broad bands?

We therefore agreed with the (then) Institute of Personnel and Development (since July 2000 the Chartered Institute of Personnel and Development) that, under its auspices, we should conduct research based upon a questionnaire completed by 190 members of the IPD's compensation forum and visits to 27 organisations. This book also refers to the research carried out in Europe by Towers Perrin, and the experience of organisations and consultants in the USA and research carried out there by the American Compensation Association (now WorldatWork) and Hewitt Associates.

The book is divided into four parts:

Part 1 includes an overview of the new dimensions in reward management that our research and experience have identified, a description of the features of pay structures that are emerging in this context, a summary of the points to be considered when introducing a new or revised structure (this is expanded in Part 4), and a summary of the outcomes of the 1999/2000 IPD research, and various other research projects.

Part 2 describes the current features of broadbanded pay structures, how they are managed and how they can be introduced.

Part 3 describes in a similar manner job family structures.

Part 4 covers methods of developing, introducing and evaluating new pay structures.

A total of 17 case studies are included in the book.

Although our book concentrates on the design and management of pay structures that provide the basis for financial rewards, we do not underestimate the importance of non-financial rewards. Pay structures and systems can support initiatives to increase organisational effectiveness. They can deliver messages about what the organisation values. They can help to achieve culture change, and they are the means through which achievements in terms of results or higher levels of competence can be rewarded tangibly. If pay systems are wrongly conceived or badly managed they can do a lot of harm. But longer-term motivation and commitment is achieved by building on this sound foundation with processes that ensure that people are recognised for what they achieve, are provided with a reasonable amount of autonomy, are given the opportunity to develop their careers, and are helped to increase their skills, competencies and employability.

PART I

THE BACKGROUND

1 CHANGING TRENDS IN REWARD SYSTEMS

The pressure on organisations to add value, achieve sustained competitive advantage, and respond and adapt quickly and flexibly to new challenges and opportunities are relentless. The responses to these pressures have taken many forms, including new types of organisations – 'lean', de-layered, flexible, process- or project-based – increasing reliance on information technology, and an emphasis on continuous improvement in terms of performance, quality and customer service. The quality of the human or intellectual capital possessed by organisations is seen generally as the key factor in differentiating them from their rivals and achieving superior results. The focus is on the development of business strategies to achieve longer-term goals, and the part played by human resource strategies in general, and reward strategies in particular, in supporting their achievement is now well recognised.

As a result, significant changes in the ways in which pay systems are developed and managed are taking place, as summarised in Table 1 (overleaf). We comment in turn on the most significant of these trends in this chapter, concluding with developments in pay structures.

Focus on total reward

The total reward concept, as illustrated in Figure 1 (overleaf), focuses on the interlinked and cumulative impact of various forms of reward – base pay, variable pay, benefits and non-financial rewards. It hypothesises that the aim of reward strategy should be to develop an integrated and mutually

Table 1
CHANGING TRENDS IN REWARD SYSTEMS

Old	New
• Focus on financial reward	• Focus on total reward
• Reactive pay	• Strategic pay
• Administered pay	• Business-driven pay
• Bureaucratic pay systems	• Flexible pay systems
• Stand-alone pay systems	• Integrated pay and HR processes
• Hierarchical structures	• Lateral/continuous development focus
• Pay-for-performance	• Pay-for-contribution
• Priority given to internal equity	• Market-driven
• Job-centred	• People-centred
• Imposed 'best practice'	• Contingency/cultural fit
• HR control	• Devolution to the line
• Pay spines/multigraded structures	• Broadbanded/job family structures

Figure 1
THE COMPONENTS OF TOTAL REWARD

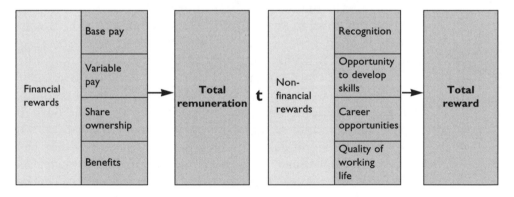

supporting range of processes which in conjunction with one another will make a much more powerful and longer-lasting impact on individual, team and organisational effectiveness.

The significance of pay as a means of attracting, retaining and providing tangible rewards to people is not underestimated. It is important to get it right – much harm can be done if it is wrong. But as a means of generating long-term commitment and motivation, pay has to be regarded as only part of a whole. It is the non-financial rewards that will ultimately make the difference. These include recognition, scope to achieve and exercise responsibility, opportunities for growth and development, the intrinsic motivation provided by the work itself, and the quality of working life provided by the organisation. The new dimensions in pay structures – broad-banding and job families – are as much, if not more, concerned with providing the framework for total rewards as for delivering pay.

Strategic pay

In the past, pay practices generally reacted to business and market pressures to produce short-term panaceas. In 1990 Ed Lawler exposed the limitations of this approach when he wrote:

> The starting-point for any reward system design process needs to be the strategic agenda of the organisation. Thus the first step in designing the reward system for an organisation is to focus on the individual and organisational behaviours that are needed in order for the organisation to be successful.

In 1995 Lawler enlarged this statement to cover all organisational systems when he wrote:

> The business strategy, in particular, serves as a crucial guide in designing organisational systems because it specifies what the company wants to accomplish, how it wants to behave, and the kinds of performance and performance levels it must demonstrate to be effective.

Lawler's message was reinforced by Schuster and Zingheim (1993) who pointed out that: 'Reward strategies provide a road-map from where the organisation is presently to where it wants to be in the future.'

Reward strategy definition

Reward strategy is a business-focused statement of the intentions of the organisation concerning the development of future reward processes and practices, which are aligned to the business and human resource strategies of the organisation, its culture and the environment in which it operates.

Rationale for a strategic approach to reward

A strategic approach to reward is required in order to:

- ❏ clarify what the organisation values and is prepared to pay for, and what it wants to get in return
- ❏ provide a sense of purpose which ensures that a coherent approach is taken to the development of reward policies and practices thus avoiding mixed messages and uncoordinated activities
- ❏ provide a common framework for the design of reward processes
- ❏ clarify accountabilities for the strategy and its operation
- ❏ ensure that results and behaviour are consistent with key organisational goals and values and that the achievement of goals and behavioural standards are rewarded appropriately.

Strategic reward areas

Reward strategies emerge in line with the development of business strategies. As Richter (1998) points out:

> Compensation, like any strategic HR function aimed at shaping a culture, can travel neither ahead of the business nor very far behind it. It has to be sufficiently conversant with the vision of the business to continuously produce solutions and/or improvements as the business evolves . . . compensation must constantly interact with the leadership, rather than exist as a downstream activity.

As James Bray, Manager GB Total Pay at Xerox, comments: 'We focus on what the business requirement is. Formerly, pay was a niche specialisation in Xerox; now it is part of the business operation.'

Many of the organisations included in the (former) Institute of Personnel and Development's 1999/2000 survey adopted a strategic approach to reward which was integral to the business strategy. (The IPD became the CIPD, or Chartered Institute of Personnel and Development, in July 2000.) The strategies were typically concerned with meeting business needs arising from the pressure to increase shareholder value, achieving competitive advantage through innovation, quality or cost leadership, improving performance, or responding to the new circumstances arising from a merger or acquisition. Business strategies may set out the need to change direction (eg the demutualisation of the Halifax Building Society), to respond to global competition through diversification or the development of new products or services (eg Xerox) or to respond to fundamental changes affecting the business such as market consolidation and restructuring, the use of new technology, and shifts in consumer demands (eg Yorkshire Building Society).

Strategies may be developed to ensure that a new vision for the services provided by the organisation and its values is realised (the Children's Society) or as part of an organisational transformation programme (Yorkshire Water). The business strategy may indicate that a fundamental shift in the corporate culture must be achieved (IBM), or that significant changes in the skills base are required (BT).

These and other business imperatives are associated with a variety of reward strategy innovations. Typically, these can consist of one or more of the following:

❏ *changing the pay structure* – eg AXA Insurance, IMS Health, the Prince's Trust, the Royal Bank of Scotland
❏ *developing new contingent pay schemes* – eg Bass Brewers, the Children's Society, Nuclear Electric, Pfizer Central Research
❏ *developing new performance management processes* – eg Texas Utilities, Yorkshire Water
❏ *introducing flexible benefits* – eg PricewaterhouseCoopers
❏ *increasing flexibility/reducing bureaucracy* – eg IBM
❏ *devolving more responsibility for pay to line managers* – eg IBM.

The following are some examples of strategic approaches to reward.

At *Halifax plc* the process of demutualisation meant that its business operation, structure and culture had to be transformed. A strategic reward review played an important part in this process. The aims of the review were to:

❏ make the reward strategy much more business-focused, supporting the delivery of business objectives

❑ reinforce a performance culture throughout the organisation (a particular requirement of the chief executive, James Crosby) – the fundamental question was: 'How can pay support a performance culture?'

❑ ensure that the pay system supported a more flexible approach to running the business.

At *IBM* the compensation strategy was evolved to ensure that IBM could survive and thrive in a networked world very different from the context in which it had come to near failure. As Andrew Ritcher, Director Global Employee Compensation, explained in 1998, compensation's response to the demands for change was threefold:

1 *Marketplace rules* – The focus was shifted from internal comparisons to external comparisons, different pay actions being taken for different job families.

2 *Fewer jobs evaluated differently in broad bands* – Job titles were reduced from more than 5,000 to fewer than 1,200. The old point-factor plan was replaced by a classification approach with three factors (skills, leadership requirement and job scope) and the 24 grades were reduced to 10 broad bands. Mid-point management techniques and compa-ratios are no longer used.

3 *Letting managers manage* – Managers get a budget, some coaching and a tool they can use in many different ways. This is a spreadsheet which lets managers rank employees on a number of factors (skills and results) before deciding how to carve up a budget. Which factors managers use is up to them. If they do not want to use ratings, they can simply input salary increases directly with an explanation comment of one or more sentences that records their rationale.

At *Littlewoods Retail* the restructuring of Littlewoods' retail businesses into a single organisation afforded the opportunity to develop a new and unified pay and benefits package for senior management (see case study in Chapter 2).

At the *Royal Bank of Scotland* a strategy of improved business focus in response to diverse customer demands is supported by business-driven changes to reward practices which are now aligned with the differing needs and characteristics of some 40 distinct business units (see case study in Chapter 8).

At *Nortel and Bay Networks* a major change in Nortel's business strategy and the resulting acquisition of Bay Networks in late 1998 has led to the development of a new reward strategy and substantial changes to the pay management practices in the company (see case study in Chapter 6).

At *IMS Health* a review of the pay structure was initiated, as explained by Angela McCorriston, Director of Human Resources, in order to 'evolve a system which could be flexible enough to cope with the ever-changing business environment we were in' (see case study in Chapter 8).

At *Xerox (GB)* aggressive growth targets and the urge to develop and market new products has resulted in significant changes to the skills required. The reward strategy as explained in the case study outlined in Chapter 8 has responded to these demands.

Business-driven pay

The new dimensions in pay structures we describe in the rest of this book have generally resulted from the adoption of a more strategic approach to reward management. In each of these cases and many others covered by the IPD research HR generalists and reward specialists have acted as business partners. Reward is no longer an isolated function, it is part of the strategic business process. This contrasts with the traditional 'salary administration' approach in which pay specialists lived an isolated life as technical designers, running bureaucratic systems and dealing on a day-to-day or annual pay review basis with immediate job grading or pay level issues. Many of the case studies contained in this book demonstrate the heavy involvement of line managers in the process of introducing broadbanding and/or job family structures, as well as extensive communication with employees. They have in the main been initiatives designed to address 'real' and 'live' business issues.

Flexible pay systems

Salary administration was traditionally associated with bureaucracy in the shape of elaborate, paper-intensive and time-consuming job evaluation schemes and forms and ratings-dominated performance appraisal systems. Multi-graded pay structures and pay spines with fixed service-related increments were managed rigidly. They were originally developed in large hierarchical and bureaucratic organisations, mainly as control tools. Merit payments were governed by quotas and the forced distribution of ratings. No recognition was given to the fact that organisations were moving to faster and more flexible methods of operation, that different situations within organisations required different solutions and that people were increasingly carrying out more flexible roles rather than conforming to lists of duties contained in prescriptive job descriptions.

These administrative and control-oriented approaches persist in many organisations, but increasingly the tendency is to 'free-up' reward structures and processes. Hence the development of broadbanding and job families and the relegation of job evaluation in many businesses to a support role rather than one which dominates grading and therefore pay decisions. What is also now being recognised is that pay practices may vary within organisations. For example, Coventry Building Society (case study in Chapter 8) has team pay for some staff whereas others participate in a corporate bonus scheme based on growth and cost control. Line managers may be given more scope to vary pay practices to suit their circumstances or inclinations as at IBM, or may be allowed to vary their approach to pay management as long as they adhere to certain general principles, as in a financial services company we visited.

Integrated pay and HR processes

Pay systems and supporting processes such as job evaluation and performance appraisal used to stand alone apart from other HR processes. They existed in their own right and had little or no contact with other HR processes. Sandra O'Neal of Towers Perrin forecast in 1994 that:

In the 21st century, pay and reward systems will need to support the development of intellectual capital, customer relationships, universal use of information technology, strategic alliance, continuous learning, and employee populations that come and go.

This is now happening:

Broadbanded and job family structures are no longer treated simply as vehicles for delivering pay and are often seen as being complementary to competence and career development policies. The main aim is to provide information on development opportunities and career paths that, as part of a performance management process, can contribute to personal development planning.

(Armstrong 2000)

In fact, organisations are often focusing initially on the business need for such policies and the processes required. Only then do they consider how reward systems can support them, frequently basing pay structures on competence frameworks and profiles.

At *Coventry Building Society*, for example, a holistic approach was adopted to the development of a new reward system so that from whatever angle staff looked at the elements of performance, development and reward, they were consistent. The programme was underpinned by a competency framework related to recruitment, training and career development. This was fed into the reward system. A new vocabulary was introduced, centred on the concept of a performance, development and reward system.

At *Southern Focus Trust* a broadbanded structure is being introduced to replace a traditional pay spine, but equal emphasis is placed on the new structure as a framework within which performance management, continuous development and career planning can take place. It is the developmental aspects of performance management rather than links to pay decisions which are emphasised in such organisations as the Victoria and Albert Museum, Great Ormond Street NHS Trust, New Forest District Council and Halifax plc.

So broadbanded and job family structures, as research has found, are generally concerned with much more than just pay.

Lateral/continuous development focus

In what was once the typical multigraded pay structure the emphasis was on the hierarchy: the only way ahead was upwards, through promotion or re-grading. The pressure on upgrading contributed to grade drift and a reduction in the credibility of job evaluation which was often manipulated to provide the justification for a higher grade even if the motivation was to recognise high individual performance, or pay appropriate market rates in areas of high demand.

In de-layered, 'lean' organisations, the opportunities for promotion have been reduced but the scope for lateral development has expanded. Roles are more flexible and people not only grow within their roles but also grow their roles. Linda Holbeche (1998) suggested that to cater for the impact of flatter structures on careers, organisations could introduce career bands in which opportunities for lateral growth would be specified. This proposal fits the concept of broad-based pay structures and the notion of career development pay as people move laterally through the band. Horizontal progression is often based on increases in competence and contribution and does not depend on grabbing more job evaluation points to achieve an upgrading.

In the brief to employees prepared by Yorkshire Water Services, one of the key reasons given for moving to a structure of six broad bands was 'to remove the focus on hierarchical progression and provide greater potential for development [and] encourage movement across roles and teams'.

Pay-for-contribution

As Brown and Armstrong commented in 1999: 'The goals of performance-related pay schemes were often not clear, agreed or accepted (nor even performance-related in some cases), and even more critically, the schemes did not operate in practice as intended.'

Another objection to performance-related pay was that it was solely concerned with outputs. The belief that people should be rewarded for their skill or competence (their inputs) led to the interest in competence-related pay.

More recently, however, it has been recognised that people

should be rewarded for both their outputs (results) and their inputs (competence) – in other words, not only for what they do but how they do it. This approach is termed contribution-related pay. The reasoning behind this move was explained by a compensation and benefits manager in the finance sector as follows:

> Performance in our setting is much more complex than a decision relating to five SMART objectives. Often the most measurable is not the most meaningful ... Contribution talks to a broader series of outcomes, is easier to relate to corporate values, encompasses enthusiasm, future capability and teamwork ... It relates to discretionary effort, rather than the sort of narrow-minded, individual, short-term results focus which stifles innovation in many organisations.

At *Xerox GB*, as James Bray noted: 'There is a default for people who are performing steadily in their jobs, but we also want to recognise people who are making an excellent contribution in terms of their performance *and* improvements in skills and competencies; both these are key metrics.'

At *Coutts & Co*, both output and competence are taken into account when reviewing pay. The requirement was to find a balance between rewarding for results and rewarding for behaviour. Competence is used as the major component in determining base salary and outputs govern cash bonuses, although they contribute to base pay decisions.

The new dimensions in pay structures that we are describing aim generally to provide greater scope to reward and develop contribution.

Market-driven

At one time, organisations tended to give more attention to considerations of internal equity than those of external competitiveness. But now businesses such as BT, IBM and Xerox GB are recognising that they have to compete for scarce skills in the labour market, which means that their pay levels have to be market-driven. As an HR manager in a finance sector business told us, 'Internal equity is nice to have – but it is second.' Almost without exception, the companies covered by the IPD research had adopted market-driven pay policies, often associated with a broadbanded or job family structure. Correspondingly, the relative emphasis on job evaluation and detailed, common standards of internal job measurement and grading have in most cases been reduced, and in many cases removed altogether.

People-centred

In 1986 Ed Lawler wrote that job evaluation tends to de-personalise people by equating them with a set of duties rather than concentrating on what people are and what they can do. He advocated a people-based rather than a job-based approach, and this has become an important aspect of the philosophy underpinning broadbanded and job family structures – that it is people not jobs that add value, and that people should be rewarded for their contribution, rather than because they happen to have been given certain things to do. The focus is on roles – the part people play – rather than on jobs – the tasks they are given as prescribed in a job description. Role defini-tions – defining accountabilities in terms of outcomes and competence requirements – are becoming the basis for perfor-mance management and reward, rather than job descriptions which concentrate narrowly on job content. This is illustrated in many of our case study write-ups.

Best fit

Reward management was governed for many years by the concept of 'best practice' – that there are universal ways of doing the 'right' thing. Other organisations had broadbanded pay structures, so your organisation needed to have them. What is now appreciated is that 'best fit' is more important. Reward strategies and practices should be contingent on the circumstances of the organisation. They should fit the needs of the business and its culture as it is now or as the organisation wants it to become. Unfortunately, the new dimensions in pay structures we describe have been interpreted in some quarters as the new best practice, which in some organisations will not be the case simply because they will not fit the circumstances. Failure of innovations such as broadbanding or performance-related pay can often be attributed to misunderstandings about the extent to which they were appropriate to the organisation, however well they worked elsewhere. This does not mean that 'good practice' should be ignored nor that lessons cannot be learned from the experiences of other organisations. But the good practice and the lessons need to be adapted to the particular requirements of the business. For example, in a case study in Chapter 6 the oil company in question did not install the radical broadbanding of some of its competitors but utilised a more structured and intermediate approach which better suited its requirements.

Devolution to the line

The HR function has traditionally controlled the implementation of pay policies and practice. Line managers have tended to do what they are told. Some managers have been known to shelter behind HR decisions and are glad to blame them for pay problems. Others lack the skills or inclination to spend time managing pay in their own departments. The tendency now is to devolve more responsibility for pay decisions to line managers as part of a broader policy of empowerment and decentralisation of decision-making and responsibility within the organisation.

Devolution of pay decisions is often associated with broadbanded pay structures because the increased flexibility of such structures means that managers who are on the spot are best equipped with the information to manage pay and rewards.

Broadbanded and job family structures

Most of the factors mentioned above have contributed to the shift away from hierarchical multigraded structures and pay spines. The most important of these have been the need to:

❑ achieve greater flexibility in pay management

❑ reduce the bureaucracy associated with multigraded structures and job evaluation

❑ reward lateral development and continuous improvement

❑ clarify career paths

❏ respond to the changing nature of work

❏ provide for more management involvement in pay.

These are the considerations which have led many organisations to introduce broadbanded and job family structures, or a combination of the two, which have now become the norm rather than the exception as the primary method of organising pay management in UK organisations.

Conclusion

The reward practices described in the rest of this book should be designed to underpin the business strategy. Why this should be done and how it should be done was explained to us admirably by Karen Moir, HR director at Yorkshire Water, as follows:

❏ Rewards are symbolic, radical and reinforcing.

❏ They are *disablers* if they reward behaviour that you don't want.

❏ They are *enablers* if they reinforce the behaviour that you do want.

❏ It is necessary to define what you want – people performance requirements.

❏ It is necessary to know how you are going to measure performance.

❏ Put in checks and balances (stabilisers) to help if it goes wrong.

❏ Implement and improve *through* implementation – gradually take the stabilisers off.

2 PAY STRUCTURES: FEATURES AND CHOICE

Definition

Pay structures provide a framework for managing base pay and often other aspects of reward. The main types, as described later in this chapter, are:

- traditional graded structures
- broadbanded structures
- job families
- mixed model (broadbanded and job family)
- pay spines
- individual job structures.

Some organisations do not have a formal structure and instead use 'spot rates' – specific rates for individual jobs or people without any defined scope for pay progression to or beyond the rate. For example, Thistle Hotels adopts a market-driven spot rate approach (see the case study at the end of this chapter). The majority of organisations in the UK with fewer than 100 employees have no formal pay structure but simply pay individuals what they think they are worth. However, most organisations with more employees do use formal pay structures which:

- establish pay ranges or scales for jobs grouped into grades, bands or job families, generally by reference to market data and often guided by the results of job evaluation
- provide scope for pay progression in accordance with performance, skill, competence, contribution or service through these pay ranges or scales

❏ specify the basis upon which jobs and/or individuals can move between levels, grades or bands in the structure.

There may be a single, integrated pay structure covering the whole organisation or, in large organisations, there may different structures at different levels, with one structure for managerial, professional, technical, sales and administrative staff, and another for manual workers. Executive directors are often also treated separately.

Organisations sometimes have separate parallel structures for different occupations. For example, there may be 'technical ladders' for scientists or research and development engineers, which recognise that progression can sometimes depend more on professional competence than the assumption of managerial responsibility for people and other resources. This principle may be extended to setting up separate structures for different job families, as described later, which may create distinct 'market group' structures to cater for categories of employees whose levels of pay are heavily influenced by market pressures and who may therefore have to be treated differently from other groups of people.

Parallel and market group structures may appear to be inconsistent with the principle of internal equity in pay management, but, as perceived by companies which adopt this policy, it is an inevitable requirement if high-quality staff are to be recruited and retained in a competitive labour market.

Rationale for pay structures

Pay structures are needed to provide a logically designed framework within which equitable, fair, consistent and transparent pay policies can be implemented. They enable the organisation to determine levels of pay for jobs and people and are the basis upon which the effective management of relativities and of the processes of monitoring and controlling the implementation of pay practices can take place. The pay structure is also a medium through which the organisation can communicate the pay opportunities available to employees. Other reasons that we were given for the use of pay and grade structures by the organisations in the research we have conducted included:

- ❏ to organise pay management
- ❏ to simplify the determination of pay levels, which would take far longer and be more contentious if every individual's pay level was set separately
- ❏ to control the growth in pay costs, ensuring that range maxima are not exceeded
- ❏ to link pay and other rewards to the organisation's structure and career paths
- ❏ to provide a rational and objective basis for the allocation of benefits such as company cars.

Types of pay structures

Graded pay structures

Although broadbanding has come to the fore, graded pay structures remain the most typical types in the private sector. These consist of a sequence of job grades into which jobs of broadly equivalent value are slotted, usually on the basis of job evaluation scores. A pay range is attached to each grade. The maximum of each range is typically set at a rate between 20 per cent and 50 per cent above the minimum. For example, a '40 per cent' range for a grade with a minimum of £20,000 would span from £20,000 to £28,000. Pay ranges are also described as a percentage of the mid-point; for example, the range could be expressed as 80 per cent to 120 per cent where the mid-point is £25,000 and the minimum and maximum are £20,000 and £30,000 respectively. The mid-point may be regarded as the rate for a fully competent individual and aligned to market rates in accordance with company policies on the relationship between its pay levels and market rates for similar jobs (this is sometimes called the 'market stance'). The pay range provides scope for pay progression.

There may be 10 or more grades in a structure, generally depending on the size and degree of hierarchy in the structure of the organisation. Grades may be defined by job evaluation in points terms, by grade definitions or simply by the jobs that have been slotted into the grades. Differentials between pay ranges are typically around 20 per cent and there is usually an overlap between ranges, often of up to about 50 per cent. Ranges are often designed to be wider at more senior levels, on the assumption that there is more scope to deliver different levels of performance at these levels and such differences should be rewarded accordingly. What are sometimes called 'mid-point management' techniques are often used to analyse and control pay progression by comparing actual pay with the mid-point. 'Compa-ratios' measure the relationship between actual and policy rates of pay as a percentage: if the two coincide, the compa-ratio is 100 per cent.

Broadbanded pay structures

Increasingly, however, *broadbanded* structures are replacing traditional graded structures. In such structures, the number of grades is compressed into a relatively small number of much wider 'bands' in which pay is managed more flexibly than in a conventional graded structure and increased attention is paid to market relativities. The band widths may be as much as 100 per cent, although more typically they are between 50 per cent and 80 per cent. There may be only five or six bands in the structure. The band boundaries are often defined by job evaluation. Roles may be placed in the bands purely by reference to market rates or, more commonly, by a combination of job evaluation and market rate analysis. Bands can be described in general terms by reference to the types of roles allocated to them. Reference may be made to generic roles or clusters of roles, and these can be used as benchmarks against which other roles are matched when decisions have to be made on the band into which they should be placed.

Although 'zones' may be defined in a band to indicate normal progression patterns, there is much more scope in a broadbanded structure for additional 'career development pay' by moving horizontally through the band (and indeed beyond the notional band limits), on the basis of increases in the scope of activities, contribution and competence. Pay progression and career development are not simply a matter of getting promotion to a higher grade.

The aims of broadbanded pay structures are commonly:

❑ to achieve more flexibility in pay management

- ❏ to fit the pay structure to a de-layered organisation
- ❏ to reflect an emphasis on horizontal processes in such organisations
- ❏ to create a strong relationship between pay and contribution and de-emphasise the status-based nature of rewards
- ❏ importantly, to provide a framework within which people can be rewarded for lateral development.

Broadbanded structures are more likely to be introduced in flexible organisations which do not operate with extended hierarchies and believe wholeheartedly in continuous development. Such organisations have often been through a restructuring exercise which looks at the fundamental processes of the business from a cross-functional perspective and aims to break away from the constraints of conventional organisational boundaries and from traditional hierarchical, functional and job divisions of labour.

Job family structures

Job family structures cater for separate groups or *families* of jobs. Families consist of roles in a function such as research, finance or HR which are related through the activities carried out and the basic skills used, but are differentiated by the level of responsibility, skill or competence required. Each job family has its own structure of levels which may be defined in terms of accountability, skill or competence. Levels may have their own finite pay range, as in a conventional graded pay structure. The pay levels in different job families may vary to reflect market rate pressures.

Job family structures are used because it is felt that some occupations need distinct treatment from both the reward and the career development points of view. One of their perceived advantages is that career progression on the basis of increases in skill or competence can be planned, and individuals can be made aware of the development opportunities available to them in their own and other job families. They are popular in organisations which have a high proportion of professional and knowledge workers.

They may also be set up for 'market groups' where the occupations concerned are subject to particular market pressures.

The market rates for such jobs are higher than those for other occupations which would be placed in the same grade on the basis of internal relativities alone. However, the creation of market groups means that there is increased risk of gender discrimination and job families can also create barriers to lateral development across the organisation.

The mixed-model broadbanded/job family structure

It is possible in a common broadbanded structure to cater for job families within bands. It is equally possible to use broad bands in a job family structure. Essentially, this allows for some flexibility to reward and progress the pay of individuals separately in the different families but still maintain a common structure of bands and the ability to 'read across' throughout the organisation. This maintains an element of consistency and equity, and enables lateral development across the organisation to take place. How it can be effected is discussed in Parts 2 and 3 of this book.

Pay spines

Pay spines consist of a series of incremental points extending from the lowest- to the highest-paid jobs covered by the structure. A pay spine increment may be standardised at, say, 3 per cent from the top to the bottom of the spine, or the increments may be wider at higher levels. Progression up the spine is based on service in the post, usually at one increment per year, but if performance-related pay is introduced, individuals can be given accelerated increments. Jobs may be placed at fixed points on the spine, or ranges for different job grades may be superimposed on it.

Pay spines are found in the public sector or in agencies and charities which have adopted a public-sector approach to reward management. There has recently been a trend in some of these organisations to replace pay spines with a broadbanded or job family structure.

Individual job structures

Individual job structures simply define a separate pay range for each job. The rates for jobs and the relativities between them are often governed by market rates – job structures can often be described as 'market-driven'. For example, Littlewoods Retail (see the case study at the end of this chapter) rejected broadbanding to adopt this freer approach.

Relativities between jobs can be determined by point-factor job evaluation, which may in effect convert points to pounds by the application of a formula, as was the case at the Peabody Trust before its new job family structure was introduced in 2000. A broadbanded or job family structure, such as the 'mixed model' structure introduced to replace the old arrangements at Peabody Trust and at Lloyds TSB, may incorporate 'zones' which are in effect individual job ranges in a band.

Selecting a structure

Understanding the organisation

Before selecting any new type of pay structure or modifying an existing structure, you must have a clear understanding of the organisation, its people and the current pay arrangements. This can be achieved by considering the following questions.

1 What are the strengths and weaknesses of the current pay arrangements in terms of reward policies, the pay structure, methods of rewarding staff for performance, competence, skill or contribution, performance management processes, and employee benefit packages?

2 In the light of the answer to Question 1, why is it believed that a new or revised structure is necessary?

3 In general, how would a new or revised structure meet the needs of the business as defined in the business strategy?

4 In particular, what should be the aims of a new or revised structure?

5 What are the characteristics of the organisation which should be taken into account in order to ensure 'good fit'? These characteristics could include the type of business, its culture, the organisation structure, and the type of people employed.

6 How might any pay structure developments support proposed organisational or cultural change and reinforce other HR policies and practices?

7   How ready is the organisation to introduce a new or changed structure?

8   What issues will have to be addressed in the process of developing and introducing a new structure?

The information that is required to afford answers to these questions can be obtained by a diagnostic review, as described in Chapter 9.

Making the choice

Every organisation will have different answers to the above questions. As a result, there is no such thing as a model structure or 'best practice' in broadbanding or job families. As our research has established, there is a wide diversity of approaches; every organisation adopts its own type of pay structure to suit its circumstances. While the general trend in large organisations is towards flatter, broader and more flexible structures, we have worked with a number of fast-growing technology companies which have recently introduced more grades in their pay structures as part of the professionalism of management in the organisation.

Generally, however, companies and institutions with formal, hierarchical organisation structures have tended to prefer conventional graded structures which permit orderly administration and make for ease in managing internal relativities. Organisations that want to achieve more flexibility but within a defined framework may opt for a broadbanded or job family structure or a mixed model. More flexibility is possible if greater freedom is given to line managers to make pay decisions in different parts of the organisation. Even more flexibility can be achieved if an individual job grade or spot rate system is used. The disadvantage of the latter two approaches is that internal equity considerations may be neglected and the danger of paying unequally for work of equal value is increased. They may also be more complex and difficult to administer.

A comparison of the features and advantages and disadvantages of the most typical structures is summarised in Table 2.

More details of the main alternatives – broadbanding and job family structures – are given in Chapters 4 and 7 respectively. These should be studied before an initial choice is

Table 2
COMPARISON OF PAY STRUCTURES

	Traditional graded	Broadbanded	Job family	Mixed model	Pay spine
Features	• A sequence of job grades – 12 or more • Narrow pay ranges – eg 20% to 40% • Progression usually linked to performance	• A series of, often, five or six broad bands • Wide pay bands – typically between 50% and 80% • Progression linked to contribution and competence	• Separate pay structures for job families containing similar jobs • Progression linked to competence and/or contribution	• Either job families inserted into a broadbanded structure OR • Broad bands inserted into a job family structure • Progression linked to competences and/or contribution	• A series of incremental pay points covering all jobs • Grades may be superimposed • Progression linked to service
Advantages	• Clearly indicates pay relativities • Facilitates control • Easy to understand	• More flexible • Rewards lateral development and growth in competences • Fits new-style organisations	• Clarifies career paths • Facilitates pay differentiation between market groups	• Can combine the merits of broadbanded and job family structures	• Easy to manage • Pay progression not based on managerial judgement
Disadvantages	• Creates hierarchical rigidity • Is prone to grade drift • Is inappropriate in a de-layered organisation	• Creates unrealistic expectations of scope for pay rises • Seems to restrict scope for promotion • Difficult to understand	• May inhibit lateral career development • May be difficult to maintain internal equity between job families	• Can incorporate the disadvantages of both broadbanded and family structures • Can be complex to operate and understand	• No scope for differentiating rewards according to performance • May be costly as staff drift up the spine
When appropriate	• In a large bureaucratic organisation with well-defined hierarchies • When close and rigid control is required • When some, but not too much, scope for pay progression related to performance is wanted	• In de-layered, process-based flexible organisations • Where more flexibility in pay determination is wanted • Where the focus is on continuous improvement and lateral development	• Where there are distinct groups of jobs in families • When it is believed that career paths need to be defined more clearly in terms of competence requirements • When there are distinct market groups who need to be rewarded differentially	• When the conditions for either broadbanding and/or job families are favourable, and it is felt that the advantages outweigh the disadvantages	• In a public-sector or voluntary organisation where this is the traditional approach • Where it is believed to be impossible to measure differential levels of performance fairly and consistently

made. A more comprehensive process of analysis and diagnosis and the preliminary design work as described in Chapters 6 and 7 may lead to a decision to adopt a job family rather than a broadbanded structure or vice versa. What often transpires is that the eventual structure is a mixed model, incorporating aspects of job family, broadbanding and, sometimes, traditional pay structures. This is all part of the process of tailored design that is currently occurring in UK organisations. It is always possible that the development process will indicate that the present system should not be changed or should be only subjected to minor modifications – for example, reducing the number of grades from, say, 14 to 10 to produce a broader-graded structure.

Case studies

The following three case studies illustrate how organisations can adopt a less conventional, freer approach because it suits their operation. They can be contrasted with the case studies at the ends of Chapters 4, 5, 6 and 8 which describe how a number of different organisations went along the broadbanding or job family route (or a combination of the two) because they wanted *some* structure.

Case study

INDIVIDUAL RECOGNITION AND REWARD AT LITTLEWOODS RETAIL

Background

A restructuring of Littlewoods retail businesses, and their integration into a single organisation – Littlewoods Retail – afforded the opportunity to develop a new and unified pay and benefits package for senior management. The business employs approximately 27,000 people and has a turnover of £2,200 million. Approved by the executive remuneration committee, this new package is, according to Group HR director Juris Grinsbergs, a critical component of its 'customer-focused people vision and business strategy', with an emphasis on individual contribution and flexibility. Interestingly, the reforms involved consideration, but ultimately rejection, of broadbanding.

Past arrangements

Until May 1999, Littlewoods senior managers were paid within a hierarchical grading structure, supported by a traditional job evaluation system, with five pay grades, and corresponding salary ranges and benefits allocations. Managers received an annual cost-of-living-related pay increase. According to Rod Rees, director of Remuneration and Benefits, the 'restrictive and inflexible' pay zones 'encouraged people to focus almost entirely on the package of benefits available on promotion, rather than the contribution they could make to Littlewoods'. The Group chief executive explained the new approach in terms of encouraging employees to 'use personal development rather than status as the yardstick by which to measure success'.

Choice of new pay system

Encouraged by the flatter structure resulting from the reorganisation, the company initially looked at a system of broadbanding in order to reduce the hierarchical and inflexible nature of the five zones. But this was felt not to place enough emphasis on the prime objectives of reform: emphasising individual contribution and market worth. As Rees explains, 'We didn't feel broadbanding would take us down the road we wanted' because it would still involve grouping roles for pay management purposes, even within wider pay ranges. More fundamental reform was required.

Reflecting a looser and flatter organisation structure, with more scope for each manager to develop and grow his or her own role, the five pay zones have been replaced by individual salaries for senior management roles. These are based on a combination of market rates, background, skills and competencies, and contribution to the company.

The process for establishing indicative market salaries was extended down from the top 60 executives to cover all senior managers, using a range of market data sources. According to Rees, this now enables Littlewoods to 'better attract and retain' managers, while placing 'more emphasis on external value and less on internal relativities'. Individual pay levels typically fall within a range of +15 per cent around the indicated point – the indicative market salary – but there are no fixed job rates or ceilings as under the old structure.

In the past, directors had felt they were restricted in rewarding their most talented managers, and that promotion was the only means to recognise them effectively. As the communications materials to managers emphasise, 'Benchmarks primarily will act as a guide and not as a "rate for the job".' Now directors set the appropriate salaries, using the data supplied by HR, and related to the wide range of relevant factors. These include:

❑ the scope and influence of the job
❑ the individuals' skills and experience
❑ the individuals' personal development and acquisition of new skills and competence
❑ their overall contribution to the company's success.

Function directors are the key people who determine the value of the contribution which individual managers make, with an appraisal system that assesses both quantitative and qualitative individual goals.

Finally, the company also introduced in May 1999 a 'Lifestyles' flexible benefits programme, to further reinforce the move away from status to contribution-based reward. Managers can now select or trade their level of car, life assurance, medical insurance, PHI and holidays, buying additional benefits or taking a lower entitlement with a cash payment.

Learning points

The move to more flexible, individual market and contribution-driven rewards has, according to Rod Rees, been a complete change of management approach, not just a pay redesign exercise. Simply broadbanding existing grades, he feels, would have eased some immediate problems but not achieved the fundamental change in pay philosophy required. The new process, he explains, is not 'HR running a bureaucratic salary structure which dictates what people will earn. Rather, senior directors have bought into the process, taken ownership of it and are committed to the salaries they are paying their people ... If someone is making a significant contribution over and above satisfactory performance, then directors can make the case for a special adjustment at any time in the year.'

While it is too early yet to fully assess the success of these changes, Littlewoods is already looking at how to extend these principles of rewarding contribution and reflecting the market down through the entire organisation.

MOVING TO A BUSINESS AND MARKET-DRIVEN EMPLOYMENT PACKAGE AT STANDARD LIFE INVESTMENTS

Background

Standard Life Investments (SLI) is the investment management division of the large Edinburgh-based financial services mutual company. SLI employs approximately 700 staff performing a range of front, middle and back office services for its customers. The focus of the changes documented here, involving a move out of the corporate reward and grading structure to a flexible and person-based approach, was for the 500 support staff, engaged in administration, communication, IT and secretarial activities.

Current systems and the need to change

Historically, since being set up as an independent division, the pay and rewards of SLI's support staff had been managed within a common set of policies and pay structure which applied across the whole of Standard Life. The pay structure, established in the early 1990s, had 20 grades, with nine grades below management levels, to which a variety of differentiated conditions and entitlements – such as holidays, overtime and car parking – were attached. The standard work week is, for administrative and support staff, 35 hours, with a flexitime scheme in operation.

Standard Life pay scales are comparatively broad by external standards at 80–100 per cent+ from minimum to maximum, and a system relating pay increases to the appraised contribution of each individual employee was introduced in 1996. However, the overall annual pay scale movement continues to have a large effect on the increases individuals actually receive, and the vast majority of staff are paid within 10 per cent of the mid-point of their band. Pay bands overlap considerably by up to two-thirds, and so although there is a strong focus on achieving promotions up the grade structure, promotion-based increases are typically in the range of 2 per cent to 5 per cent. In addition, a discretionary bonus scheme operates across Standard Life in which payment opportunities vary by grade and level.

The application of this approach, driven by the needs and market of a large life assurance company, created some significant recruitment, retention and motivation issues in SLI. A project team sponsored by the head of the division was set up to investigate the situation. It consulted with staff on a wide range of people, business and customer issues, as well as investigating the practices of competing investment houses. A number of factors led them to recommend reward changes, including:

❑ lack of market-alignment with the packages on offer in other investment houses, which was found to be a significant factor contributing to the high staff turnover rate in the organisation; the financial services labour market in Edinburgh has become increasingly tight in recent years, following a number of new entrants' coming into the marketplace; of particular concern was the loss of high-performing staff and the inability to recruit from competitors

❑ the existing grading structure was felt to be unduly restrictive from a career development as well as a pay perspective, with a strong emphasis on vertical promotions and general inappropriateness for a non-hierarchical, compact, flexible organisation

❑ the current working practices often did not match with the demands of customers, who expected to be able to deal with staff outside the normal 9–5 working day; the existing 35-hour week and flexitime system, combined with the growing volumes of work, meant that in addition to vacations, most staff took their full entitlement of 18 flexitime days off, and overtime costs were considerable.

Achieving the Vision: the reward changes

Under the banner of 'Achieving the Vision', and supported by a well-orchestrated communications and briefing programme, the new employment and reward package in SLI was introduced between May 1997 and February 1998. The declared philosophy was one of paying leading and market-aligned salaries for high performance, and key features of the changes included:

❑ moving to a 40-hour flexible working week, averaged out on an annual basis and based on business needs, which removed the requirement for overtime working; staff salaries were increased proportionately to reflect the five-hour increase

❑ adopting a new contractual bonus for all support staff, of up to 15 per cent of base pay, based on a mix of company performance and individual contribution

❑ abandoning the corporate grade structure and moving to job-based salary levels in line with peer group investment houses, which for many positions has also resulted in a salary increase.

In moving out of the corporate grade structures, SLI considered a move into broader pay bands. However, this option was rejected because the nine existing grade ranges were already fairly broad at over 80 per cent from top to bottom. The key issues were therefore more to do with how individuals' salaries were set and moved in relation to the market and their contribution. Fewer broad bands in themselves would not have created this essential flexibility and greater differentiation in relation to specific market worth and contribution.

Instead, SLI has moved to a system of job-based market value ranges. Good market data amongst competitors for similar jobs is available relatively easily in Edinburgh, and line managers are now provided with a 'market value range' for each of the jobs they manage. This is the range between the upper and lower quartile levels of the market data within which the majority of market incumbents are paid. However, this is merely an indicative range, with no fixed ceiling. Using this information and their own assessed levels of the individual contribution of their staff, managers then recommend appropriate increases for them. There are no fixed increases or matrices to restrict the increase recommended. The overall pay bill increase for SLI is then agreed, taking account of all managers' recommendations and the overall performance of the division, before individual increases are confirmed and communicated.

Individual development has also been a key component of the changes. Individual role profiles were written specifying the duties and competencies of each position. All staff now have an individual development plan and two hours a week is allocated for self-development activities.

Learning points

Summarising the reasons why both line managers and staff supported their reward and employment changes, HR manager Gordon Teasdale explains, 'We had been rewarding our people like life insurance people. We wanted to recognise they had a value in their own right, and to pay our best people in line with the highest salary levels in the industry.'

The focus was very much on achieving these ends, not on implementing 'best practice' designs that wouldn't meet their needs. Hence broadbanding in his view would have achieved little; they needed to go further: to change the mindset and move to job-, market- and person-based pay. A read-across with the rest of the organisation, even of a less hierarchical and a more flexible nature, simply wasn't the issue.

The new approach to pay management is not an easy option in any sense. Managers have required a lot of briefing, coaching and support to help them determine and explain salary decisions to staff, without the 'crutch' of a pay structure or salary matrix to lean back on. An extensive communication and briefing campaign was essential, in Teasdale's view, to achieve the necessary understanding and trust in the new approach amongst staff. Some information systems problems at the time of the implementation of the changes didn't help.

Two years on from the changes, in 1999, staff turnover is still relatively high and the local labour market has become even tighter. SLI is now working on improving the 'softer' side of staff recognition, and a team of employees recently went to receive an industry customer service award which the business had won. Yet Teasdale and his management colleagues are confident that their pay budgets are being more effectively invested to reflect people's real value and contribution, and that a more flexible and motivated workforce is now better able to achieve what the business strategy requires.

'It is vital that the pay methods were integrated into the broader employment relationship we wanted to create to support our business vision,' according to Teasdale, and he is confident that significant progress has been made in this direction. It is perhaps a measure of the success of the changes that other parts of Standard Life are looking at adopting a similar approach involving a move to broad job-family-based and more market-aligned pay ranges.

A FLEXIBLE APPROACH AT THISTLE HOTELS

The main features of the pay and benefits system used in Thistle Hotels are as follows:

- There is a simple five-grade structure covering all 7,500 workers, developed by identifying the largest jobs at the top and the smallest jobs at the bottom. Those jobs next to the top and the bottom categories were then identified and the rest were placed in the middle grades. The purpose of this grade structure is only to indicate benefit levels.

- Job evaluation is not used to allocate jobs to the benefit grades. They usually fall naturally into place. If a director wants to move a group of staff into a higher level, he or she is shown which jobs are in the higher level and asked if the responsibilities of the jobs under review match the higher-level ones.

- There are no pay ranges or scales. The structure is market-driven in the sense that the pay rate for the job is the market rate for that job in a sector where there is a great deal of market information. General managers usually know perfectly well what that rate is. There is no point in having a scale below that rate because people are not recruited below the market level.

- The aim of the whole re-design exercise was to keep it simple and to align the way pay and benefits are managed with the way in which the business is managed. This does not mean that it is not a good thing to bear in mind certain basic principles, and a logically justifiable and consistent approach is necessary.

- All staff are eligible for some form of bonus related to company or hotel performance, but the type of scheme varies at different levels.

- Newly appointed staff are told that they have the opportunity to progress their careers and that pay progresses in line with career progression.

- Managers determine base pay increases annually within a budget. They will take account of the individual's performance (but there is no mechanical rating formula to determine the link between performance and pay). Guidelines will be issued that pay increases within that budget should range from 0 per cent to 10 per cent. A separate 'pot' of typically 0.5 per cent is retained centrally to deal with exceptions. There are individuals who may have fallen behind market rate levels. (As is common in many organisations, the salaries of existing staff can lag behind market rates.) Managers submit recommendations to the centre on these exceptional cases. The situation does not normally arise with non-managerial staff because of the closer link to market rates and a higher level of labour turnover.

❑ Mark Geary, director of human resources at the time of the interview, believes that 90 per cent of managers can be expected to make sensible and logical decisions about pay. The other 10 per cent may need some guidance.

❑ Attitude survey results have shown improvements in staff satisfaction, which supports the view that these arrangements seem to be working satisfactorily.

3 PAY STRUCTURES IN ACTION

Much of the point of this chapter is that it may be useful as a means of benchmarking a reader's own organisation. This book, after all, is largely based on the outcome of the research into pay structures we carried out on behalf of the (then) Institute of Personnel and Development (now the Chartered Institute of Personnel and Development) in 1999/2000. But a number of other relevant research projects have been carried out in the UK and the USA, and the results of these are summarised later in this chapter. (The order in which such information is presented is intended to reflect British events before American.)

The IPD 1999/2000 research

The IPD survey of developments in base pay structures and pay management was conducted by means of a questionnaire which was completed by 193 organisations. Of these, 69 per cent were in the private sector, 25 per cent in the public sector and 6 per cent in the voluntary sector. Forty per cent of them had 1,000 employees or less, while 23 per cent had between 1,001 and 3,000 employees, and 37 per cent had over 3,000 employees.

We followed this up with 27 case study interviews, held primarily with pay and benefits managers. These were carried out with a balanced sample of large, medium-sized and small organisations in the private, public and voluntary sectors, including AXA Insurance, the BBC, BP Amoco, Bristol Myers Squibb, BT, the Children's Society, Halifax plc, IMS Health, an international oil company, Lloyds TSB, the Ministry of

Defence, the National Gallery, Nationwide Building Society, a global communications company, Norfolk County Council, Perkins Engines, Peabody Trust, the Prince's Trust, the Royal Bank of Scotland, the Royal National Lifeboats Institution, Thistle Hotels, Xerox (UK), Yorkshire Water and Zurich Financial Services.

Broadbanded pay structures

The research confirmed that there is no generally accepted definition of what a broadbanded structure is, except that it comprises fewer and wider bands than a traditional graded structure. The textbooks describe broadbanded structures as having fewer than six bands, each with a pay span of at least 70 per cent to 100 per cent above the pay range minimum. In practice, some organisations refer to their structures as being broadbanded when there are seven or eight grades each with spans of 50 per cent or so. These might better be called 'fat-graded' structures, while those that are truly broadbanded could be termed 'career-based' structures. The latter term is appropriate because it underlines the principle adopted by a number of the organisations surveyed, which is that broad bands are as much, if not more, about career development as the delivery of pay. 'Fat-graded' structures, on the other hand, have largely come about as a move away from traditional structures to provide marginally greater individual pay flexibility, but maintaining the emphasis on pay equity and cost control.

Number of bands

The proportion of organisations with various numbers of bands for senior executives, managerial/professional staff and other staff is shown in Table 3.

Table 3
NUMBER OF GRADES/BANDS

Number of bands	Senior executives %	Managerial/professional %	Staff %
3 or fewer	64	40	23
4 to 5	19	34	26
6 to 9	12	18	34
10 or more	4	8	17

As might be expected, broadbanded structures with three or fewer bands were most common for senior executives, although a good proportion of organisations (40 per cent) had this type of structure for managers and professional staff.

At the other end of the scale, only 8 per cent of managerial/professional staff and 17 per cent of other staff were in a narrow-graded structure. This indicates that such structures, which were typical in the 1970s and 1980s, are now much less popular. Broadbanded structures (five or fewer bands) have become the most common form (60 per cent for managers, professional and other staff). Just under half of the broadbanded structures (47 per cent) have been in place for at least three years.

Width of grades/bands

The information provided by respondents on the width of grades (the pay span in percentage terms) in their structures is summarised in Table 4. This shows that nearly half of survey participants (48 per cent) had structures with bands of 50 per cent or more.

Grade and band widths were greater for more senior and higher paid positions, but in the main it can be seen that broader bands rather than very wide bands might be a better description of this important trend.

Use of job evaluation

One of the issues associated with broadbanding is the use of job evaluation as a means of defining bands. Initially, it was thought that broad bands would mean the end of analytical job evaluation as we know it. The survey showed that this is

Table 4
WIDTH OF GRADES/BANDS

Width of grade/band	percentage of respondents
Narrow grade (25% or less)	24
Broad grade (26–49%)	28
Fairly broad band (50–79%)	30
Very broad band (80% or more)	18

generally not the case. Although simpler forms of job evaluation are gaining in popularity, 42 per cent still relied on
analytical job evaluation, which is the basis for assigning jobs
to broad bands adopted by 34 per cent of organisations.
However, much simpler job matching was used to place jobs in
bands by 24 per cent of respondents.

Progression through bands

Broadbanding was generally designed to provide greater scope
for progressing individual pay according to contribution. The
focus was on lateral careers and continuous development
rather than on progressing upwards through the hierarchy of
grades. This concept originally raised some concern in the HR
community because it implied untrammelled growth and esca-
lating costs, a viewpoint that ignores the equally objectionable
phenomenon of grade drift often associated with a conventional narrow-graded structure. However, the majority of
respondents to the survey (78 per cent) have decided that some
control in the form of a bar to pay progression within each
band is necessary. A large proportion of respondents (43 per
cent) incorporated zones within bands that indicate the normal
range of pay for someone in a particular or generic role. These
zones were frequently (37 per cent of survey participants)
located around market reference or anchor points that indicate
the rate of pay for a fully competent individual in a role and are
often aligned to market rates. So in most cases staff are not
able to progress through the whole of the broad pay ranges
associated with each band.

This contradicts the original American concept of broadbanding which envisaged potential for progression without any
limitations. Where there are zones, the question might be
asked: what is the difference between – as in one of our case
studies – 15 grades in the previous pay structure and five broad
bands, each with three 'zones' in the new structure? Zoning
companies would respond that the new structure is much
flatter and less hierarchical, with only five levels. Movements
between zones at any particular level are rare and do not
depend on gaining more job evaluation points. The zones
purely represent different market rates for jobs in their level.

Objectives for introducing broad bands

The objectives given by organisations for introducing broad bands are set out in Table 5.

It is interesting to note that the most significant reason by far was the desire to provide more flexibility. However, few respondents wanted to get rid of job evaluation altogether and the desire to retain some element of order and control is still evident.

Achieving the objectives

Some 14 per cent of the survey respondents believed that their objectives for introducing broadbanding have been entirely achieved, and 58 per cent thought that they had been mostly achieved. Where the objectives were only partly or not very well achieved, the most important reason for this was inadequate performance management processes (26 per cent). Another frequently mentioned cause of failure was ineffective training of managers (18 per cent). Thus the problems were to do with managing the progression of pay in the new flatter structures rather than with the move to fewer and broader bands *per se*.

Problems in controlling the pay progression or the pay bill were reported by only 13 per cent of respondents and very few (6 per cent) thought that the problem was the suspicion or hostility of staff. Where employees were hostile, the main reasons were perceived lack of promotion prospects (39 per

Table 5
OBJECTIVES FOR INTRODUCING BROADBANDING

Objectives	percentage of respondents
To provide for more flexibility in rewarding people	29
To reflect changes in organisational structure	18
To provide a better base for rewarding growth in competence	14
To replace an over-complex pay structure	12
To devolve more responsibility for pay decisions to managers	11
To provide a better basis for rewarding career progression	11
To reduce the need for job evaluation	8
To simplify pay administration	7
To eliminate the need for job evaluation	2

cent) and the belief that broadbanding lacks structure (22 per cent).

Broadbanding developments

Less than 1 per cent of organisations proposed to abandon broadbanding, although 16 per cent wanted to modify it. Around one in five organisations (22 per cent) covered by the survey intended to introduce broad bands. The popularity of broadbanding continues.

Job family structures

Job family structures existed in far fewer of the responding organisations (16 per cent). However, 17 per cent were planning to introduce job families within the next two years, possibly to address the problem mentioned above of staff perceiving a lack of structure in broad bands. Over half of these organisations (55 per cent) have placed all occupations in job families with separate pay structures. A high proportion (42 per cent) have fitted job families into a common broadbanded pay structure. Levels in job families were mostly (60 per cent) related to job size as determined by job evaluation. The remaining 40 per cent had graded job families on the basis of levels of competence or skill.

Objectives

The most commonly mentioned objective set by respondents with job families was, interestingly, 'to map out career paths'. Flexibility came next, and pay – in the shape of an aim to identify market groups – came third. Job families are by no means only about money.

The prominence given to career paths is interesting. This suggests that organisations which introduced broad bands to replace hierarchical structures that overemphasised promotion are now contemplating the introduction of job families as alternative means of demonstrating career and pay progression opportunities to their staff.

A large majority of the respondents (71 per cent) believed that these objectives have been mostly or completely achieved. The most prominent reason for failing to achieve objectives (22 per cent) was the difficulty of assessing internal relativities, which might explain the move to combine job family and broadbanding approaches. The next most frequently mentioned cause is inadequate market data (17 per cent).

Contingent pay

Method

Respondents were asked what method of progressing base pay existed in their organisations. Their replies are summarised in Table 6.

Performance-related pay is by far the most popular, and in many cases broad bands were introduced to provide more scope to vary pay in relation to individual performance. Hardly any organisation had pure competence-related or skill-based pay, although 8 per cent combined performance and competence pay (which is sometimes referred to as contribution-related pay). The proportion of organisations with service-related increments is surprisingly high at 22 per cent, but it is declining.

Developments

A number of organisations (15 per cent) proposed to introduce competence-related pay. No organisation intended to abandon performance-related pay, though 38 per cent wanted to modify their scheme.

Rating

Of those organisations with performance- or competence-related pay, 22 per cent do not use ratings, relying instead on

Table 6
CRITERIA FOR PROGRESSING PAY

Method	percentage of respondents
Wholly related to performance	67
Wholly related to competence	2
Wholly based on skill	1
Wholly related to a combination of performance and competence/skill	8
Service-related increments	22

an overall assessment. This shows little change from the findings of the IPD research into performance management in 1998, which found that 24 per cent of respondents with performance-related pay did not incorporate rating in the process.

Control

The control of contingent pay increases is mainly through pay budgets (75 per cent). A pay matrix is used to determine increases in relation to a performance rating and position in the pay range by 31 per cent of respondents.

Case study findings

The findings from the field visits are summarised below.

Diversity

The most striking outcome of the visits is the diversity of practice. Certain basic principles are often followed, such as flexibility and integration of pay systems with competence, skill and career development processes. But each organisation applies these principles in accordance with its own culture and context. This research has quashed once and for all any idea that there is such a thing as 'best practice' when applied to pay systems. It is *best fit* that matters, and a contingency approach is the one usually adopted. Broadbanding is definitely not right for every organisation, as our case studies illustrate.

Competence and career development

Broadbanded or job family structures are increasingly being treated as a basis for planning and implementing competence and career development processes. They are no longer regarded simply as vehicles for delivering pay. In fact, organisations are often focusing initially on the business need for competence and career development and the processes required. Only then do they consider how these processes can be supported by reward structures. These may not be labelled as 'broadbanded' or 'job family' at all. They simply represent the preferred way to integrate employee development and reward. Thus the 'bundling' of HR practices which some experts regard as critical to the delivery of effective HR and reward strategies is actually taking place in this area.

Both broadbanded and job family pay structures are often based on competence frameworks and profiles. Job size is only one consideration. The primary aim is to provide information on development opportunities and career paths that can be fed into personal development planning processes as part of performance management.

Use of job evaluation

The research confirmed yet again that the death of job evaluation has been greatly exaggerated. Job sizing is still regarded as a necessary basis for supporting the design of the structure and, importantly, ensuring that a reasonable degree of internal equity is maintained, subject always to market rate considerations. However, placing jobs in fewer bands is easier, so the job evaluation system can often be simpler. Re-grading decisions are no longer so crucial in a broadbanded or job family structure. Thus, once the structure has been established, job evaluation is being relegated to a support and validation role. Although the bands or levels may be defined in terms of job evaluation points, the band and level definitions (often phrased in accountability and competence terms) provide enough information to enable jobs to be matched accurately. Organisations often make use of generic job descriptions as the basis for matching or 'slotting' jobs into grades as illustrated in some of the case studies.

The role of job evaluation is becoming one of validating decisions on band or level gradings if circumstances have changed significantly or if there is cause for concern. A few organisations are using job evaluation purely as an audit tool to ensure that equal pay for work of equal value considerations are taken into account.

Market-driven pay levels

The tendency is for pay levels to be more market-driven, although the extent to which this happens will depend on the degree to which the organisation is competing to attract and retain scarce skills in the labour market. Within broadbanded structures the reference point or target salary for a fully competent person is often aligned to the market rate in accordance with company 'pay stance' policy. In the absence of reliable market data, job evaluation may be used to interpolate a rate between the market rates established for other roles in the band. But priority may well be given to external competitiveness rather than internal equity. Job family structures in particular are giving much greater freedom to pay different rates in each family according to the market.

Integration with the business strategy

New pay structures are frequently being introduced as part of a business strategy for cultural change. In a number of the organisations covered by the field work, the importance of integrating reward and business strategy was fully appreciated so that reward processes supported, even led, cultural change as described in Chapter 1.

Change management

Perhaps the most impressive finding of the case studies was the recognition by a number of organisations that the introduction of a new pay structure presented a major change management challenge. The response was an emphasis on the importance of involvement, communication and training as means of giving understanding, ownership and acceptance of the new arrangements. The old idea that involvement is simply a matter of setting up a project team has been replaced by much wider arrangements for the participation of line managers and staff generally in workshops and focus groups to consider design, development and implementation issues. What often emerges from such discussions is that concepts that seemed perfectly clear to HR and their consultants are much more difficult to grasp by those facing them for the first time. The lesson the writers have learnt the hard way as consultants is that any proposals should be simple and easy to understand and expressed in English rather than consultant-speak. HR professionals must also avoid 'manager-ese'.

The importance of bringing line managers into the picture at an early stage as well as staff representatives was underlined by many organisations. The point was made several times that it is too easy to underestimate the need to get line managers involved and to fail to appreciate the assistance they can provide. In our experience, the very fact that line managers are not HR or pay specialists means that they can bring to bear a refreshingly practical and common-sense perspective. Involving line managers is particularly important when more responsibility for pay decisions is going to be devolved to them, as is frequently the case.

Conclusions

The case studies generally supported the survey finding that a wide diversity of approaches to pay structures exists. Perhaps the only principle emerging from the research that could be regarded as 'best practice' is the need for involvement, communication and training.

Whatever the many forms broadbanding takes, it seems to be here to stay. The traditional structure of 10 or more grades exists in a relatively small proportion of the respondents' organisations, as shown in Table 3, while broad bands (five or fewer) are used by a much greater percentage of participants. Pure job family structures are much less common, although some interest is being expressed in extending their use, and, in general, organisations are differentiating more strongly on the basis of market worth, performance and competence.

Perhaps the most important point confirmed by the survey and the field visits is the need for a contingency approach to developing pay structures. It may therefore be unhelpful to label a structure 'broadbanded' or 'job family'. It is better to start by asking how rewards can be delivered in ways that support the achievement of the business strategy, are congruent with the organisation's culture and structure, and are integrated with other human resource management policies and practices.

Institute of Personnel and Development 1996 research

The 1996 IPD research in the UK indicated that organisations were most likely to introduce broadbanding when they are:

❑ undergoing swift and pervasive change
❑ developing new strategies for pay delivery which support the achievement of their business goals, reflect their changing operational environment and help to change or reinforce its culture

- ❑ determined to integrate their employee reward and other employment and development processes as a means of achieving improved business results
- ❑ aware of the need to develop levels of competence and define career paths in de-layered structures
- ❑ disenchanted with the inflexibility of their present system and the bureaucracy and costs associated with it
- ❑ devolving more authority to line managers to make pay decisions.

The following are the reasons given by the organisations covered in the survey for introducing broad bands:

- ❑ *Bass Brewers* – as part of a major change programme which was concerned with both structure (de-layering and greater emphasis on horizontal processes) and culture (sharper commercial perspective, enhanced customer orientation and increased operational and role flexibility)
- ❑ *Citibank* – to simplify the pay structure, to minimise maintenance and to provide room for lateral development
- ❑ *Glaxo Wellcome* – to achieve greater emphasis on development and continuous improvement, less complexity and movement across functional boundaries
- ❑ *IBM* – as part of a major organisational transformation process which involved globalising the business, 'right sizing, and reduction of management layers'
- ❑ *the Inland Revenue* – as a means of helping to achieve greater cohesion
- ❑ *the Midland Bank* – because the existing grade structure was seen as inflexible and expensive
- ❑ *RAC Motoring Services* – because it had become increasingly clear that the existing grade structure and remuneration approach was inappropriate to the present needs of the business. In particular it was felt that multiple grades emphasised status rather than contribution or performance, and that this was a barrier when contribution, teamworking and an integrative approach were vital. It was also believed that narrow grade structures inhibited lateral career moves between divisions, functions and work groups

❏ *Reckitt & Colman* – 'to deliver flexibility and to reflect new organisation structures and career paths'.

❏ *Volkswagen* – following the introduction of a lean structure in which jobs had become more flexible than ever, a means had to be found to reward staff for taking on added responsibilities in the flat structure.

Research by Duncan Brown

The main reasons given for introducing broad bands by the seven UK companies surveyed in 1996 by Duncan Brown – a UK retail bank, a public sector corporation, a UK high-technology company, a fast-moving consumer goods company, a UK subsidiary of an international telecommunications company, a Scottish bank, and a brewing company – were to:

1 support broader business and organisational changes
2 align personal and career development patterns
3 improve the administration of pay.

His conclusions from the research were that:

❏ a strategic approach is necessary for the development of broad bands: 'Broadbanding initiatives will almost certainly fail if they are treated as one-off, quick-fix pay re-design exercises'
❏ a clear business purpose is essential
❏ successful broadbanding relies heavily on changes to related pay programmes and other HR practices, which are generally difficult to achieve
❏ the changes required to operate broadbanding systems effectively have to be pursued over many years.

Towers Perrin 1997 Survey

A survey of over 300 European companies conducted by Towers Perrin in 1997 established that 32 per cent of them had introduced broadbanding in the previous two years, whereas 49 per cent proposed to introduce them in the following two years. The pay restructuring objectives and the degree to which those objectives were met are shown in Table 7. The degree of satisfaction is consistently high, which contradicts the assumption made by some commentators that broadbanding has generally failed to live up to its promises.

An analysis of the reasons respondents to the survey gave for not meeting objectives is given in Table 8. Lack of support systems such as performance management and pay budgeting were two of the most frequently mentioned reasons for failure. But ineffective communication was also important, as was lack of top management support. A number of organisations commented that the problems arose because the number of grades was inadequately validated (10 per cent) or the bands were too broad (9 per cent).

Table 7
BROADBANDING: OBJECTIVES, PRIORITIES AND ACHIEVEMENTS

Objectives	percentage of companies who say:	
	it is a top priority	the objectives have been met
To enable better pay differentiation based on performance	21	77
To reflect flatter organisation structure	15	83
To respond more rapidly to organisational change	15	80
To reflect broader roles rather than jobs	14	75
To enhance the ability to value individual skills/competencies	14	64
To increase the flexibility of base pay	13	85

Table 8
REASONS FOR NOT MEETING THE OBJECTIVES SET FOR BROADBANDING

Reason for failure	percentage of respondents who gave it as the reason
Lack of support systems	28
Inadequate market data	24
Lack of communication	21
Lack of senior management support	14
Number of grades inadequately validated	10
Bands too broad	9

Participants with broad bands managed individual pay within bands in various ways, as set out in Table 9. By far the most popular is the use of market reference points, as described in Chapter 4.

The approach used to assign jobs to bands is summarised in Table 10. Traditional job evaluation is still the most frequently used method, although a fairly high proportion of organisations use market pricing, band descriptions or organisational role level.

In the 150 UK companies covered by the survey it was found that in the main they had broader bands rather than true broadbanding. Only 19 per cent had bands with a width of more than 60 per cent for management, and even fewer (15 per cent) had bands of over 60 per cent for non-management staff.

Table 9
PAY MANAGEMENT PROCESS IN BROADBANDED STRUCTURES

Pay management process	percentage of respondents with broad bands who use the process
Market reference points	47
No control points	25
Formal zoning segments	14
Skill/competency blocks	10
Informal segments/zones	6

Table 10
ASSIGNING JOBS TO BROAD BANDS

Method of assignment	percentage of respondents with broad bands who use the method
Traditional job evaluation	46
Market pricing	21
Slotting, using job descriptions	20
Organisational role level	18
Competency/skill level	15

American Compensation Association

The 1998 survey conducted by Hewitt Associates for the American Compensation Association asked participants to list their top five reasons for implementing broadbanding, with the results shown below:

❏ To create more organisational flexibility   78 per cent
❏ To support a new culture   61 per cent
❏ To de-emphasise traditional structure/
   hierarchy   51 per cent
❏ To foster a flatter organisation   47 per cent
❏ To emphasise career development   38 per cent
❏ To encourage skill development   33 per cent
❏ To respond to changes in job/work design   31 per cent

The interesting thing about these reasons is that none is concerned with pay delivery. They all relate to organisational or career/skill development concerns.

An analysis of the reasons contributing to the degree to which broadbanding was judged to be effective is shown in Table 11.

It seems that problems are associated with the introduction of broadbanding, such as inadequate testing, rather than because of intrinsic design faults or operational difficulties. Yet again this survey confirmed that lack of attention to communications and training is a major cause of failure.

Table 11
FACTORS INFLUENCING THE EFFECTIVENESS OF BROADBANDING

Too little organisation time/resources committed to:	percentage of companies judging broadbanding to be effective	percentage of companies judging broadbanding to be less effective
Feasibility study	19	50
Programme design	3	42
Programme testing	50	82
Development of communication materials	36	56
Development of training materials	46	61
Conducting management training	39	68
Conducting employee training	51	56

Conclusions

The research findings in the UK, Europe and the USA all indicate that broadbanding is here to stay and is in fact on the increase, although it may often be in the form of broader bands than a true broadbanded structure. In spite of some problems over its introduction, companies with broadbanding seem to be reasonably satisfied. Approaches to introducing a broadbanded structure which help to minimise the problems are discussed in Chapter 6.

PART II

BROADBANDED PAY STRUCTURES

4 FEATURES OF BROADBANDED PAY STRUCTURES

Definition of broadbanding

Broadbanding is the process of compressing a hierarchy of pay grades or salary ranges into a number of wide bands. The number varies, but may be no more than four or five. The range of pay in each band is therefore wider than in a traditional graded structure. Each of the bands often spans the pay opportunities previously covered by several separate grade and pay ranges. However, in rapidly growing organisations such as One-2-One, broadbanding can be the first form of pay structuring. The focus in a broadbanded structure is on lateral career movement within the bands and on competence growth and continuous development in the role. The move from a conventional graded structure with, say, 12 grades where the span of each grade from bottom to top is 30–50 per cent to a broadbanded structure with four grades and a span of 60–80 per cent in each band is modelled in Figure 2 (overleaf).

Varieties of broadbanding

Broadbanding means different things to different people and is applied in many different ways. Gilbert and Abosch (1996) distinguish between broad grade and career band structures.

Broad grade structures

A broad or 'fat' grade simply collapses a number of salary grades into fewer grades or bands, although it retains the traditional features and controls of conventional graded structures.

Figure 2
CONVERSION OF A TRADITIONAL GRADED STRUCTURE INTO A BROADBANDED STRUCTURE

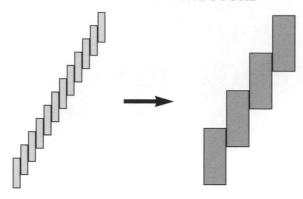

Typically, these include 'mid-point' management in which the mid-point of the range is aligned to market rates and used as the control point.

Pay in such structures may be managed through the use of compa-ratios which represent the rate of pay for an individual or the whole or part of the population of an organisation as a percentage of the mid-point. The compa-ratio for individuals defines their position in the pay range compared with the mid-point and indicates where their pay should be positioned in accordance with that relationship. A group compa-ratio indicates the relationship of the sum of actual pay in a population to the sum of the mid-points. It establishes how pay policy is being implemented and how budgets are being controlled.

A broad grade structure might have seven or eight grades with range spreads of 50 per cent and differentials of 20 per cent, while a typical traditional structure might have 14 or so job grades with pay range spreads or spans ranging from 20 per cent to 40 per cent and 15 per cent differentials between adjacent ranges. The Towers Perrin research found that a 50 per cent reduction in the number of grades was typical in organisations moving towards broad bands, but the increase in range widths was often marginal.

Career band structures

Career band structures depart much further from conventional pay structures. Fewer bands are used – say, four or five – but more importantly, the emphasis is on flexible roles, individual career development and competency growth, rather than progression based on position in the range. Career moves are more likely to be horizontal in the organisation and therefore take place within the same band. There is much less emphasis on movement upwards through a hierarchy. There is no such thing as a mid-point and compa-ratios are therefore not used.

The term 'career bands' has not been generally adopted in the UK although it does describe an important feature of broadbanding – the focus on lateral growth. In the UK, and in this book, when reference is made to broad bands, these are assumed generally to have the characteristics of a career band. However, this does not mean that there is any such thing as a standard broadbanded structure, as research has shown.

Why broadbanding?

Broadbanding has emerged as the leading approach to pay structuring because it fits the ways in which organisations are developing and how they believe employees should be rewarded. Abosch (1998) suggests that: 'In many cases principles supported by broadbanding – re-engineering, flattening and speed – are playing a significant role in human resource stratcgics to succcssfully compctc in today's markct placcs.' Broadbanding, as Abosch and Hand (1994) claim, 'is regarded by some as the future of compensation'.

The IPD 1996 research found that the increased incidence of broadbanding could be attributed to the following causes:

❑ the growth of the 'lean' organisation and the widespread de-layering of organisation structures which has meant fewer levels of management and supervision and a considerable reduction in promotion opportunities to higher grades, resulting in lateral rather than vertical career development

❑ the thrust for 'boundary-less' organisations involving the abolition of functional 'chimneys' and an increased emphasis on horizontal processes that cut across organisational boundaries, fostered by business process re-engineering exercises and characterised by the use of cross-functional project teams

- ❑ the consequent pressure for increased organisational flexibility accompanied by role flexibility – the concept that many people now have to use a wider range of skills within their capabilities as members of multidisciplinary teams or in response to new challenges and opportunities
- ❑ a recognition of the fact that in flexible and adaptive organisations people can grow their roles as well as grow in them – they are no longer confined to the rigidities set out in conventional job descriptions (which are rapidly being replaced by less constricting role definitions which emphasise outcomes and competence requirements)
- ❑ the focus on employee development to enhance continuous improvement and role flexibility and to facilitate lateral career moves
- ❑ the general use of competence profiles and frameworks as the basis for employee resourcing and development
- ❑ the increasing use of competence as a factor for consideration in performance management processes and as an influence on pay decisions
- ❑ disillusionment with traditional job evaluation systems as being over-rigid and bureaucratic
- ❑ pressure to devolve more responsibility for pay decisions to line managers
- ❑ disenchantment with multigraded pay structures as being no longer appropriate, insufficiently flexible and conducive to grade drift.

Perhaps the most common reason reported to us in 1999/2000 was the last one. As we were told by one head of remuneration: 'There were more grades than the army has ranks.'

Our 1999/2000 research established that *the need for a more flexible approach to managing pay* was by far the most commonly mentioned reason for broadbanding. This, together with the second most frequently reported factor (*to reflect changes in organisation structure* such as de-layering), indicates that the development of broadbanding can be associated with a belief in the importance of 'freeing up' the ways in which organisations are managed. The emphasis is on horizontal processes and lateral careers. A frequently expressed aim was to replace an over-complex and inappropriate pay structure.

The objective of *providing a better base for rewarding growth in competence and career progression* also featured prominently, as did a policy aim of *devolving more responsibility for pay decisions to line managers*. However, the need to reduce or even eliminate job evaluation was not a particularly important factor. Other research projects in the UK and the USA have identified similar or related objectives.

As stated in Chapter 3, the reasons given for introducing broad bands by the seven UK companies surveyed by Duncan Brown (1996) fell into three, often overlapping categories:

- ❏ *business and organisational change*
  - responding to competitive/cost pressures, as in a public body and a brewer that he studied
  - supporting a changed business strategy and culture, as in a major bank
  - reflecting a de-layered, downsized organisation, also relevant in the bank
  - attacking status distinctions and a 'top-down' culture, as in a privatised utility
  - reinforcing teamworking and breakdown job rigidities, eg a brewer
- ❏ *pay management*
  - introducing greater flexibility to respond to market pressures, particularly relevant in the public sector
  - simplifying and reducing the emphasis on job content and evaluation, as was the case in a multi-product manufacturing company
  - supporting an individual performance-related pay approach in many of the organisations
  - moving the responsibility for pay management away from HR onto the line, another objective in the manufacturing company
- ❏ *developmental*
  - addressing the overemphasis on vertical careers progression/promotion as a reward vehicle, particularly in the two manufacturing companies

- developing and rewarding individual competence, skills and performance – for example, in the IT company
- fearing the lack of depth/specialisation due to the pressures to upgrade.

It was found that those businesses driven by an *organisational change* rationale had been the most radical in reducing the number of grades, and those with more of a *pay management* focus had generally adopted the most measured approach.

The Watson Wyatt survey (1996) of broadbanding in the UK revealed that it was perceived as a key tool to support a *more flexible organisation*. Broadbanding was intended to allow greater flexibility in managing pay and benefits by reshaping the link between grade and pay levels, put a *greater emphasis on the individual* rather than the job, promote individual development and lateral growth, and *encourage multi-skilling/tasking* rather than focusing on specific tasks.

The survey by Hay Management Consultants (1996) showed that the most common reasons given for introducing broadbanding were that it allows *more flexibility in making and administering pay decisions*, it recognises that careers are more likely to develop within homogeneous levels of responsibility rather than by progressing up a number of steps in a hierarchy, and it *reduces the problem of grade drift and the preoccupation with grade status* common in conventionally graded structures.

A US survey by William Mercer (1995) of 3,400 organisations established that the main reasons for broadbanding were *to foster a flatter organisation, encourage a broadly skilled workforce, support a new culture/climate and promote career development opportunities*. These goals were expressed in varying terms such as: reduce emphasis on promotions and grades, create a boundary-less company, facilitate lateral job moves, provide flexibility to respond to changing business needs, break down barriers to teamwork and co-operation, and place more human resource decisions in the hands of managers.

Some of our most recent consulting work has revealed another reason driving the use of broad bands in large multinational organisations such as BP Amoco, Shell and Unilever.

This is *to provide a global framework for pay and career development* while allowing the flexibility to local businesses to reflect their specific needs and market characteristics.

Characteristics of broadbanding

The term 'broadbanding' is often used loosely. It can take many forms. Many organisations with what they describe as broadbanded structures have in fact simply reduced the number of grades and produced a structure which loosely conforms to the 'fat-grade' model referred to earlier. There are, however, certain features which can be used to define a structure as being broadbanded, namely:

- often no more than five or six bands for all the employees covered by the structure, although some organisations describe their structures as being broadbanded when they have as many as eight or nine grades; the total size of the organisation and the level of hierarchy in the existing structure help to define what each organisation regards as broadbanding
- wide pay spans, which can be 80 per cent or more above the minimum rate in the band
- emphasis on external relativities; market pricing may be used to define reference points or 'target rates' for roles in the band, and to place jobs in the band
- less reliance on conventional and rigidly applied analytical job evaluation schemes to govern internal relativities
- focus on lateral career development and competence growth
- increased devolution of pay decisions to line managers who can be given more freedom to manage the pay of their staff in accordance with policy guidelines and within their budgets by reference to information on market rates and relativities within their departments
- less emphasis on hierarchical labels for bands
- generally, less concern for structure and rigid guidelines, and more concern for flexibility and paying for the person rather than the job.

Variations

But there are a number of variations on these basic themes, for example:

❏ In some organisations such as the Yorkshire Building Society and Zurich Financial Services there are no pay limits for bands; others only define the starting point in pay terms.

❏ 'Zones' or sub-bands may be defined within bands which define, or at least provide some guidance on, the pay range for different roles in the band.

❏ Analytical job evaluation processes are abandoned completely in some systems, while others define band limits in evaluation point-score terms and, to greater or lesser degree, use job evaluation to underpin, or at least monitor, internal relativities across the organisation and to deal with borderline or equal pay issues.

❏ Some broadbanded structures rely on whole job comparisons (internal benchmarking or matching), often using generic role definitions; others rely on band definitions or 'descriptors' as the basis for allocating jobs to bands.

❏ Pay levels in the structure may be entirely market-driven or only subject to general scrutiny in relation to market trends – the emphasis might edge towards being externally competitive rather than internally equitable.

❏ Progression in the band may be governed or at least influenced by competence and/or performance – the links between these criteria and pay may be clearly defined or there may be only broad guidelines for line managers on progression.

❏ Positioning people into bands and decisions on pay increases may still largely be governed by internal equity considerations through comparisons between the pay of people with similar roles in job clusters or job families.

❏ The extent to which the responsibility for managing pay is devolved to line managers varies in accordance with the degree to which organisations trust managers to make equitable and consistent decisions and the perceived need to exercise control to achieve what is regarded as a proper degree of equity and consistency.

These variations are largely a product of the organisation's culture, structure, operational processes, management practices and prevailing management style. It is because these are always different that all broadbanding systems are different.

A contingency approach to the design, development and introduction of broadbanding is required, just as it is for any other HR or reward innovations. And the most important factors to be taken into account will be the business strategy of the organisation, its culture, technology and work processes, its structure, and the type of people employed.

Theory v practice

The research carried out on broadbanding in the UK and the USA during the last five years has confirmed that the theory of broadbanding as originally propounded in the USA is not applied in practice. Brown (1996) summarised this as set out in Table 12.

Table 12
COMPARISONS BETWEEN THE THEORY AND THE PRACTICE OF BROADBANDING

Aspect of pay	Broadbanding theory	Broadbanding practice
Placement into bands	Job evaluation is dead	Simplified job/role evaluation continues
Number of bands	Five to 10	Five to 12
Pay band width	80% to 200%	40% to 80%
Pay structures	Single, harmonised band structure	'Bands within bands' and some separate structures most commonly on a job family basis
Use of market data	For individual pay decisions	To develop pay structure and to influence individual pay decisions
Range progression	Free movement within bands	Progression limited by performance zones or job family bands (narrower rather than full bands)
Individual pay increases	Pay budgets for line managers to allocate on a discretionary basis	Guidelines, formulas and matrices for managers; HR heavily involved, but guiding, not controlling
Career moves	Removal of notion of set increases for promotion; career development managed within total pay budget	Defined increases for job/career growth and lateral development provided
Pay budgets	Held by line managers to cover all types of regular and one-off adjustment	Held by line managers but generally split into annual reviews, market adjustments and developmental increases

Designing broadbanded structures

When designing broadbanded structures, the following factors must be considered:

❑ the number of bands
❑ the width of bands
❑ overlap between bands
❑ the definition and description of bands
❑ band structure.

The number of bands

The number of bands is related to the number of distinct levels of responsibility in an organisational hierarchy of roles. A broadbanded structure may contain as few as four or five bands if it covers managerial and staff roles. Businesses with integrated structures which include shop-floor and distribution workers may have no more than six or seven bands. But there are no rules. The number depends on the perceptions of the organisation about how many distinct but broad levels of responsibility or 'value-adding tiers' exist, and on the extent to which it is necessary to differentiate between those levels. The only certain feature of a broadbanded structure in the proper sense of that term is that each band will cover the pay opportunities previously covered by more than one pay range.

Our 1999/2000 research showed that broadbanded structures with five or fewer bands have become the most common form of pay structure. For example, the Yorkshire Building Society has four 'role levels'. The pan-European survey of reward challenges and changes conducted by Towers Perrin in 1999 established that in the UK the average number of grades for senior executives in large organisations was 3.3, while for managers and professional staff it was 4.3 and for non-managerial staff 6.4. Watson Wyatt found that the median number of bands in the companies covered by their 1996 survey was 5.0.

IPD research in 1996 and 1999/2000 revealed the following information on the number of bands in the organisations surveyed:

❑ Bass Brewers – 5 (all staff)

❑ BP – 3 (top managers)
❑ Citibank – 6 (all staff except senior managers)
❑ Glaxo Wellcome – 6 (all staff)
❑ Inland Revenue – 5 (all staff except senior management)
❑ RAC Motoring Services – 5 (all staff in management grading structure)
❑ Reckitt & Colman – 6 (global senior executives)
❑ Volkswagen UK – job family structure, each with its own band
❑ Zurich Financial Services UK Life – 8.

Duncan Brown found the average reduction of grades in organisations introducing broadbanding was 50 per cent, the largest reduction being 66 per cent.

The width of bands

Like the number of bands, the width of bands (the pay span in percentage terms) in a broadbanded structure can vary widely, although it is generally smaller than the original broadbanding model in which widths of 100 per cent were said to be typical. The Towers Perrin 1999 research revealed that 26 per cent of respondents had bands of between 51 per cent and 80 per cent, and only 18 per cent had bands of more than 80 per cent. This distribution was substantially confirmed by our 1999/2000 research which indicated that 30 per cent of survey participants had structures with bands of between 50 per cent and 79 per cent, and 18 per cent had bands which were more than 80 per cent wide.

The research conducted by Brown (1996) showed that the width of the pay bands in the seven organisations studied varied between 40 and 80 per cent, the widths increasing with seniority. Widths were previously between 25 and 35 per cent. As he remarked, this is much narrower than the band widths other commentators describe, and so his research found 'broader rather than truly broadbanding'.

The band widths in the following organisations covered by the IPD research were often wider:

❑ Bass Brewers – 55 per cent to 100 per cent
❑ Citibank – 100 per cent

- ❑ Glaxo Wellcome – 100 per cent plus
- ❑ Inland Revenue – 74 per cent to 101 per cent
- ❑ Reckitt & Colman – 50 per cent
- ❑ Volkswagen UK – variable, typically 85 per cent or more.

When designing a broadbanded structure organisations often adopt an empirical approach, first deciding on the number of bands and the allocation of roles into them and then establishing market rates. The range of the latter determines the width of the band, which will therefore vary. Some organisations such as IBM UK, the Prince's Trust, the RAC, the Yorkshire Building Society and Zurich Financial Services go even further and have no fixed limits. The dimensions are governed by the span of market rates for the jobs in the band as guided by the lower and upper quartile rates.

Overlap between bands

There is often an overlap between the pay ranges of adjacent bands. Thus the range in one band could be £15,000 to £30,000 while that of the next higher band could be £20,000 to £40,000. This provides for more flexibility in pay provision by recognising that people in roles in one band may deliver more added value than some in the next higher band. For example, if there were separate bands for team leaders and individual contributors, the levels of responsibility and competence that are required of a professional or technical individual contributor could be higher than those required of a team leader in an administrative department and would be rewarded accordingly. Broadbanding can therefore provide the scope to recognise that individual contributors could be worth more to the organisation than people in managerial or supervisory positions.

Definition and description of bands

Bands may be named by means of descriptive labels which refer to the generic roles that have been allocated to them – for example, managers, team leaders, individual contributors (technical and professional), individual contributors (administration and support). This underlines the message that a broadbanded structure is not the same as a traditional graded structure in that it does not emphasise the hierarchy by desig-nating bands with numbers or letters.

Bands may be defined simply by reference to their labels and the roles they contain. More specifically, they may be defined either in terms of the main features of the roles placed in the band, as at the Automobile Association, or in terms of generic competences. At Glaxo Wellcome, for example, generic compe-tence profiles have been developed for each band. At Citibank, the broadbanded structure is essentially defined by means of what are in effect band definitions into which jobs are slotted on the basis of whole-job comparisons.

When defining bands the typical aims may be:

1 To enable jobs to be placed in the bands by a process of internal benchmarking using whole-job comparisons, often by reference to generic role definitions as at the Children's Society

2 To provide a natural link between the band descriptions and the information needed for career development and planning.

Broad band definitions may therefore differ from the grade definitions in a traditional job classification scheme. Bands are frequently defined by reference to generic role definitions, while grade descriptions usually mirror conventional job eval-uation factors (eg knowledge and skills, responsibility, decision-making). In some systems, such as that at Glaxo Wellcome, bands are defined by means of job evaluation points so that all roles with a score of between, say, 500 and 800 points, are placed in one band. However, Brown's 1996 research established that those organisations who moved to broad bands but retained detailed point-factor job evaluation found that the flexibility goal of the former was being restricted and frustrated by the latter.

Band structure

As noted earlier, the original concept of broad bands was that they should be unstructured, allowing scope for career progres-sion and rewarding increases in contribution and competence through the whole width of the band. In practice, most organ-isations that have introduced broadbanding covered by the IPD

1999/2000 survey (78 per cent) have balked at so much flexibility and introduced some form of control within bands. A large proportion of respondents (43 per cent) incorporate zones within bands that indicate the normal range of pay for someone in a particular or a generic role. These zones are frequently (37 per cent of survey participants) located around reference or anchor points that indicate the rate of pay for a fully competent individual in a role and are usually aligned to market rates in accordance with company policy.

The 1997 Towers Perrin survey produced similar results. The majority of respondents (75 per cent) used some form of control, the most popular being market reference points (47 per cent) and formal zones or segments (14 per cent). These approaches and the incorporation of job families into bands (a form of zoning) are described below.

Market reference points

Market reference points (sometimes called anchor rates or target rates) within bands indicate the rate of pay for an individual or generic role or for a group of roles. They are 'referenced' to market rates at a level dependent on the organisation's policy for relating internal rates to the market. This rate is often assumed to be the rate appropriate for a fully or highly competent individual in the role. A band with reference points is illustrated in Figure 3.

Figure 3
A BROAD BAND WITH REFERENCE POINTS

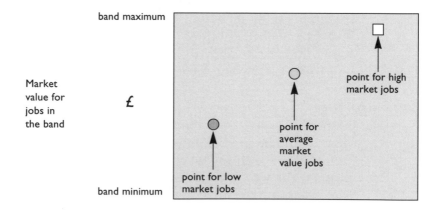

Reference points look like spot rates except that they are located within a band on the basis of comparisons with market rates, and internal relativities may also be taken into account. Some flexibility may be allowed in deciding the extent to which individuals can be paid below or above the rate depending on their competence and performance, although it is usually assumed that the rates of most if not all holders of the role will cluster around the reference point.

Zones

Zones add more structure by defining the extent to which pay can range below and above the reference point. Pay progression within the zone will depend on levels of competence, performance or both (contribution). The lower level of pay could be 10 per cent below the reference point, while the higher level could be 10 per cent above that point. Typically, there might be two or three zones in a band. Lloyds TSB, for example, uses three zones according to the 'low', 'medium' or 'high' market worth of each job. Unilever has two zones in each band. A band with three zones is illustrated in Figure 4.

As we have seen elsewhere, zones may be regarded as 'bands within bands', and the question is sometimes asked about whether there is really a difference between a broadbanded structure with five bands, in each of which there are three zones, and a conventional graded structure with 15 grades.

Figure 4
A BAND WITH ZONES

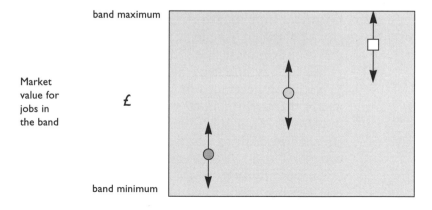

The answer is that zones operate more flexibly. In a traditional graded structure the grades are predetermined and are set out as a hierarchy which is defined in terms of job evaluation points or a grade description. Upgrading depends on promotion or a re-evaluation of the job.

In contrast, zones in bands are defined primarily by reference to market rate data although internal relativities may also be taken into account. The reference point for a zone, and therefore its lower and upper limits, may be altered in response to market rate changes so that the zone occupies a new position within the band. Pay ranges in a graded pay structure are more rigid. They do not move differentially in response to the impact of market forces on levels of pay for individual jobs or clusters of jobs.

In a zoned band, movement to a higher zone takes place when it is evident that the role an individual is carrying out matches the role carried out by people in that zone. It is not dependent on the evaluation score of the individual's job, and re-evaluations are not required unless matching is difficult or there are equal pay considerations.

Zones of the type described above are not usually defined as a hierarchy within a band. In some broadbanded structures there is scope for creating a special zone for individuals whose role has enlarged significantly but not enough to justify allocation to a higher zone in the band.

An example of market zoning in an insurance company is shown in Figure 5 (opposite).

Segmented bands

Segmentation means dividing bands into a number of levels through which people can progress as their competence and contribution increases. The different segments resemble zones in that a pay bracket is attached to each of them but, subject to satisfying certain criteria, employees can advance progressively through the band rather than moving from one zone to another, as in a zoned band. A segmented broadbanded structure, as in Halifax plc (see the case study at the end of this chapter) and Volkswagen UK, is designed to encourage employees to increase the breadth and depth of their skills and competences by providing them with rewards linked to the

Figure 5
A MARKET-ZONED STRUCTURE

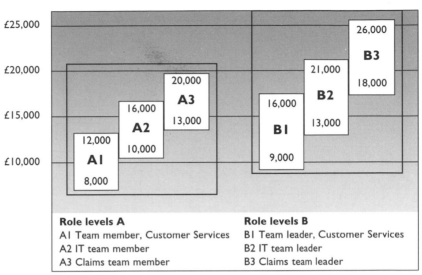

Role levels A
A1 Team member, Customer Services
A2 IT team member
A3 Claims team member

Role levels B
B1 Team leader, Customer Services
B2 IT team leader
B3 Claims team leader

NB: Progression most commonly A1 to B1 etc, rather than A1 to A2.

levels they achieve. A segmented broadbanded structure based on a developmental competency model is illustrated in Figure 6 (overleaf).

Job family zones

Zones within broad bands can be reserved for job families. For example, as illustrated in Figure 7 (overleaf), a band could have separate zones catering for operations, finance, IT and professional services, each with its own pay range. Reference points may be incorporated in the job family zones for roles at different levels of expertise and market worth.

Case studies

The different ways in which broadbanding works in practice are illustrated by the following five case studies:

❑ *The BBC* – The structure covers all staff and therefore has 11 grades, which means that it could be regarded as a conventional graded structure but the grades are broad (150 per cent maximum) and the number of grades has been

Figure 6
A SEGMENTED BROADBANDED STRUCTURE

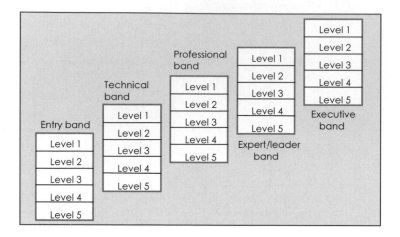

Figure 7
JOB FAMILIES IN A BROAD BAND

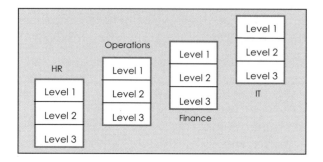

designed to cover a wide range of jobs at different levels. Progression is related to personal progress, responsibility and performance.

❑ *BP Amoco Exploration* – There are seven bands: four of 70 per cent and three of 73 per cent. Pay levels are market-driven and level descriptors are used to provide guidance on positioning jobs in the band.

❑ *Bristol Myers Squibb* – There are eight bands with an average width of about 100 per cent. A fairly loose system of job evaluation is used to allocate jobs to bands.

❏ *Halifax plc* – There are five segmented bands with ranges varying from 55 per cent to 75 per cent.

❏ *RNLI* – A 12-grade common structure was initially introduced to replace a somewhat complex mix of pay structures after a large-scale job evaluation exercise, and this has been subsequently reduced to eight bands.

Case study

THE BBC

Fundamental principle
The fundamental principle underpinning the BBC pay structure is: 'the introduction of modern, flexible and fair pay systems which will help to attract, retain and reward the best talent with the most competitive pay and create a closer link between pay and performance'.

Key changes to the pay structure
The number of grades was reduced in 1995 from 20 to 11, following an earlier reduction from more than 40 grades. Each grade has a wider salary range to allow for more flexibility to reward staff who are consistently high performers. Jobs are graded using a tailor-made computer-aided job evaluation system, which has considerably reduced the administrative burden of detailed point-factor job evaluation in a rapidly changing organisation.

The salary management policy
The salary management policy is to have a corporate pay and grading structure which will:

❏ attract and retain staff with the skills and experience necessary to produce programmes of quality

❏ reward staff on the basis of achievement of objectives and performance in their jobs

❏ demonstrate to employees that their pay is being dealt with fairly and consistently

❏ deliver consistent decisions on salary

❏ enable an annual review of basic pay to take place at corporate level with the trade unions

❑ be capable of being monitored in order to ensure adherence to these principles and consistency and equity of application.

Salary structure

The maximum of each range is about 150 per cent above the minimum, but this is not described as a broadbanded structure. Progress through the range is on the basis of one or more of the following factors:

❑ growth in the job, particularly in the early years
❑ increased responsibility within the same grade
❑ assessment as a consistently high performer.

Salary adjustments can also be made:

❑ on completion of a pre-agreed training programme
❑ to ensure appropriate consistency of salaries in work groups
❑ to ensure equal pay for work of equal value
❑ to respond to market pressures.

Progression within a job

Newly appointed or promoted staff develop into a job as they acquire the skills and experience to be fully effective. Following appointment to a new job a member of staff will, subject to remaining in the same job throughout, reach at least 110 per cent of the salary range minimum for the grade within three years and reach at least 115 per cent of the salary range minimum after six years. Progression to these salary levels is subject to the individuals' ability to demonstrate that they have performed at a satisfactory level and achieved their objectives consistently throughout the time periods.

The time period within which each individual progresses to the 110 per cent and 115 per cent levels will vary by job and will depend on the individual's skill, experience and entry point into the salary range as well as subsequent performance. Some staff, because of previous experience or particular expertise, may be appointed beyond the salary points specified above.

Case study

BP AMOCO EXPLORATION

Background

The recently introduced broadbanded structure consists of seven bands: four of 70 per cent and three of 73 per cent. The pay levels are driven by market rates.

The structure was developed in the following stages:

- The levels were defined – these are associated with Hay points ranges which are wider than in the previous structure.
- Benchmark jobs were selected.
- By reference to the discipline, the benchmark jobs were allocated into a level.
- The benchmark level allocations were checked against Hay points.
- The allocations were checked by the unit business leader.
- A check was carried out across business units by 'network leaders' as an assurance that horizontal relativities were appropriate.

Outcomes

Descriptors have been produced for each level in terms of knowledge, skills and accountabilities. The following is an example of one of the eight sections of the description for level F.

> Requires highly advanced technical knowledge of own professional/ technical discipline. Incumbent in job is viewed as an expert in a specialist area. Requires extensive understanding of how to create business opportunities through application of knowledge. Works on technical or broad policy developmental/implementation projects, usually in lead capacity.

Pay progression bands are determined by managers within their budgets subject to monitoring by HR and peer review. There are no appraisal ratings. Individuals are informed of how well they have done in an appraisal discussion. This is linked back to performance discussions which have taken place throughout the year. Individuals know how they have been performing and there are therefore no surprises and no need for ratings.

Case study

BRISTOL MYERS SQUIBB

Background

Bristol Myers Squibb is an American-owned pharmaceutical company with 2,400 employees in the UK engaged in research, marketing and manufacturing. There are, in effect, six different businesses.

A decision to adopt a global broadbanded structure was made by headquarters in the USA. The aim was to ensure that people would be rewarded for their competence, skills and growth as well as for their performance. Another factor was to have a structure which would prevent people fighting for promotion.

The structure

The structure consists of eight bands. Each band is broadly 100 per cent from minimum to maximum but salary ranges are not used to manage pay. Rates of pay are fixed by market pricing for benchmark jobs.

Roles are allocated to bands by a fairly loose system of job evaluation based on three factors: internal scope (including impact, job size and accountability), complexity, and external operating environment. Essentially, however, the basis of allocation is that it 'feels right'.

Managing pay

Managers, who are 'treated as adults', propose pay increases taking into account four factors:

1   market rate data with which they are supplied
2   the employee's current rate of pay
3   the employee's performance
4   relevant internal comparisons.

Considerable importance is attached to qualities of leadership in assessing people and, therefore, to leadership development.

Pay is reviewed within a budget. An additional 0.5 to 1 per cent is available for market rate adjustments (relatively few). Managers are not aware of market rates for jobs because that would mean that they might become 'fixated about paying above or below the rate'.

The three approaches to deciding on performance-related increases adopted in different areas are:

1   increases based on ratings of performance in three categories –
    below, at, or above expectations
2   across-the-board increases plus eligibility for two more defined
    levels of increase
3   guidelines on the range of increase without any prescriptive
    levels.

Managers make the decisions and HR has a 'partnership' role. Help
and advice is given to managers, but their decisions are not vetoed.

Outcomes
The structure is flexible and fits the culture. Staff understand it and
it has helped to encourage people to move laterally within a band.

Case study

HALIFAX PLC

Background
Halifax plc employs about 25,000 people in its core retail banking
business. Since it de-mutualised it has transformed its business operations, structure and culture. The 'Halifax Way' describes the
company's mission as being to:

- delight the customer
- support each other
- do it superbly.

The strategic reward review – the results of which were implemented
in 1998 – played an important part in this process of transformation.

The strategic reward review
The aims of the strategic reward review were to:

- make the reward strategy much more business-focused, supporting the delivery of business objectives
- reinforce a performance culture throughout the organisation (a
  particular requirement of the chief executive, James Crosby) –
  the fundamental question was: 'How can pay support a performance culture?'
- ensure that the pay system supported a more flexible approach
  to running the business.

As set out in the booklet *A Fresh Approach to Reward*, the new approach was designed to:

- 'change the emphasis from measuring the job and its accountabilities to recognising the person and the contribution they make to the business
- reflect the way the organisation is changing by encouraging us to be more responsive and flexible to customers' needs
- improve reward for excellent performance by freeing up salary ranges'.

As Mike Braithwaite, remuneration research manager, said: 'Previously, pay systems followed the business; there is now a recognition that they ought to be central to business decisions.'

The new pay structure

The pay structure introduced in June 1998 is broadbanded. It replaced the previous grade structure of four clerical and nine management grades which was believed to be restrictive and inflexible. The changes were designed to improve recognition for people whose performance was judged to be very good.

To free up the structure, the existing grades were assimilated into five broad and overlapping pay bands: A, B, C, D and E. Each band contains jobs of a similar nature in the Network (branches), Head Office and the Regions. A number of target salaries are incorporated in each band. The old grade minima, mid-point and maxima no longer apply.

The bands contain between four and six target salaries. The top two target salaries are the 'headroom' salaries which are used only for staff who sustain a high level of performance which exceeds expectation. A minimum target salary is also defined which is 15 per cent below the target salary.

The range of target salaries in the bands is from 55 per cent to 75 per cent and there is an overlap between bands B and C, C and D and D and E corresponding to the two 'headroom' bands (an overlap of only one headroom band exists between bands A and B).

Placing jobs in bands

Within bands there are different target rates for jobs related to median market rates. Job evaluation (Hay) was used to allocate jobs to bands and to indicate where they should be placed in the band in terms of the target rate.

Progression within bands
As Shirley Marsh, Group remuneration and benefits manager, pointed out:

> We make people aware that their target salary is their ceiling in the present situation. But if over time they show that they are performing at a higher level, they can increase that ceiling to another target salary. So the band is designed in steps, rather than being unstructured.

Progression to the next target salary in bands B to E can take place when an individual has been at least three years at the same target salary and performance has exceeded expectations in two of these three years, including the last year. In band A, a move can be made when performance has exceeded expectations in two successive years. At higher target levels a different and more demanding set of objectives will be agreed. In effect, what an individual has to do to exceed expectations at one level is what has to be done to meet expectations at the next higher level. Progression stops when it is clear that someone has reached his or her level of competence and is unlikely to be capable of achieving the more demanding objectives at a higher level.

Performance-related pay
Staff who are below the target rate can expect to move to the rate within five years. The rate accelerates if performance exceeds expectations. When on the target rate they can qualify for a non-consolidated bonus if their performance exceeds expectations.

Promotion within a band
Staff can be promoted to a higher target salary range within a band if their current job changes and grows significantly – ie additional responsibilities and accountabilities are assumed on a permanent basis. They can also apply for and be promoted to a role with a higher target salary in the band.

Promotion to a new band
Promotion to a new band can take place if the job changes and grows significantly – ie additional responsibilities and accountabilities are assumed on a permanent basis. It can also, of course, happen when individuals apply for and are promoted to a role with a higher target salary in the next band.

Performance management
Objectives
The objectives of the performance management process are stated as being to:

- 'improve the way our business is managed by adopting a common approach to managing performance and personal development
- ensure everyone has an agreed set of challenging performance objectives
- provide a closer link between individual performance and reward
- encourage personal development to enhance each individual's skills'.

Process
The process is based on a balanced scorecard approach which is used for planning, managing and measuring performance. There are two strands to the process: performance planning ('about what we need to deliver') and personal development planning ('about developing the skills we need to help us to deliver, now and in the future'). The performance management cycle is illustrated below:

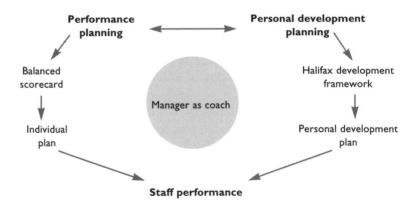

The annual appraisal
It is explained to staff that: 'The annual performance appraisal is the final review and assessment of your performance over the past year. However, because you and your manager will be having regular coaching sessions throughout the year, you should be aware of how your performance is viewed. There should be no surprises when it comes to annual appraisal.'

The levels of performance appraisal are: fulfilling expectations, exceeding expectations and not fulfilling expectations. The definitions of these categories as explained to staff are:

Fulfilling expectations
In order to fulfil the expectations agreed for your role, you and your manager will agree at your appraisal how you have:

❑ worked with others and developed yourself
❑ followed through processes and made improvements
❑ met the needs of internal/external customers
❑ achieved key financial and business results.

The expectations are stretching and demanding, and if you achieve them you will have done well and made a full and balanced contribution which has delivered the requirements of the business.

The majority of staff achieve what we expect of them and are currently assessed at this level – we expect this to continue in the future.

Exceeding expectations
People who exceed the expectations agreed for their role will be exceptional for two reasons:

❑ expectations of all of us are generally stretching and rise over time, so to have exceeded them denotes an approach which has added value beyond these normal high standards
❑ performance is assessed not only in the job but also compared to colleagues doing similar jobs, so a clearly differentiated contribution will have been made.

People who exceed expectations can therefore expect higher pay awards and faster salary progression.

Not fulfilling expectations
We hope that there will not be many people who do not fulfil expectations. Such people will be counselled and supported to improve their performance – but if, in the end, their contribution has not met the requirements of the business, they can expect to receive a smaller pay rise or no pay rise at all.

As stated in the booklet for staff: 'The key to performance

management is an effective partnership between you and your line manager.' Throughout the year your manager will work with you at regular coaching sessions to:

- agree the objectives and the standards of performance expected of you
- ensure that your performance and development objectives are stretching but achievable
- provide regular, balanced feedback on your performance
- coach, counsel and support you when required.

Lessons learnt

The main lessons learnt as spelled out by Mike Braithwaite and Shirley Marsh are that:

- You need to be certain of what you are paying for and what your principles are.
- It takes time – you cannot expect people to recognise overnight that the new driver is performance: they will hark back to the old system and put their own labels (ie grades) on the new one.
- The development of flexible systems requires the definition of more flexible and generic role profiles.
- It is essential to have a well-defined development project plan, starting from clearly stated aims as to what is to be achieved and why.
- If you don't communicate flexibility, you will not achieve flexibility.
- A good deal of time has to be devoted to educating people in the new processes.
- The amount of support managers need should not be underestimated.

Case study

THE RNLI: BRINGING PAY AND REWARD ARRANGEMENTS INTO THE TWENTY-FIRST CENTURY

Background

The Royal National Lifeboat Institution is one of the world's leading offshore rescue services. With the compelling mission 'to save lives at sea', it carries out many operations and saves thousands of lives each year. It manages to successfully combine 175 years of history and tradition with being at the leading edge of technology in boat design, fund-raising and rescue services. It is totally financed by charitable donations and legacies.

The bulk of the rescue staff on boats are actually volunteers, but the organisation employs nearly 1,000 full-time staff. Its headquarters are in Poole, Dorset, and the staff there are employed across a range of professional, engineering, boat-building, fund-raising and administrative activities.

The series of reward changes that have been undertaken in the last few years, including pay restructuring, demonstrate both the importance of such changes as means of reinforcing a much broader need for cultural change, and also the need to move at a manageable pace, which reflects both the existing organisation and the vision of where it is heading.

Reviewing job evaluation and pay arrangements

In many ways, the scale of reward changes now evident at the RNLI might surprise even the architects of those changes themselves. They began with the introduction of a new job evaluation scheme designed to support a move to simpler and more harmonised reward structures in 1997. Existing arrangements were a complex mix of different pay structures and systems for various staff groups, with many historical anomalies and allowances. The exercise took much longer than planned, but on completion all but the manual staff were moved into a common structure of 12 pay grades on the basis of their job evaluation scores.

However, in many ways the job evaluation exercise raised as many questions as it answered, and so a second phase of work began in late 1998 with a review of all pay, grading and allowance arrangements. The review included consultation with senior managers and staff groups, a review of external market trends, and in-depth analysis of current schemes. An internal advisory group reviewed the findings and recommended a series of changes as a result to the senior management and governing bodies of the organisation.

The study's findings, presented in mid-1999, showed major differences in perceptions and issues between, say, the IT function in Poole and the front-line staff around the coast. However, significant consistent points to emerge included:

❑ The RNLI was an organisation which, despite a relatively low staff turnover, was undergoing significant changes and in which staff generally felt that their efforts and effectiveness were not being adequately recognised and rewarded.

❑ Strong perceptions of inequalities and inconsistent pay arrangements, which the job evaluation exercise had brought into focus, also existed.

❑ There was an evident general lack of understanding of reward policies and, more broadly, of how the employment relationship in the organisation was shifting.

The external analysis highlighted the dilemmas confronting many of the major charities as they face business-style pressures to become more efficient and performance-oriented organisations. Thus the relatively high size of pay awards given at the RNLI compared to the UK market in general in recent years was becoming increasingly difficult to justify externally, and not fully appreciated by staff.

Staff received a general pay award, supported by service-based progression with quite significant incremental increases up relatively narrow pay scales: 20 per cent of staff were on their pay ceiling, and an existing ex gratia bonus scheme was largely used to recognise these 'capped' employees. A relatively archaic system of subsistence allowances and expenses, differentiated by grade, also operated and accounted for over 10 per cent of the total pay budget.

In summary, therefore, the reward systems suited a steady-state paternal organisation with a uniform, passive workforce, rather than the modern needs of a dispersed organisation with demanding service and efficiency goals. And despite generally competitive reward provisions, the impact of these on staff motivation and recognition was relatively slight.

The new reward policy

Supported by the introduction of a new director for the organisation, Andrew Freemantle, who regarded the previous NHS unit he led as 'the highest-paid and highest-performing' unit in the country, the RNLI's pay changes were detailed in late 1999 and implemented in April 2000. They were introduced as part of a clear, communicated strategy to staff, with the aims of:

❑ clearly setting out the goals of pay and reward practices

❑ recognising the contribution and development of staff

❑ providing greater flexibility to meet the changing needs of the organisation and its various parts

❑ improving the management of pay structures

❑ continuing at the same time to maintain competitive and equitable practices.

The main changes have included:

❑ all staff being moved into a new flatter pay structure of eight grades, in April 2000, with wider, market-related pay ranges

❑ in the lower grades staff retaining a general pay increase, but there is now the flexibility to reward high performers with an additional sum; in the higher grades pay increases are entirely merit-related, through the operation of an equity-shares-type scheme, which will operate from April 2001

❑ the new pay adjustment system's being supported by the introduction of a new performance development and review scheme, in which all managers and staff are being trained.

Other changes include:

❑ the replacement of the subsistence and allowances system with a much simpler and less differentiated system of a single disturbance allowance, and expenses paid on receipt

❑ targeting the bonus scheme on the recognition of specific and defined achievements and behaviours by staff throughout the year

❑ the harmonisation of working hours between staff and hourly paid employees.

A few remaining aspects of rewards – including the possibilities of introducing flexibility in benefits provision – has also been under review and consideration in 2000.

Learning points

As head of personnel Terry Clark (whose personnel team led the changes) explains, the project started out as a fairly limited review of the grade structure. 'We had considered reducing the number of grades at the time of the evaluation work,' he says, 'but it was generally agreed to be a step too far.'

However, once the 12-grade structure was analysed in detail, 'We realised there were a whole range of related issues, such as the incremental pay progression and grade-related differences in allowances [which were] driven by the militaristic-style of organisation of the past,' rather than the 'modern, efficient, merit-based organisation of the future'. The inconsistencies became so apparent that the early worries of some managers at the disruptive effect of pay reforms was soon forgotten amidst strong general senior management support for these changes.

Line management commitment is another point which Clark and his director emphasise to have contributed towards making the pay restructuring and other reward changes work. Considerable time was invested in consulting with their key managers at all stages in the process. Staff were also heavily involved in group discussions and through regular communications. Terry Clark credits them with having achieved the successful introduction of the new structure in April 2000 with virtually a 100-per-cent sign-up by staff to the new contracts.

5   MANAGING BROADBANDING

The processes and procedures used for managing a broad-banded pay structure are:

- using job evaluation
- allocating roles to bands
- positioning roles within bands
- progressing pay within bands
- achieving equity and consistency
- controlling costs.

Using job evaluation

Is job evaluation necessary?

Some proponents of broadbanding claim that it eliminates the need to use traditional analytical job evaluation schemes. Rightly or wrongly, these have become associated with rigidity, bureaucracy, numerous appeals, point-grabbing through creative job-description-writing and the facilitation of grade drift. Others do not disown job evaluation entirely but attach much less importance to it. A technology company executive told Brown (1996) that: 'We wanted the emphasis to be on personal development and performance rather than on point-scoring to achieve a promotion.'

Broadbanding cannot eliminate the need for procedures to value jobs which still have to be allocated into the right bands and into appropriate positions in those. And internal equity and equal value considerations must not be ignored. The

1999/2000 IPD survey established that job evaluation may still be necessary in a broadbanded structure, but what method is appropriate?

Analytical job evaluation

Analytical job evaluation may be used to define the boundaries of bands and to support decisions on allocating roles into bands. In the design stage, analytical job evaluation can help in making decisions on relativities within bands. It can be used to check that internal equity and equal pay considerations have been properly taken into account.

Thereafter, job evaluation may be held in reserve to assist in resolving equal pay issues and to provide some guidance on the positioning of new roles within bands. This is essentially a *support* role. In a broadbanded structure job evaluation is not generally used to make decisions on placing jobs or people within bands. This is simply because there are no grades in the traditional sense within bands, and if there are zones, they are not usually defined in terms of job evaluation points. While job evaluation points may be used to define band boundaries, job evaluation points scales are seldom attached to individual bands to determine relative positions within the band. Neither are they normally linked to zones within bands. If they were, the whole purpose of broadbanding would be defeated – it does not involve paying 'pounds for points'.

Analytical schemes are closely associated with conventional graded structures and extended hierarchies, and there is often constant pressure to use them to justify re-grading. This is one reason why their application can be both time-consuming and expensive, and why some organisations with broad bands either relegate analytical job evaluation to a supporting role or do without it altogether.

Broadbanding is essentially about providing the means to reward people for growth within their roles *and* for growing their roles. It offers rewards for continuous improvement and career development. It acknowledges that flexible organisations need flexible reward processes. Such organisations do not consist of job-holders locked into finite jobs whose only hope for the future is to be re-graded following a job evaluation exercise, or promoted into another finite job in a higher grade into which they will be locked until a further promotion opportunity, if any, occurs. If organisations are uncomfortable with this concept of broadbanding, then it is not for them.

However, it should be recognised that using an analytical job evaluation scheme, even in a supporting role, is a good way of meeting equal-pay-for-work-of-equal-value requirements. The nature of a point-factor scheme and the fact that staff are often involved in evaluations and that there is generally a formal appeals system means that the process feels fair, even if it is not as effective and scientific as some people may think.

Competence-related analytical job evaluation

If an analytical method of job evaluation is felt to be necessary, possibly in a supporting role, consideration can be given to making the language of the scheme (ie the factor plan) consistent with the language used in most broadbanded structures, where the focus is on competence development.

An analytical competence-related scheme will include headings in the factor plan which refer to the core or generic competences included in a competence framework. The levels at which the generic competences can be applied in roles are defined, and scores are allocated to each level. The competence-related factors may not be weighted. Individual role competence profiles are defined, and these are compared with the generic competence level definitions and scored in exactly the same way as in a conventional point-factor scheme.

Some organisations have developed hybrid schemes which include:

❑ traditional input factors such as knowledge and skills
❑ output factors referring to impact on end results
❑ competence-related factors covering competence areas such as interpersonal skills, flexibility, leadership and teamworking.

A case study at the end of Chapter 6 describes how this was done in the Portsmouth Housing Association, now the Southern Focus Trust.

Non-analytical forms of job evaluation

Broadbanding systems can avoid the use of analytical job evaluation altogether and rely on non-analytical methods such as market pricing or matching (job classification). A non-analytical competence-related approach can be adopted which matches roles to band definitions expressed in competency terms or overall comparisons between the competence profiles of the role to be evaluated and generic role competence profiles.

Analytical methods of placing roles into bands may not be necessary where there are a limited number of bands, each of which is clearly defined. For example, there is not likely to be much difficulty in allocating roles to bands in a four-banded structure covering, for example, managers, team leaders, professional/technical individual contributors and administrative/support individual contributors. In any case, if the pay span of the band is elastic enough to accommodate all the roles in the band and allow room for growth and market rate adjustments, banding decisions will not be so critical. In these circumstances it can be argued that it is unnecessary to use an analytical scheme to define band boundaries in terms of evaluation points.

It can also be argued that analytical job evaluation schemes are unnecessary in broad bands in which progression depends on competence and contribution rather than on acquiring extra job evaluation points. The essence of the broadbanding concept is that upgrading in the traditional sense does not occur within bands.

But it can be argued equally strongly that it is useful to have an analytical job evaluation scheme in reserve to be brought out when there is an issue concerning internal equity or when it is thought that an equal pay audit is necessary. And this is the approach adopted by such companies as Halifax plc, Nationwide Building Society and Glaxo Wellcome.

Examples of approaches to job evaluation

- ❏ *Bass Brewers* uses analytical job evaluation to define the grades and to determine job grading.
- ❏ *BP* does not use job evaluation for its top management grades. Senior managers are grouped into clusters based on broad assessments of comparability.

❑ *Citibank* uses band definitions into which jobs are slotted on the basis of whole-job comparisons.

❑ *Glaxo Wellcome* uses analytical job evaluation plus a common-sense review to check whether or not a grading feels right.

❑ *IBM* places jobs in the bands by the non-analytical process of internal benchmarking.

❑ *The Midland Bank* still regards analytical job evaluation as being necessary in its broadbanded structure, but on a job family basis.

❑ *Reckitt & Colman* uses a home-grown job evaluation system which is much more flexible than the traditional 'pay for points' approach but is still sufficiently robust to control costs.

❑ *Volkswagen* defines the band boundaries in terms of job evaluation points but does not use job evaluation for grading decisions within bands.

Allocating roles to bands

The 1999/2000 IPD survey found that the methods used by respondents to assign roles to bands were:

❑ traditional point-factor job evaluation	35 per cent
❑ job matching/slotting	25 per cent
❑ competency/skill level	17 per cent
❑ role level	14 per cent
❑ market pricing	9 per cent

Competency and role level approaches are a variation on job matching, and although market pricing is seldom used alone, it has a major influence on decisions concerning reference points in bands and the dimensions of pay ranges.

The job evaluation approach

Roles are traditionally graded in conventional pay structures through analytical job evaluation – points brackets are attached to each grade and individual roles are 'sized' and allocated into grades by comparing scores with the points brackets attached to them. The design of the structure therefore involves evaluating a selection of benchmark jobs and deciding how the rank order produced should be divided into bands, exactly as in a conventional grade structure design process.

The difference when developing a broadbanded structure is that an *a priori* decision may have been made on the number of bands and how they should be described and defined. In these circumstances, job evaluation is simply used to determine points dimensions for the bands as a guide to where roles should be allocated. This is the approach adopted by Halifax plc (see the case study in Chapter 4) although many organisations such as Zurich Financial Services (see the case study in Chapter 6) and the Children's Society use a matching or slotting process. The result is that job evaluation is much simpler and less time-consuming because detailed measurement is not required. The approach is being increasingly adopted, which means that although the original concept of broadbanding as not needing any form of job evaluation has proved not to be the case, at least it correctly hypothesised that job evaluation would no longer dominate grading decisions.

The matching (job classification) approach

At the design stage, matching means allocating benchmark roles to bands by comparing their characteristics as expressed in a role definition with the previously prepared band definitions that define the role level and may be expressed in skill or competency terms. 'Matching' is becoming the preferred term as an alternative to 'job slotting' because the latter implies a mechanical approach, whereas matching suggests that more care is taken to ensure that the characteristics of jobs are compared systematically.

Matching is in essence the non-analytical job evaluation technique of job classification, but it is easier to make matching decisions if broad generic definitions exist for a small number of bands than to make the decisions based on a multigraded structure. The band definitions described in accountability terms used by a large not-for-profit organisation are shown in Table 13 (opposite) and a generic role definition used to assist the matching process is shown in Table 14 (on page 94).

Table 13
BROAD BAND DEFINITIONS IN A NOT-FOR-PROFIT ORGANISATION

Band	General level	Competences and work/role requirements
1	Administrators and support workers	• Provide basic and administrative support services • The work is largely prescribed, freedom to act fairly limited • Role requirements are clearly defined.
2	Senior administrators and support workers	• Provide fairly complex administrative and support services • The work is generally standardised • Freedom to decide on methods and priorities is limited.
3	Team leaders and specialists	• Lead a small team of administrators or support workers, or provide specialist/basic professional services • There is some diversity in role requirements • Activities are within specified policy and procedural guidelines.
4	First-line managers and senior specialists	• Manage certain operations within function, or provide professional services in a key area, or lead a small team of specialists • The work is diverse • Activities are within broad policy guidelines.
5	Middle managers	• Manage a function or department within an operational or technical area, or be the main provider of professional advice and services in a key aspect of the organisation's activities • The work is highly diverse • Activities are within broad policy frameworks.
6	Senior managers	• Act as head of a major function or department, making a major and strategic impact on the performance of the organisation • The work is complex and involves making a wide range of highly diverse decisions • A considerable amount of independent activity is required within the framework of organisational strategies and plans, and subject only to general guidance.

When benchmark roles have been placed in bands, more precision can be obtained by comparing and matching individual role definitions (which could include their competence profiles) with generic or individual definitions for the benchmark roles, especially when these include a competence profile.

Table 14
A GENERIC ROLE DEFINITION IN A NOT-FOR-PROFIT ORGANISATION

Generic role definition: Specialist level 3	
Overall purpose of role	To provide effective and efficient services to internal customers in a major area of the organisation's activities
Key result areas	1 Provide high-quality practical and relevant advice and services on matters relating to area of responsibility 2 Keep closely in touch with internal customers to ascertain their needs 3 Innovate new practices and develop new or improved procedures to meet needs 4 Organise pilot tests of new procedures 5 Help internal customers to implement and manage new practices/procedures 6 Keep in touch with new developments through research, benchmarking and reading 7 Set up and manage efficient work systems within function 8 Provide reports and information as required by internal customers 9 Control expenditure within budgets
Competency requirements	
Manage performance	Determine and work to demanding goals Take initiative to solve problems Work with only general supervision
Manage self	Generate practical solutions Confidently apply knowledge and skills
Manage others	Take a leadership role when appropriate, giving direction and support Lead task forces and project teams as required
Manage relationships	Build good relationships with colleagues and internal customers Exert influence on internal customers Develop effective networks with internal customers
Manage communications	Communicate clearly and persuasively orally or in writing to internal customers
Manage customer service	Contribute to the development and maintenance of high standards in customer service
Manage continuous development	Set targets for improvement Develop and manage programmes for implementing change Contribute to the development of quality assurance and control processes and ensure that they are implemented
Manage resources	Contribute to the setting of budgets Manage budgets and allocate resources within them Manage projects

Positioning roles within bands

Roles may be positioned within bands on the basis of market pricing (external value), job evaluation (internal value), or both.

Job evaluation

What Gilbert and Abosch (1996) call the 'internal value-based model' may focus on the measurement of internal relativities through job evaluation. The aim is to be able to demonstrate that internal equity has been achieved. Account is also taken of the need to be externally competitive, but internal equity considerations are paramount. Use can be made of an analytical job evaluation process – a conventional point-factor scheme, a 'proprietary brand' or, as in organisations such as Thomas Cook and the Southern Focus Trust, a role evaluation system based on core competences. The latter approach ties in the positioning process with the developmental aspect of broadbanding where this is based on competence assessment.

Relative internal values may, however, be measured much more broadly by reference to competence level assessments and/or by making 'whole role' comparisons between roles or clusters of roles placed in a band described generically or individually. This process is sometimes called matching or internal benchmarking. A non-analytical system, as used by BP Amoco and Citibank, depends on a very careful review of positioning in the bands by reference to assessments of the individual worth of people in those bands. It is a people- rather than a job-centred approach and is therefore in accord with what some commentators would regard as an essential feature of broadbanding.

However, an issue with the use of job evaluation to define positions within bands is that it really makes it difficult to explain to staff the difference between the broadbanded structure and a traditional multigraded structure.

Market pricing

Market pricing or, as Gilbert and Abosch (1996) describe it, the 'external value-based pay delivery model', relies on market rate data to determine benchmark role values. The data can be collected for individual roles, for clusters of related roles or for job families. This approach depends on the availability of reliable market rate data for the key benchmark roles. Like all job evaluation market pricing techniques, it assumes that the relativities in the external labour market are appropriate. It takes no account of internal labour market relativities. Neither does it provide the analytical job evaluation process required to demonstrate that work of equal value is being paid equally. Reliance on market pricing will not necessarily result in inequalities but it might be difficult to prove that equality exists. The RAC Motoring Services and Zurich Financial Services structures are examples of ones driven by market relativities.

Where market rate information is not available for roles, they may be slotted into the pay range for the band by means of whole-role comparisons (internal benchmarking). Alternatively, the rate is fixed by interpolation between two existing rates by comparing job evaluation scores. Thus, if the market rates for jobs A and B were £30,000 and £40,000 respectively, and their evaluation scores were 400 and 450, the market rate for a job with a score of 425 would be £35,000.

External and internal values

This method takes into account both external and internal value considerations. It acknowledges that concentrating entirely on market rate data may produce results which are difficult to explain or justify to employees and could result in internal inequities. It also recognises that internal pay levels and relativities are affected by both external market and internal considerations. It can be argued that it is unrealistic to pretend that internal factors are the only influence on relativities – external relativities will also make an impact. However, the extent of that impact and the degree to which the organisation will emphasise internal or external factors will depend on how much it relies on the external labour market and the scope that the market offers valued employees to move elsewhere (ie attraction and retention factors). Another factor which has to be taken into account is that the market worth of individual employees is strongly influenced by the level of competence they have attained. This is a good reason for paying attention to competence criteria in grading, assessing and rewarding employees.

The external/internal value approach selects a representative sample of 'benchmark' roles for which both external and internal comparisons can be made. Published and private or special market rate surveys generate the external data, and this should be updated regularly to ensure that rates remain competitive. Concurrently, the benchmark roles may be evaluated using a point-factor scheme, possibly incorporating competence-related factors. Alternatively a non-analytical method of job evaluation may be used.

The external/internal value method using market rate surveys and analytical job evaluation may be compared with the conventional technique for designing graded structures as described by Armstrong and Murlis (1998). But this method involves analysing the distribution of points scores against market rate data *before* deciding on the grade structure. In contrast, the usual method for developing broadbanded structures is to decide on the design of the band structure first and then to determine the relativities within that structure.

Matching within bands

The process of matching as described earlier in relation to allocating jobs to bands can also be used to determine where jobs should be placed *within* bands.

Progressing pay within bands

General considerations

Perhaps the most important feature of broadbanding is its emphasis on lateral and in-job progression rather than vertical career growth. Opportunities for career and therefore pay progression are more likely to take place by moving horizontally through a band than by climbing a promotion ladder. As Gilbert and Abosch (1996) point out: 'The unstructured nature of broadbanding, especially career bands, helps employees understand that their economic growth is only limited by their ability to continually increase their impact on the organisation.' The emphasis in broadbanded structures is on rewarding people for value-adding behaviour, and this can be achieved through lateral growth rather than by moving up a hierarchy.

In contrast, traditional graded structures were designed to fit an extended hierarchy in which it was usual to have rigid or prescribed methods such as increments or a pay matrix for progressing pay through the relatively narrow grades. Pay spines, of course, operate by relating pay progression to length of service.

A much more flexible approach can be adopted in the wider and less tightly structured ranges typical of fully broadbanded systems. Progression is based on judgements about an individual's performance, competence, contribution and ability to continue developing laterally. This reflects the fact that in today's flexible organisations the set of responsibilities assumed to form a job as closely defined in the traditional approach may no longer be stable. Roles become more dynamic as employees – especially the increasing proportion of knowledge workers – have greater scope to influence the content of their jobs. Progression is people-oriented rather than job-oriented.

However, a challenge facing many organisations moving into broad bands has been that with severe pressure on pay cost increases in many sectors, and with historically low levels of price and wage inflation, the general rate of pay progression and pay increases in organisations has declined. Particularly in the public sector, people have therefore moved into broad bands yet do not have any realistic opportunity to progress significantly up the band. In one government department we calculated that it would take a high-performing assistant psychologist over 40 years to progress from the minimum to the maximum of his or her scale! This has encouraged the use of structured and segregated approaches such as zones and segments.

But there is still the issue of how different such methods are from those used in conventional narrow graded structures. As we explained in Chapter 4, the difference is that movement between zones and segments in a broad band are managed more flexibly. In a zoned band, movement to a higher zone takes place when it is evident that the role an individual is carrying out matches the role carried out by people in the higher zone. It is not dependent on the evaluation score of the job, and re-evaluations are not required unless matching is difficult or there are equal pay considerations. Zones are not usually defined as a hierarchy within a band. However, this feature of broadbanding can be difficult to explain, which reinforces the need to communicate the purpose and methodology of broad bands with great care.

Criteria for progression

The four criteria that can be used as the basis for pay progression decisions are:

- performance only
- competence only
- performance and competence (contribution)
- service.

A full description of the first three approaches is contained in Brown and Armstrong (1999). Most organisations responding to the 1999/2000 IPD survey use performance only; a few use competence; and a smallish proportion (8 per cent) use contribution. But the number adopting the latter criterion is growing, as our 1999/2000 research showed.

Performance criteria

This familiar and much criticised approach involves simply assessing performance in achieving objectives. Targets and standards are agreed and the results attained are assessed and, frequently, rated. The ratings are converted into a percentage increase and the payment may be consolidated into the base salary. However, many businesses are now applying performance-related pay as variable pay or pay-at-risk by making lump-sum bonus payments rather than consolidating increases. In such cases there is no progression along the band on the basis of performance alone. In the Inland Revenue, progression through the bands takes place on the basis of annual performance-based pay awards delivered through a pay matrix for each band.

If this approach is used, it is essential to have effective performance processes in place and to involve staff in its development. Effective communications and training are also vital.

Competence criteria

Competence is not frequently used as the sole criterion except in heavily knowledge- and research-based activities. Where it is used, progression within a band may be related to competence development, although the focus is always on the output aspects of competence – ie the use of competence to deliver or exceed the required standards of performance. It is necessary to emphasise that progression within a band is not simply based on the acquisition of skills and competence or qualifications. Instead, it should be linked to their effective use. At Volkswagen, the principle underlying their whole competence-based process is that 'people are paid for what they can influence'. And Glaxo Wellcome state: 'Movement along a salary band is based on the development and consistent application of the competencies required within the role which the individual is performing. Movements will be based on the demonstration of competences rather than as a result of time in the grade.'

Competence-related payments are usually consolidated into base pay, the implied assumption being that the achievement of a certain level of competence predicts that performance will be at least maintained at the level. (It is an assumption that may, in the fullness of time, turn out not necessarily to be justified.)

Contribution criteria

Organisations are increasingly using contribution as a criterion, which means assessing both performance and competence – outputs and inputs. The assumption made is that progression should be related not only to what people do but also to how they do it.

Service

Service-related incremental systems persist in some public sector and voluntary organisations. This approach does not really fit the broadbanding philosophy of progressing people for what they contribute and how they make their contribution. Organisations may, however, retain fixed increments in zones or in the lower portions of the band in a broadbanded structure as an interim measure while they develop the performance management processes required for the successful operation of any form of performance, competence or contribution pay.

Methods of managing pay progression

There are many methods of progressing pay in broadbanded structures. Pay progression can be totally unstructured where bands have no form of framework such as reference points, zones or segments as described in Chapter 4. Where such a framework does exist, pay progression can be semi-structured. Fully structured pay progression related to incremental scales is seldom found in broadbanded structures.

Unstructured pay progression

Unstructured pay progression takes place where there are no mandatory limits or guidelines on how far or how fast individuals may progress within a band. Conceptually, people can progress at any speed through the band and to any point within the limits of the band (if these are defined), although a move in the direction of structuring may be achieved by providing guidelines on normal progression paths. For example, in Bass Brewers there are no zones in the bands but a pay policy line is used as a guide to the rate for a job. Formal job evaluation will not be used in an unstructured band to locate roles within it.

Decisions on where individuals are placed in the band and the rate at which they move through it will, however, be based on the following considerations:

❑ their market worth – ie the market rate of pay for people at broadly the same level of pay as influenced by supply and demand factors

❑ the level of competence they have achieved in their own role in comparison with the competence levels of other people in similar generic roles

❑ their contribution or delivered performance in their role, again in comparison with other people in similar roles.

Unstructured pay progression processes may allow line managers a considerable degree of freedom within their budgets to determine rates of pay and pay increases for their staff. They will act in accordance with assessments of the market worth, contribution and competence of individual role-holders and in relation to any increases in the latter's range or level of responsibility. They will also be expected to take into account relativities with other people in similar roles.

However, while all the organisations covered by the IPD research emphasised that their policy was to devolve greater responsibility for pay decisions to line managers, they also recognised that the HR function must provide managers with the information required to make such decisions. This includes data on the distribution of pay amongst existing role-holders in the department and on market rates, together with guidelines on how competence levels and performance should be assessed. Line managers need to be encouraged to consider carefully pay relativities between members of their staff occupying similar roles before making proposals on individual rates of pay or increases. They may be asked to explain or defend the rationale for their pay proposals to the HR department and/or to their peers.

Information for managers on the pay of their staff may include details of actual salaries, where people are placed in the band, and data on market rates. The information can be presented graphically, as in Figure 9 (opposite) in which the actual pay of clusters of people in similar roles is charted according to their assessed levels of competence and contribution. A policy progression line is incorporated in this example but it could be for guidance only. Market rate data is also shown.

Managers assess the level of competence or contribution of individuals – but may not rate them formally – and then compare their rates of pay with the pay progression guideline, the rates paid to other people in similar roles, and market rates. By reference to this information they then make an assessment of the total rate of pay that is ideally appropriate for the individual. This 'holistic' approach is adopted by BP Amoco Exploration. The initial proposals may, however, have to be modified to ensure that the pay review is kept within the budget. Spreadsheets can be used as at Bass Brewers and Zurich Financial Services to model alternative awards and, after a series of 'what ifs', achieve the optimum distribution of the budget to individuals, and therefore the increase in pay that should be awarded to them.

Figure 9
DISTRIBUTION OF PAY IN AN UNSTRUCTURED BAND

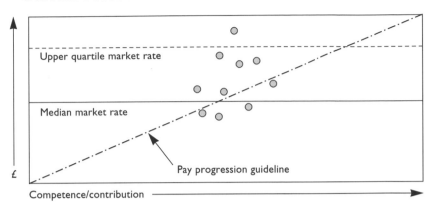

This approach can work well in spite of the lack of structure, but only if:

❏ good market rate data are available

❏ managers are capable, well-briefed and trained

❏ assistance to managers in the form of computer modelling is made available, with guidance on its use as necessary, provided by HR

❏ departmental managers discuss with one another their proposals

❏ the HR department provides good information on pay distributions and market rates together with hands-on guidance, and also monitors the whole process

❏ there is strict budgetary control, not just for pay reviews but for the total payroll expenditure of individual budget centre managers

❏ staff understand and accept the system and fully trust their managers to apply their considerable discretion fairly and consistently – which is perhaps the greatest barrier to this approach.

Semi-structured pay progression

Semi-structured progression related to increases in competence, performance or contribution can take place within zones or within and between segments. It can also take place when the role carried out by a role-holder expands (or the role-holder expands the role), but there is no justification for moving the role-holder to a superior reference point or zone – ie there has been a progressive expansion of what the role-holder contributes rather than a 'step leap' to a higher level. The rates of pay of individuals could progress beyond the upper limit of their zone if they show that they are capable of extending their contribution by enlarging their role and taking on new responsibilities, which may be deliberately planned as part of a career development process. Individuals would be eligible for such increases even when they had not moved to an entirely new role for which the reference point or target rate in the band is higher than that for their present role. This could be described as a personal reference point. They could also be eligible for what may be termed a career development pay increase if they assumed responsibilities normally carried out in roles where the reference point rate is higher. The main approaches to managing semi-structured pay progression are described below, and the criteria that can be used are considered.

Progression in a zoned band

A zone incorporates a range for a role or a cluster of roles through which the pay is progressed. There could, for example, be scope for progression from 90 per cent to 110 per cent of the reference point. Because there is more scope to move flexibly to higher reference points, the span of the pay ranges in zones is often fairly small. A band with a number of zones placed in it, each with different reference points and its own range was illustrated in Figure 3 (Chapter 4).

There are a number of methods of progressing pay in zones. The following examples are drawn from voluntary sector organisations.

1   The zone extends 10 per cent on each side of the reference point, and progression through the zone is based on assessed contribution (no ratings).
2   The pay range in the zone is 10 per cent and staff progress through that range on the basis of assessments of their competence, but their progress can be barred if they do not

prove themselves to be highly competent. The top of the zone is the 'target rate', which represents the rate of pay for a highly competent role-holder and is set between the median and upper quartile market rates. If and when the target rate has been reached, individuals are eligible for bonuses for exceptional contributions.

3   The pay range below the reference point is 10 per cent, and the criterion for progressing through this range is competence. Above the reference point, staff are eligible for a bonus for exceptional contributions. If they are assessed as making an exceptional contribution for two successive years, the second year's bonus is assimilated into the base rate. The cycle then begins again – ie the bonus is only consolidated if contribution is exceptional for two successive years. The base rate can increase through consolidation up to 10 per cent above the reference point. This is known as the exceptional maximum rate (EMR).

Progression in a segmented band

Progression in a segmented band as described in Chapter 4 is determined on the basis of assessments of performance or contribution. This is the approach adopted by Halifax plc (see the case study at the end of Chapter 4).

Alternatively, the segments may be defined as competence levels, and what is in effect a process of accreditation has to be undergone before progressing to a higher segment. This is the method used at Volkswagen UK in its broadbanded job family structure.

Movement to new roles within bands

In a banded structure without zones, individuals who move to a new role within their band can be placed at a point in the band which corresponds broadly with their contribution/competence levels in relation to other people carrying out a similar role within a job family. This is a matter of judgement. Where zones exist, individuals would be positioned in the zone for their new role at a point which broadly corresponds with their level of competence.

Movement to new roles in higher bands

Individuals who are promoted to a role in a higher band can also be paid on the basis of their level of contribution or competence in relation to the zone for the new role, if there is such a zone, or, in unstructured bands, by exercising judgement. In the latter case, positioning in the new band would be determined by reference to where people carrying out similar roles are placed in that band. The decision to move someone to a higher band could be made simply by a process of internal benchmarking, but if band boundaries are defined in terms of job evaluation points, the job evaluation scheme may be used to check on decisions in borderline cases or where there are equity considerations.

These moves – the equivalent of promotion in traditional grade structures – are typically accompanied by significant pay increases. This is because the pay and responsibility jumps between bands are usually larger than in narrow-graded structures. The actual size of the increases can be left to managers, or minimum or guideline increases can be set or recommended.

Achieving equity and consistency

Achieving equity and consistency is an important concern when designing a broadbanded structure, but the broadbanding concept incorporates fundamental beliefs about the need to:

❑ devolve responsibility for pay decisions to line managers
❑ avoid or at least minimise the use of traditional bureaucratic or rigid job evaluation systems.

However, the implementation of processes in line with these beliefs creates the possibility of inequities in pay delivery. In particular it may be difficult to ensure that equal-pay-for-work-of-equal-value requirements are met unless special steps are taken to ensure that, as far as possible, consistent and equitable pay decisions are made.

To avoid these problems the following steps are desirable:

❑ *Train* managers on the principles governing the system and their role in operating it. The training should cover such aspects as defining and assessing competence, making use of market rate data, conducting pay reviews, and taking steps to ensure consistency and fairness.

❑ *Provide guidance on* the size and distribution of pay increases, on relating pay increases to competence, performance and career development, on dealing with anomalies (staff who are paid considerably more or less than the target rate for their role or the rates paid to equally competent colleagues), on the circumstances in which pay can advance beyond the upper limits of a zone, and on fixing rates of pay when appointing staff to roles.

❑ *Monitor* pay increase proposals to ensure that the recommended awards are sensible and fair. The distribution of awards will have to be studied with care to avoid anomalies. Managers may be required to justify extra-high increases and explain why any staff in similar roles are paid considerably more or less than others. Line managers who propose much the same increase to all their staff might be asked to explain why. (Such a 'central tendency' in pay increase proposals is a fairly common phenomenon: some managers lack the confidence or courage to deviate much from the norm.) Monitoring is always necessary, but it should be carried out judiciously. Line managers will not exercise their devolved powers effectively unless they are given a reasonable degree of freedom to make pay decisions within their budgets. It will be necessary to monitor managers' pay decisions quite closely when broadbanding is introduced, but it should be progressively relaxed, except for newly appointed managers and those who continue to need close guidance (in the latter case their competence as managers should be questioned).

❑ *Moderate* decisions – line managers can moderate each other's decisions by meeting to exchange information on their proposed pay increases and the distribution of pay amongst their staff. They can be challenged by their peers to justify anomalies and exceptional rates of pay or proposed increases. This means that their decisions are monitored by their colleagues, which reinforces the process of devolving pay decisions to line managers.

❑ *Evaluate* jobs – use job evaluation as required to check on anomalies.

❑ *Audit* periodically – carry out periodical audits to ensure that inequities are identified and dealt with, especially those which indicate that work of equal value and people with similar levels of competence in their roles are not being paid equally. An analytical job evaluation scheme could be used for this purpose.

One pharmaceutical company trained a number of line managers to act as coaches to their colleagues to help build quality into the pay management process. Another company ran 'simulation' workshops with managers in advance of implementing broadbanding to help develop the effective use of their new responsibilities for pay management.

Controlling costs

Broadbanding relaxes or even removes clearly defined and absolute limits for pay progression. The scope for increases may be increased from, say, 40 per cent above the minimum of the grade to 100 per cent or more. There may even be no upper limits to the band. The tendency in traditional pay structures has been for most staff to progress inexorably to the top of their grade. What is to stop this happening, at great expense, in a much broader band?

The starting point for the prevention of 'band drift' when broadbanding replaces a conventional graded structure is to make it absolutely clear to all concerned from the word go that no one should expect to move to the upper reaches or top of a band unless they have earned it through increased competence, career development, the assumption of greater responsibilities and the delivery of higher levels of contribution and added value. It should not be too difficult to convince people that their pay spans have not magically increased from, say, 30 per cent to 100 per cent. But it would also be necessary to emphasise that they should not expect to move inevitably to the upper limit of their zone. Such moves have to be earned.

The experience of the UK companies which have introduced broadbanding, as established by the IPD and Towers Perrin research, is that it can be cost-neutral. (Surprisingly few report cost escalation.) But this will only take place if the guidelines and monitoring processes referred to above are implemented thoroughly, and – importantly – as long as a strict budgetary control is exercised over pay reviews and, possibly, total payroll costs. American experience is similar.

Pay review budgets

Pay review budgets for managers set out the overall increase in their payroll that they are allowed to recommend for their departments to cover the cost of competence- or contribution-related awards. This is the basic control mechanism, and managers must be required to keep strictly within their budgets.

In Bass Brewers control is exercised mainly through the pay review budget, but managers are also expected to use their judgement in controlling progression by reference to a pay policy line and the rates of pay for people carrying out similar jobs in their departments.

Review budgets restrict the scope for managers to make excessive awards leading to unjustifiable drift up the band's pay scale. But by themselves they will not prevent drift. Additional control is required by careful monitoring of the distribution of pay in bands to ensure that anomalies and drift do not occur. Peer reviews or moderating processes can be used which enable out-of-line payments to be identified. Such reviews should specifically check that the levels of pay for people in similar roles are consistent with the levels of competence and contribution demonstrated by them.

Total payroll budgeting

Pay review budgets do not control total payroll costs within departments – these are, of course, dependent on the number of people employed in different roles and their rates of pay. Payroll costs vary as a result of changes in those numbers and increases in pay arising from general and individual pay reviews, the amount of pay offered to new, promoted or transferred staff (which, if they replace existing staff, could be higher or lower than the rates paid to those replaced), and the extra pay earned by staff on promotion or upgrading.

Pay review budgets do not control the payroll costs arising from new appointments, transfers and promotion. Full control can therefore be achieved only through total payroll budgeting.

A total payroll budget is based on present payroll costs adjusted for forecast changes in the number and mix of those employed in the budget centre and the forecast cost of general and individual pay increases. When budget centre managers are held accountable for their total payroll costs, they have to justify the numbers and types of staff they employ and any increases to payroll costs they believe are required to cover pay reviews, promotions and additional costs arising from recruitment or transfers.

Preparing a budget, managers are issued with guidelines on what they should allow for general and individual pay review increases, and they will be expected to keep within these guidelines when calculating the budget and conducting their pay review. If the financial performance of the organisation means that more money can be made available to fund competence- or performance-related increases, then these budget guidelines may state the extent to which extra pay costs arising from such increases can be included in the budget.

Submitting their payroll budget proposals, budget centre managers can make out a cost for an increase in their budget above the guidelines to cover anticipated extra staff, promotions or increases in responsibility (role enlargements). But they would have to justify these increases in added-value terms – in other words, they would have to prove that the income generated by these additions will exceed the cost of them. Increases must be self-financing. Conversely, if they are able to plan the maintenance or increase of present activity levels and outputs by reducing staff numbers, they can make out a cost for using the extra cash thus released to fund competence-related, performance-related or career development increases. These can be used to reward staff for the additional contributions they are expected to make.

This approach means that some budget centre managers might have more cash than others to reward their staff – which could result in inequities unless the awards are fully justified. Such proposals therefore need to be subjected to rigorous assessment. Subsequent rewards also need to be monitored carefully. Payroll budgets can be flexed during the year in response to changes in activity levels or new projects. Many companies have interim re-forecasts once or twice a year which require managers to review their original budget in the light of experience to date and amend it as necessary.

Control is exercised over budget expenditure by regular reports analysing variances which budget managers may be required to explain and deal with.

This type of budgeting procedure can enable effective control to be maintained over payroll costs and restrain managers in a relatively unstructured pay system from overpaying staff. But full control still requires monitoring and moderating processes.

Case study

YORKSHIRE BUILDING SOCIETY

Background

Yorkshire Building Society (YBS) is one of the most successful building societies, with a 135-year history and a strong future commitment to its mutual status. It employs approximately 1,800 staff, 800 of them based at its head office in Bradford.

Despite its record of success, with a doubling of net lending to £10 billion during the 1990s, a series of cultural, HR and reward changes have been instigated since 1996, primarily in response to the fundamental changes that have affected the financial services sector:

❑ market consolidation and restructuring
❑ the use of new technology
❑ shifts in consumer demands.

As John Davies, general manager HR and Facilities, who was recruited in 1996, puts it: 'The Society has been very successful with a very tightly-run command and control culture from the top. But in this rapidly changing environment the senior management recognised the emphasis had to shift radically, to free up the organisation and to more fully involve and develop staff, so everyone could maximise their contribution to our success.'

Existing pay and grading systems

The review of pay systems began in 1997. The demand for change stemmed from both dissatisfaction with the existing inflexible and hierarchical arrangements and from a desire to use reward methods more effectively to reinforce the business agenda, and to better manage the career and reward expectations of staff. Existing systems consisted of:

❑ an archaic 10-year-old job evaluation system, with detailed job descriptions and lengthy evaluation committee meetings, lacking any relation to external market worth and with a low credibility with line managers and staff

❑ a 12-grade pay structure, with a strong focus on vertical promotion rather than lateral and personal development, and – despite a lack of clarity on what skills were needed for jobs in a particular grade – a highly visible and differentiated structuring of grade-related status-based benefits; there was significant pressure to get jobs into Grade 2, for example, which was the lowest grade eligible for company cars

❑ a separate pay structure for IT staff, which was felt to be divisive in the organisation

❑ a highly quantitative points-scoring appraisal system which made only passing reference to personal development, and allowed very limited variability in resulting pay increases; even promotion-based increases were capped at 7.5 per cent of current pay.

The new infrastructure

The objectives in making changes to these pay arrangements, therefore, were to create greater flexibility to reward personal contribution and development without creating unnecessary complexity and bureaucracy.

The starting point was not the pay structure but the requirements and competencies for effective working and success in the organisation. A competency framework consisting of 11 core skills, each defined at four levels and described with behavioural statements, was developed in early 1997, involving widespread consultation with staff. Later in that year, a larger team of personnel staff and employees from each of the major functions developed brief profiles for each distinct role in the Society. As well as the competency requirements, the profiles list the major accountabilities and relevant performance standards.

Next, the performance management system was reformed and simplified, with the 'points out of 100' scoring replaced by a simple three-fold rating scheme. Performance is now assessed against individual objectives, with a link back to the Society's strategic objectives. However, a key emphasis in the process is now on the development of core skills up to the required levels.

On the basis of this new HR infrastructure, the 12-grade pay structure has now been removed and replaced with a new framework of four role levels. This was implemented in July 1998. To provide maximum flexibility there are no formal salary limits on each of the role types, but indicative pay levels are set using a range of external surveys. All staff were transferred across into the new structure at their existing salary levels, so no extra costs were incurred in the change.

Individual pay levels and pay adjustments are now determined locally, on a flexible basis, within a budget agreed following negotiations with the Society's staff association. Pay decisions take account of a range of factors, including personal growth and development, individual potential and contribution, and current pay compared to the market.

A gainsharing scheme also now operates to further reinforce the links between pay and the performance of the society against its key goals.

Outcomes and learning points
An immediate benefit of the new structure has been the ability to recognise and reward the skills of technical and professional staff without having to give them, or pretend to give them, traditional management responsibilities. More broadly, the greater focus on development and required skills has helped promote a doubling in the proportion of vacancies filled by internal staff, and in moves between different functions.

According to John Davies, the whole pay change process itself was used to demonstrate and support the high communications and involvement culture which the Society needed to develop. More than 400 employees were involved at various stages in the process, and staff groups helped to develop the launch communications material. This he believes has paid off, in terms of the general level of acceptance and support for what could potentially have been a highly sensitive and controversial initiative. Approximately 40 appeals against placements in the new structure of role levels were made on implementation in 1998, and in July 1999 there were just eight appeals against individual pay decisions. As Davies puts it, staff were generally realistic, understood the competitive pressures in the sector, and 'knew there was no pot of gold'.

The Society's chief executive was also visibly involved, and regarded the changes as making a key contribution to his objective 'to really liberate the Society'. But according to Davies, middle managers have been the linchpin in making the changes really work in practice, and in actually using the freedom which the more flexible pay arrangements allow.

A final learning point which the Society draws from its experiences is of the need to adopt a pragmatic approach, recognising that perfect solutions can never be delivered and that support processes need time to develop, but maintaining a sufficient pace and momentum of change so as to capitalise and build on early success.

6 INTRODUCING BROADBANDED PAY STRUCTURES

Now that we have some understanding of how broadbanding works, and how it can be made to work, it is time to see how to set about introducing the system. The decision to introduce any new pay structure, however, should be made on the basis of an analysis of the organisation's structure, culture and present pay arrangements and a diagnostic review as suggested in Chapter 2. Should it be decided that a new structure is required, the choice can then be made between the alternatives. If, on balance, broadbanding is preferred, it is then necessary to plan and implement a design and development programme. As this unfolds, the original plan may have to be modified in the light of further analysis of the pros and cons of broadbanding and the readiness of the organisation to introduce it. For example, it may emerge that a job family structure or a mixed broadbanding/job family model is more appropriate.

Broadbanding requires immense care when being introduced in order to ensure that it will work. It is not just about deciding that a 12-grade structure should be replaced with four bands. It is not an easy option, a quick fix. Methods of pay management in broadbanded structures differ substantially from those used in conventional structures. It is important not only to get the basic design right but also to ensure that the various processes required to manage it are developed systematically.

The lessons learnt by a major food and drinks firm following the development of broad bands were:

❑ get line managers involved at an early stage
❑ get visible commitment from the top
❑ have a full-time or near full-time project manager from the start
❑ isolate emotive areas – eg cars – so that they don't disrupt the whole change process
❑ achieve an appropriate balance in making changes between the over-simple and the over-complex and between market drivers and internal equity considerations.

The case study at the end of this chapter provides an example of a carefully planned introduction programme at Zurich Financial Services UK.

The chapter concentrates on the particular considerations affecting the design of broadbanded structures. General approaches to the development and implementation of pay structures are dealt with in Part 4.

The development process

The first steps in the development process are to evaluate the relative merits of the alternative pay structures as suggested at the end of Chapter 2 and to clarify and prioritise the pay objectives. The development process should include an assessment of why the organisation needs broadbanding and what it hopes to achieve by its introduction. It is as well to be aware at this stage of what can go wrong so that mistakes can be avoided. The American Compensation Association (ACA) research quoted in Chapter 3 indicated that a common reason for failure was an inadequate feasibility study, including the analysis of why broadbanding might or might not be appropriate. Lack of goal clarity has also regularly been raised in the research as a significant contributor to the failure of performance-related pay initiatives. The other main problems identified by the ACA research included paying inadequate attention to communication, involvement and training.

Overall approach

While broadbanding tends to make the job evaluation process simpler and less demanding, it requires much higher-quality and active management than traditional pay structures. Broadbanding processes have to be strong enough to cope with the increased demands that will be placed on HR and line managers. And they have to be developed and described in ways which clarify for employees how broadbanding will work, how it is different, and how they will be affected by it. The questions that inevitably emerge from employees are these:

❑ On what basis has my job been placed in a band?

❑ What market data is used, and is it relevant to my job?

❑ What is the role of job evaluation?

❑ Does broadbanding mean that my opportunities for career progression have been reduced?

❑ Where will I progress to in my band?

❑ What factors will be taken into account in deciding my progression?

❑ How can I be sure that my manager will award my pay increase on a fair and consistent basis?

It is essential to have answers ready for these and any other questions that may be raised by employees through processes of involvement and two-way communication.

Areas for attention

Our 1999/2000 research indicated that the general requirements to which attention should be given in the development programme are:

❑ achieving cultural fit – ensuring that the design and processes are aligned to the corporate culture

❑ achieving strategic fit – ensuring that broadbanding is undertaken as an integrated part of a reward strategy which in turn is an integral part of the business strategy

❑ achieving HR coherence – ensuring that broadbanding initiatives are integrated with other HR processes, especially those concerned with human resource development, performance management and competency analysis

❑ understanding precisely *why* broadbanding is needed – what it is expected to achieve and how it will achieve defined objectives

❏ providing for thorough and comprehensive communication, involvement and training processes.

The advice elicited from participants of the survey conducted by Abosch and Hand for the ACA in 1998 is outlined in Table 15.

In addition, it is advisable to ensure that the following processes are in place or will be operational in time for the implementation of broadbanding:

❏ job evaluation

❏ tracking market rates

❏ performance management

❏ competence analysis leading to the development of competence frameworks and profiles

❏ pay budgeting and review.

Development stages

The stages of the development process are illustrated in Figure 10 and discussed below. We describe the development and implementation process in more detail in Chapter 9.

Table 15
ACA ADVICE ON INTRODUCING BROADBANDING

Communicate, educate

Communicate more prior to implementation about methodology and how the system works.

Take more time to educate employees and show leadership up front.

Provide for more communication and involvement from the start.

Don't rush

Spend more time at the front end for design, testing and longer-term thinking about training requirements and phase-in scheduling.

Spend more time designing the system with input from affected areas.

Spend more time communicating why broadbanding is being implemented.

Ensure that HR systems provide support

Ensure that the merit pay budget is sufficient.

Develop a better HR database management programme.

Establish a more definitive pay administration programme before implementation.

Chartered Institute of Personnel and Development

Customer Satisfaction Survey

*We would be grateful if you could spend a few minutes answering these questions and return the postcard to CIPD. <u>Please use a black pen to answer</u>. **If you would like to receive a free CIPD pen, please include your name and address.*** IPD MEMBER Y/N

....

1. Title of book ....

2. Date of purchase: month .... year ....

3. How did you acquire this book?
☐ Bookshop ☐ Mail order ☐ Exhibition ☐ Gift ☐ Bought from Author

4. If ordered by mail, how long did it take to arrive:
☐ 1 week ☐ 2 weeks ☐ more than 2 weeks

5. Name of shop .... Town... Country ....

6. Please grade the following according to their influence on your purchasing decision with 1 as least influential: (please tick)

	1	2	3	4	5
Title					
Publisher					
Author					
Price					
Subject					
Cover					

7. On a scale of 1 to 5 (with 1 as poor & 5 as excellent) please give your impressions of the book in terms of: (please tick)

	1	2	3	4	5
Cover design					
Paper/print quality					
Good value for money					
General level of service					

8. Did you find the book:
Covers the subject in sufficient depth ☐ Yes ☐ No
Useful for your work ☐ Yes ☐ No

9. Are you using this book to help:
☐ In your work ☐ Personal study ☐ Both ☐ Other (please state)

Please complete if you are using this as part of a course

10. Name of academic institution...

11. Name of course you are following? ....

12. Did you find this book relevant to the syllabus? ☐ Yes ☐ No ☐ Don't know

Thank you!

To receive regular information about CIPD books and resources call 020 8263 3387.

2

Publishing Department

Chartered Institute of Personnel and Development

CIPD House

Camp Road

Wimbledon

London

SW19 4BR

Figure 10
STAGES FOR INTRODUCING BROADBANDING

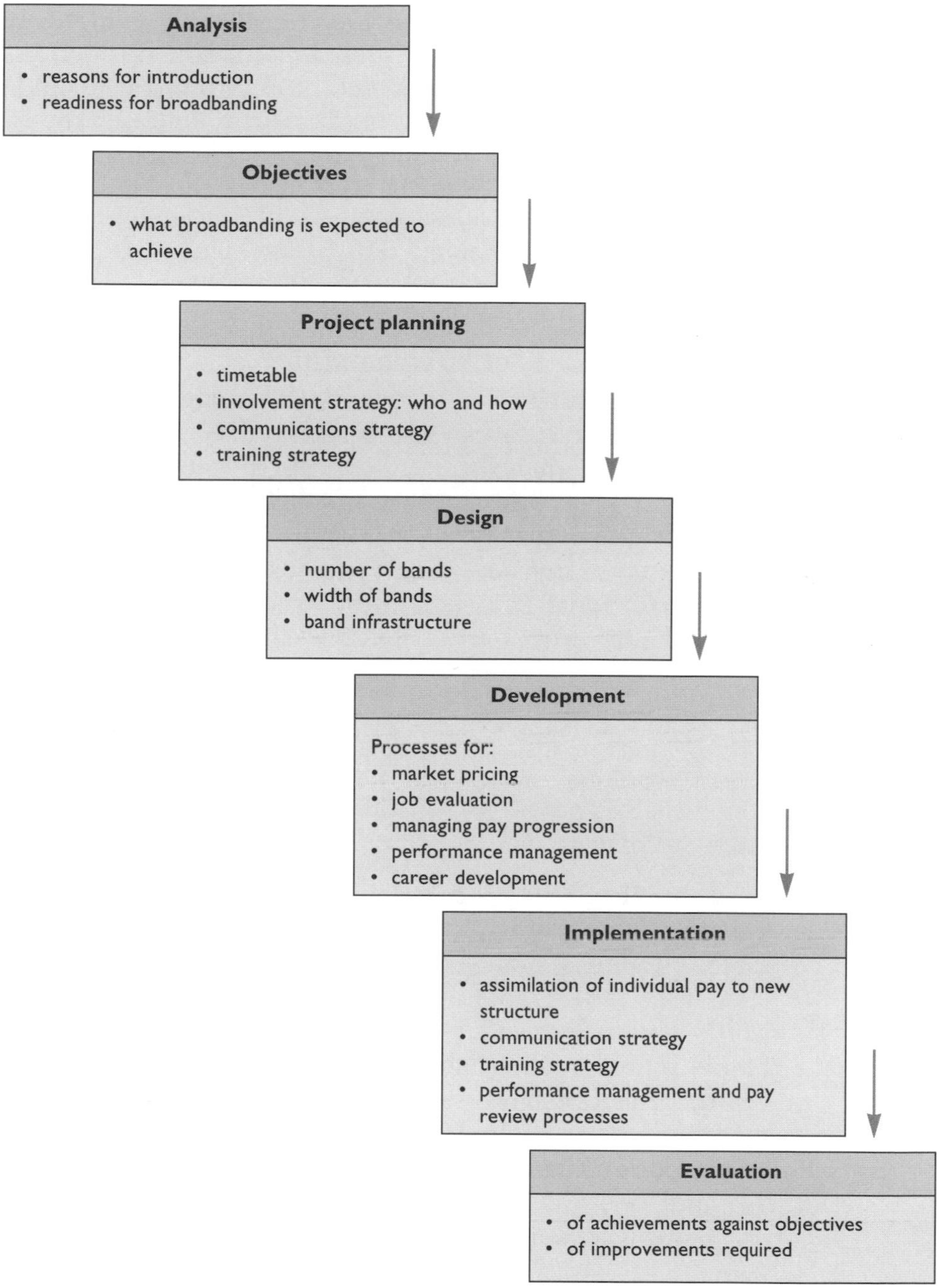

Analysis

- reasons for introduction
- readiness for broadbanding

Objectives

- what broadbanding is expected to achieve

Project planning

- timetable
- involvement strategy: who and how
- communications strategy
- training strategy

Design

- number of bands
- width of bands
- band infrastructure

Development

Processes for:
- market pricing
- job evaluation
- managing pay progression
- performance management
- career development

Implementation

- assimilation of individual pay to new structure
- communication strategy
- training strategy
- performance management and pay review processes

Evaluation

- of achievements against objectives
- of improvements required

Analysis

This is a key stage. As the research has shown, if it is neglected, the chances of success are considerably reduced. It is necessary to understand the present situation through an analysis of the pay arrangements and the environment, including the organisational culture and values, followed by a diagnostic review as suggested in Chapter 9. The pros and cons of broadbanding then need to be assessed against that background. Account should also be taken of the reasons for failure. Finally, an evaluation of readiness for introduction should be carried out.

Advantages and disadvantages of broadbanding

Before going any further, it is essential to analyse the advantages and disadvantages of broadbanding against the background of the analysis and diagnostic review as suggested in Chapter 2. The advantages of broadbanding set out below may explain its popularity, but there are many disadvantages and these must be considered before embarking on the conversion of a traditional pay structure to a broadbanded format. (Much of the information that follows constitutes summaries of material covered in detail in Chapter 4, and in not quite such detail in Chapters 2 and 3.)

Advantages

The main advantages of broadbanding highlighted by our research are that it:

❏ enhances flexibility in pay delivery, managing the reward system and adjusting pay in response to market rate variations – there is more scope for varying the rates of pay offered to new employees on the basis of their market worth, and new or wider responsibilities can be allocated to people or assumed by them (and in either case rewarded appropriately) without going through a re-grading or appeals procedure; there is also more scope to differentiate between employees on the basis of their personal contribution

❏ enables organisations to provide rewards for lateral career development, continuous learning and the achievement of increased levels of competence and contribution

❏ addresses the personal growth needs of people by offering pay opportunities for mastering new competences within the band – pay progression is not circumscribed by narrow and rigidly enforced salary ranges

❏ can reflect and support the operation of a process-based organisation with fewer levels of management and supervision

❏ supports teamworking by encouraging the development of multi-focus roles and a 'boundary-less' organisation

❏ provides a means of integrating reward and employee development strategies

❏ enhances the ability of the organisation to reward people for what they bring to and contribute to the business beyond their job descriptions

❏ reduces the time spent in analysing and evaluating jobs because there are fewer levels between which distinctions need to be made

❏ reduces the pressure for upgrading and, therefore, grade drift which is often present in multigraded structures, while still presenting ample pay progression opportunities

❏ can allow the devolution of more responsibility and accountability to line managers in different locations and parts of the organisation to make pay decisions, while maintaining an overall framework and 'read-across' for pay management and development.

Disadvantages

The disadvantages of a broadbanded structure can be that it:

❏ may be relatively easy to design but is often hard to introduce and manage

❏ can be difficult to explain to managers and employees exactly how broadbanding works and how they are affected by it; for example, they have to appreciate how pay progression within a band works and the ways in which that progression may be limited (ie that there is no promise that an individual's rate of pay will increase to the top of the band) – the traditional pay spine or narrow graded structure is much easier to understand

❏ appears to restrict the number of promotional opportunities – lateral career development pay may alleviate the problem but employees may still look elsewhere to further their careers (although it could be said that this problem is a function of de-layering rather than the broadbanding which often simply mirrors a flattened organisation)

❏ may meet with strong resistance from employees and relevant trade unions, if any – the benefits of broadbanding may be obvious to management but may not necessarily be equally compelling for employees; however, in our experience, most of the opposition appears to relate to the management of pay in the broad bands rather than being a negative reaction to fewer bands (most people find it quite easy to accept the logic of a broadbanded structure)

❏ may mean that employees formerly in higher grades feel that their jobs have been devalued by being placed in the same band as employees previously in a lower grade; for example, team leaders and their staff could be in the same band

❏ may result in employees' being concerned by the apparent lack of structure and precision – they may miss the 'career signposts' previously defined by an extended hierarchy of grades through which they could progress

❏ can build up employee expectations of much greater pay progression opportunities than may exist in a controlled structure

❏ may mean a return to the bad old days of management favouritism, subjective judgements and inequities because of the increased freedom for line managers to make their own pay decisions – the need to avoid this was the reason pay structures were introduced in the first place by many organisations

❏ can take considerable time and effort to establish and maintain

❏ requires significant commitment of training and communication resources

❏ involves HR in more work providing guidance and monitoring pay decisions – the great advantage of pay spines is that to a large extent they manage themselves, and even graded structures can be easier to control, although there is still the risk of grade drift and the excessive use of job evaluation

❏ could lead to increased payroll costs unless very careful control is exercised over the operation of the system – but there is a delicate balance to be achieved between allowing for sufficient flexibility and simultaneously maintaining the right amount of control

❏ may conflict with the culture of traditionally hierarchical organisations in which status is defined by job gradings and progress is measured by the speed and extent to which people move up the grade hierarchy

❏ may lead to difficulties in ensuring that equal-pay-for-work-of-equal-value imperatives are dealt with where analytical job evaluation is not applied extensively.

Overcoming the disadvantages

To overcome these disadvantages it is first necessary to be very clear about what broadbanding is expected to achieve. They can then be alleviated by such means as extensive consultation, communication, participation and training. And monitoring and budgeting procedures can be used to provide for consistency, equity and control. But the disadvantages could outweigh the advantages, and this is why it is important to define the objectives of broadbanding and weigh up the extent to which the organisation is ready for broadbanding *before* committing resources to developing it.

Areas of failure

Broadbanding can fail because:

❏ it is inappropriate for the organisation
❏ it is badly designed
❏ insufficient attention has been paid to communications, involvement and training.

One of the companies we visited during our research noted that insufficient attention had been paid to the training issues and that the structure was perceived by management as too complicated, requiring a lot of hand-holding.

A report by Parus (1998) on a longitudinal study of broad-banding noted that: 'Organisations using broadbanding typically have failed to carry through on career development and did not maintain effective communication with employees after introducing the program.' Nine organisations were iden-tified which had discontinued broadbanding, citing the following reasons:

❑ poor morale
❑ frustration and dissatisfaction
❑ a lack of understanding by employees and management
❑ a lack of trust in management
❑ working from the old system, using hidden grades.

However, these problems need to be seen in their full context, and business and organisational challenges continue to drive UK companies in this direction. It is interesting to note that our research identified only one organisation that had aban-doned broadbanding (an engineering company) but that was because of a change of policy in the parent company. Far more were planning to extend it. However, the head of compensa-tion at that company did comment that: 'Broadbanding provided a lot of scope for flexibility, but also huge scope for getting it wrong.'

Readiness for broadbanding

The requirements for the successful introduction of broad bands are stringent. Before taking the plunge it is essential to assess the extent to which the organisation is ready for broad-banding, or ever will be. Only then should steps to be taken to plan its introduction.

A simple readiness assessment for broadbanding which we have developed is summarised in Table 16.

Conditions favourable to broadbanding

Conditions are most likely to be favourable for the introduc-tion of broadbanding when it:

❑ is intended to fulfil a clear business purpose
❑ fits the business and HR strategies
❑ can help to attain the strategic goals of the organisation.

Table 16
A READINESS ASSESSMENT FOR BROADBANDING

Area	Criteria
Business	• increasing competitive pressures • increasing focus on added value, eg quality and customer service
Organisation	• fewer levels in organisation • emphasis on informal/matrix structures • increased emphasis on teamwork • increased role flexibility (broad role definitions)
Culture	• openness and quality of communication • level of employee involvement • trust in management
HR	• increasing focus on personal/self development • HR function playing a facilitating, not a controlling role • quality of performance management processes
Pay	• more emphasis on market competitiveness than on internal equity • less dependence on job evaluation • transparent approach to communicating pay policies and practices • harmonised pay and benefits.

The aims and operational methods of broadbanding should fit the existing corporate culture and support any necessary changes to that culture.

Broadbanding is most likely to be appropriate when de-layering has taken place: the focus is on flexibility, teamwork, multiskilling and cross-departmental processes rather than vertical, functional 'chimneys'. There should be good opportunities for in-job and lateral career development and the importance of continuous development, role flexibility and career planning should be recognised by management.

An effective and respected performance management process which assesses both inputs and outputs should preferably be in place (if not, conditions would have to favour its development) and, ideally, competence frameworks and profiles should already exist as a basis for developmental activities.

It helps if line managers have well-developed people-management skills and, with training and guidance, will be capable of operating broadbanding processes such as making fair and consistent decisions on rates of pay and assessing contribution and competence.

It is also necessary to have effective pay budgeting procedures and well-established processes for collecting valid market rate information.

Conditions unfavourable to broadbanding

Organisations are less likely to be ready for broadbanding when management and employees are content with the existing pay structure and job evaluation processes and there is nervousness about changing the *status quo*. Other unfavourable conditions include:

❏ the existence of a strong culture which values a traditional organisational hierarchy

❏ managers' and employees' attaching considerable importance to a multigraded structure and graded jobs as clear indicators of status

❏ employees' being suspicious of any changes to the existing arrangements and feeling that broadbanding is a management ploy that will work against their interests

❏ the trade union's being hostile to broadbanding, especially if it is associated with performance-related pay

❏ managers' and employees' inability to understand and/or reluctance to accept the concept of lateral development as an alternative to promotion through an extended hierarchy

❏ management's reluctance to invest time and resources in developing a new structure or in training managers and communicating with and involving staff in the matters concerning their pay

❏ even with concentrated training and close guidance, line managers' being unlikely to be able to develop the people-management skills required to operate broadbanding on a devolved basis in their departments

❏ difficulty in obtaining accurate data on market rates

❏ a situation in which performance management processes do

not exist and the traditional performance assessment scheme, if there is one, is discredited, misused or not used at all.

Introducing broadbanding

As Brown (1996) comments: 'Broadbanding initiatives will almost certainly fail if they are treated as one-off quick-fix pay re-design exercises.' There has to be a business purpose for broadbanding and it has to be integrated with other aspects of HRM, particularly those concerned with employee development and career management.

The introduction of broad bands will constitute a major culture change. The reasons for this change should be communicated in advance to employees who should be informed of how it will affect them. Obviously, the business need for broadbanding and benefits to the organisation would be emphasised, but the natural suspicions and fears of employees should be taken into account as well. Their opinions should be sought before the exercise begins through attitude surveys and focus groups, and employees should be involved at every stage in the development programme. The training required to handle the new processes should extend to employees in general as well as to managers and team leaders.

Overall, those concerned with the introduction of broadbanding should constantly bear in mind the advice of Armstrong and Murlis (1998) about any innovations in reward management:

❑ Planned and managed incremental change is easier to design and implement than quantum leaps into unknown territory.

❑ It is necessary to provide for tactical advances and retreats – you will not get it right all the time.

❑ In Voltaire's words, 'the best is the enemy of the good'; sometimes a successful future lies in agreeing what in the short term we can only get 'nearly right'.

Next steps

Assuming a favourable assessment of readiness for broadbanding, the next steps will be to set objectives and to formulate a project plan. If the result is unfavourable, alternative arrangements will have to be considered or the plans for broadbanding put on hold until circumstances change for the better.

Objectives

It is necessary to be clear about what the organisation wants to get out of introducing broad bands. Appreciating what broadbanding is *not* there to do is just as important as understanding what it can achieve. As LeBlanc and Ellis (1995) point out, banding is not a panacea for all organisational ills, a way to avoid job evaluation, market pricing or pay administration, or a de-layering or cost-cutting exercise in disguise. They go on to comment that if these are the aims of broadbanding, employees will quickly see through them and relegate it to 'an uncomfortable event that happens before people get back to their regular lives'.

Objectives could be set out under such headings as:

❑ to enhance organisational and pay flexibility
❑ to help support a new culture
❑ to de-emphasise hierarchy
❑ to emphasise career development and encourage competence and skill development
❑ to reward people for value-added results and behaviour.

Our research revealed that the most common objective was to provide for more flexibility in rewarding individuals. Other typical objectives included to reflect changes in the organisation structure, to provide a better basis for rewarding growth in competence, and to replace an over-complex pay structure. The following are two examples of objectives drawn from that research.

Glaxo Wellcome

❑ to provide a simple but practical framework for managing pay across the company
❑ to recognise and reward individuals for the development and application of the knowledge, skills and behaviours necessary for their role

- to motivate individuals to develop their core competencies to the dimensions required for their role
- to support a broadening of knowledge and skills by facilitating moves across the company
- to balance external market rates with internal comparability.

RAC Motoring Services (RACMS)

- to support the organisation through the introduction of bands which reflect the new organisational levels in RACMS
- to focus on the value-adding levels of work in RACMS, and clarify accountabilities and contribution to the business
- to assist RACMS to manage the remuneration process so that it reflects individual performance, the contribution made to the achievement of group goals and the overall financial performance of RACMS
- to streamline the grading structure in line with market practice, rationalise job titles and link these to level of contribution.

Project planning

Project planning involves deciding on a timetable and who should be involved and how. It should also incorporate the communication and training strategies and how they will be implemented.

Project timetable

Never underestimate the time taken to get broadbanding off the ground. It cannot be rushed. It is quite easy – a morning's work – to look at the existing organisation and grading structures and estimate that, say, only five bands are needed to reflect the organisation's hierarchy instead of the 12 grades existing at present. But this is only the beginning. The real challenge is to develop the band infrastructure and the various processes required and to ensure that these are understood and accepted by all concerned. This can take 18 months or more after the initial stages of analysis and diagnosis, which themselves could take three months. A typical programme is illustrated in Figure 11 (overleaf).

Figure 11
BROADBANDING DESIGN AND DEVELOPMENT PROGRAMME

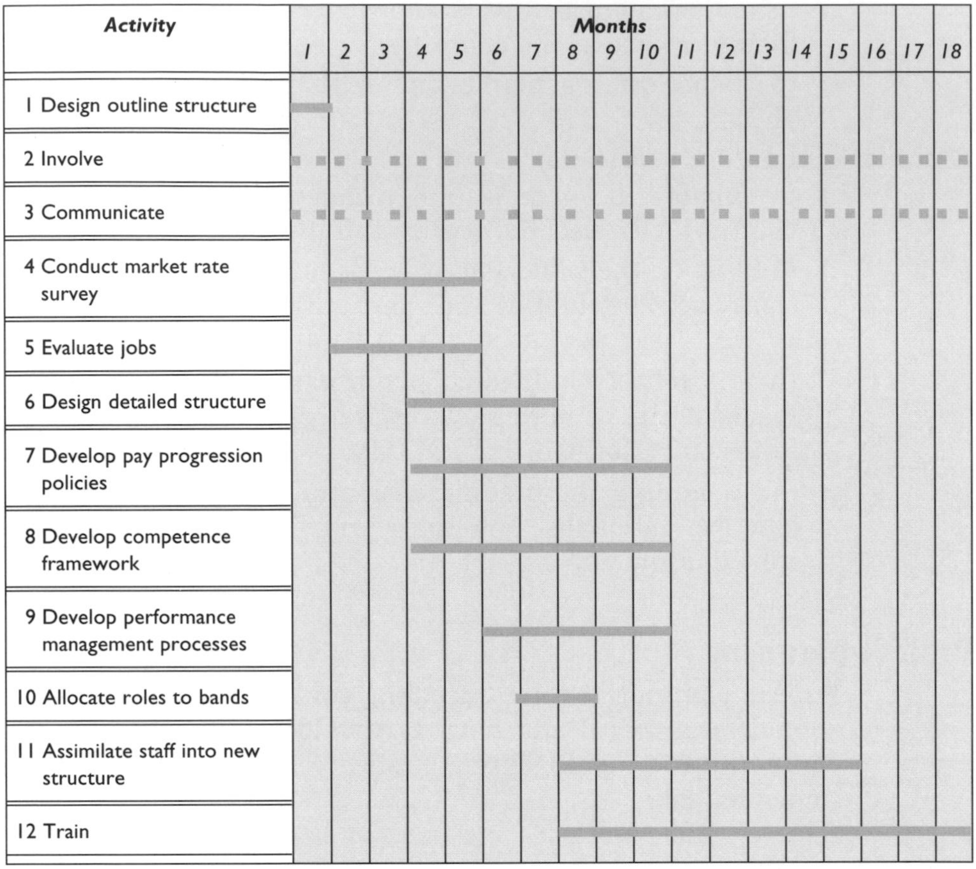

Activity	Months																	
	1	2	3	4	5	6	7	8	9	10	11	12	13	14	15	16	17	18
1 Design outline structure																		
2 Involve																		
3 Communicate																		
4 Conduct market rate survey																		
5 Evaluate jobs																		
6 Design detailed structure																		
7 Develop pay progression policies																		
8 Develop competence framework																		
9 Develop performance management processes																		
10 Allocate roles to bands																		
11 Assimilate staff into new structure																		
12 Train																		

Involvement and consultation strategy

It is essential to involve line managers, staff and, where relevant, trade union representatives, from the outset of the project. Their views should be sought on the case for developing a broadbanded pay structure and they should take part in its development. Ownership is important – by staff and their representatives as well as line managers.

The involvement strategy defines who participates in carrying out the work. This would normally include management and staff/trade union representatives, possibly advised by an external consultant. It is usual to set up a project team or task force. Much of the preparatory work will be done outside team meetings by specialists – internal and/or external consultants – but the full team will review and agree proposals. The remit of the project team is often restricted to considering the design of the structure and the supporting processes, and to carrying out job evaluations. Market rate surveys and decisions on pay ranges and individual rates of pay are usually the responsibility of management, possibly advised by consultants.

Pay levels may be subject to negotiation and trade unions normally only join project teams on the understanding that it is without prejudice – they will reserve the right to negotiate any proposed changes to terms and conditions emerging from the project. It is always sensible to sound out trade unions on their likely reactions to any possible developments, especially if they mean that existing arrangements will change significantly, or if it is proposed to introduce performance- or competence-related pay. It is advisable to hold informal discussions with full-time union officials to seek the union's views. Company union representatives will often ask for advice from their officials and it is as well to know in advance what that advice might be so that issues can be addressed in good time. It is not a good idea to carry out an extended development programme only to be greeted at the end by hostile reactions that could have been avoided. In any case, union officials can make valuable contributions based on their own experience, and a partnership approach is in line with the policies of most if not all unions.

If there is a works council, representatives should be included in the project team but consultation on changes to terms and conditions with a council may be required under its constitution. Such consultation should aim to achieve agreement, even if it does not involve negotiations.

Although the project team may do most of the basic work with the help of advisers, it is common practice to create a management steering group to review and agree proposals made by the project team and HR and to formulate negotiating policies.

Communications strategy

The communications strategy is an important part of the project planning process. The strategy should cover arrangements for what will be communicated, how it will be communicated, to whom it will be communicated and when it will be communicated. The approach to communications is dealt with in Chapter 9.

Training strategy

The training strategy will be based on a systematic identification of training needs for line managers and all other employees. These will include, as appropriate, methods of managing progression in bands, the interpretation of market rate data, the conduct of pay reviews, and the development of performance management skills. Training programmes will have to be timed carefully to ensure that everyone is prepared to implement broadbanding and its associated processes.

Designing broadbanded structures

The uniqueness of broadbanding

There is, of course, no standard pattern for broadbanded structures (this was confirmed by the recent IPD research and previous surveys). As LeBlanc and Ellis (1995) observed:

> Because all organisations have a unique structure, set of strategic goals and culture, each one approaches banding differently. Banding is more than a pay program – it is a way of managing a company's human resources. As such, it would be inaccurate to say that there are certain 'types' of banding because banding is unique to each organisation that implements it.

Best fit is more important than best practice. The structure has to be congruent with the circumstances in the company, including its organisation structure and culture. It is always interesting to observe what other organisations do but their specific practices will seldom, if ever, transfer well. That is why the initial analysis and diagnosis stage is so important. However, case studies such as those in this book provide an interesting record of experience. The features of the structure and the methods of development and operation described in these cases will provide insight into the issues to be tackled and the alternative approaches available, but they cannot be regarded as models upon which a structure can be designed in a different organisation.

Design guidelines

Although all broadbanded structures are unique to their organisation, certain design guidelines, which are at least worth considering, have emerged as a result of our research and extensive experience in helping to develop broadbanded structures. These are:

❑ Be clear about what is to be achieved and why.

❑ Ensure that whatever else is done, the structure fits the circumstances, strategies and culture of the organisation.

❑ Don't follow fashion – do your own thing.

❑ Keep it simple – over-complexity is a common reason for failure.

❑ Don't rush – it takes longer than you think.

❑ Communicate, involve and train.

The design process

The design process has therefore to consider and evaluate in the light of the circumstances of the company the alternative approaches, particularly those concerning the number and width of bands, the band infrastructure (the use of zones, segments, etc) and the basis upon which jobs will be positioned in bands.

Number of bands

As we saw in Chapter 4, the number of bands will be related to what Gilbert and Abosch (1996) refer to as 'value-added tiers', by which they mean clusters of roles that have common responsibilities and accountabilities and make a comparable impact on organisational success. Account may be taken of generic competences – for example, managerial, team leadership, and professional or technical support. Clearly, the greater the number of competence and responsibility levels to be covered by the structure, the greater the number of bands.

Decisions on bands may be based on a job evaluation exercise (as in an international oil company: see the first case study later in this chapter). However, the number of bands is often determined judgementally on the basis of an analysis of the organisation structure and the ways in which jobs are clustered in each tier of management, supervision, technical and professional staff, support and administrative staff, and employees who are involved in producing or delivering the basic services of the organisation. The number is also influenced by the pre-existing number of grades in the organisation. There should be a significant step change between bands in terms of the levels of the jobs placed within them – for example, administrative and support workers, senior administrators and technical staff, team leaders/professional staff, managers, and senior managers. The aim is to ensure that the designation of the band clearly indicates what type of jobs will be placed in it.

In *Bass Brewers* the five levels comprise, respectively:

- senior management
- management
- professional/technical
- support (1)
- support (2).

At *Halifax plc* there are five bands:

Band A

These jobs usually have contact with customers or colleagues over the telephone or through correspondence. Work focuses on services for individual internal/external customers. The impact of jobs at this level is primarily relevant to the section within which such job-holders work.

Examples of jobs include:

- administration
- typing
- supervisory support and technical support roles undertaking administration or providing advice and coaching to colleagues and customers.

Band B

Jobs at this level are accountable for work of a technical nature or the delivery of services. This may involve the implementation of policies and some input into their development. Such jobs also have a high impact on the section within which they are located, and are usually involved in supervising and coaching other members in the team.

Examples of jobs include:

❑ team leaders
❑ supervisors
❑ first level specialists.

Band C

Jobs at this level are accountable for the implementation or the development of policies and procedures or for undertaking and delivering work of significant technical nature. Such jobs make a considerable impact on the section or department within which they are located.

Examples of jobs include:

❑ managers of sections within departments
❑ specialist technical roles.

Band D

These jobs are accountable for managing the delivery of services or technical advice. They may involve the planning and co-ordination of large business or support functions and ensuring that effective technical, financial and service standards are in place. Jobs at this level may be entirely accountable for the results of their department or area or may have a high technical impact upon operations.

Examples of jobs include:

❑ department managers
❑ professional specialist roles.

Band E

These jobs are focused on and accountable for the co-ordination of a major business or support area or they may be those of significant individual advisers on a major element of the strategy and policy of the organisation. Jobs at this level have a material impact on the group's results.

Examples of jobs include:

❑ managers of large or multiple functions
❑ expert professional roles.

The *Inland Revenue* has five bands covering respectively:

❑ administrative officers, administrative assistants and support staff
❑ executive officers and the equivalent
❑ higher and senior executive officers
❑ tax inspectors and equivalent
❑ management.

See also the first and second case studies (relating to the international oil company and the global communications organisation) at the end of this chapter.

Unilever has five 'work levels' below the board that replaced the previous 17 job classes. Only one 'value-adding' tier of hierarchy is necessary at each work level.

Width of bands

As we saw in Chapter 4, the width of bands will be primarily influenced by the number of levels and the range of pay for the jobs to be covered. In general, the fewer the levels, the broader the bands. A further factor is the size of the jobs in the band – bands will often widen progressively in line with seniority on the grounds that at higher levels there is more scope for variation in responsibilities and contribution.

A variety of factors have to be taken into account, including:

❑ the types of roles allocated to bands
❑ the opportunities for pay progression the organisation wants to and can provide in a band
❑ the extent to which the band is divided into zones
❑ the range of levels of responsibility or competence requirements for the roles in the band

❏ the range of market rates for the roles allocated to the bands, which is often a key factor.

Decisions on band widths are often made judgementally, although the judgements should be informed by empirical data. When the approach is primarily judgemental, widths are determined on the basis of views about the scope for pay progression that should be provided in the band. The judgements will be influenced by the types and levels of jobs and the need to align pay to market rates.

If a number of jobs with different rates of pay are placed in a band, its width in pay terms will be determined more empirically by reference to the range of pay levels that the band has to accommodate and the allowance for pay progression up to and beyond the market pay reference points for the job. For example, if a band incorporates three roles or clusters of roles and the range around the market reference points for each was 10 per cent on each side, the pay ranges for those roles might be:

£18,000 – 20,000 – 22,000

£19,800 – 22,000 – 24,200

£23,600 – 24,000 – 26,400

The range of pay the band would have to accommodate would therefore be from £18,000 to £26,400 – ie 47 per cent. But it might be decided that more scope at either end of this empirical range should be provided, and the band width could be fixed at about 70 per cent – £16,500 to £28,000. This process could be repeated at each level and the widths determined accordingly. For the sake of neatness, each band could have a width of 70 per cent if all the jobs could be accommodated in them. Or it might be decided, on the basis of empirical evidence or arbitrarily, that widths should increase at each level from, say, 60 per cent to 80 per cent.

To overcome the judgemental or arbitrary nature of band-width decision-making as described above, some organisations do not have any fixed limits at either end of the band. Jobs are allocated to the band and have ranges attached to them on the basis mainly of market pricing. Other organisations just have a lower limit. Thus the range of pay covered by any band can vary according to the rates of pay for jobs in the band.

Examples of the varied approaches that organisations adopt include:

- *Bristol-Myers Squibb* (case study, Chapter 4) has eight bands, all of which are approximately 100 per cent from minimum to maximum.
- *BT* has seven grades ranging between 50 per cent and 74 per cent for managerial, professional and technical staff.
- *A financial services company* has six bands, but in order to increase flexibility there are no pay limits.
- *A food and drinks company* replaced a 24-grade structure with three broad bands, the pay ranges for each band and the number of levels within them varying according to functional job families.
- *Halifax plc* (case study, Chapter 4) is an example of a company which has varied band widths ranging from 52 per cent to 75 per cent to accommodate the jobs placed in them.
- *An international oil company* (first case study, this chapter) has seven job grades varying in width from 90 per cent at the top to 60 per cent at the bottom.

Band infrastructure

A decision on band infrastructure – how the band may or may not contain reference points, zones or segments (as described in Chapter 4) should be based on the benefits and drawbacks of the main alternatives, as shown in Table 17.

The choice is likely to be a balanced one between flexibility and control. The weight attached to either of these considerations will be a matter of judgement. This will be influenced by the values of the organisation, the extent to which role and operational flexibility is a factor and the degree to which it is believed that pay decisions can and should be devolved to managers.

Table 17
CHOICE OF INFRASTRUCTURE

Alternatives	Benefits	Drawbacks
No infrastructure	• Complete flexibility to reflect personal contribution	• Control problems • Internal equity problems • Creating false expectations of pay opportunities
Reference points	• Simple, easy to understand • Flexibility • Aligned to market rates	• Some control problems • Some internal equity problems • Scope for progression not defined
Zones	• Defined scope for progression • Easier to control • Aligned to market rates	• Could inhibit flexibility • 'Bands within bands' – could be a narrow-graded structure in disguise
Segments	• Limits to progression defined • Some flexibility	• Possible control problems – drift through band

Developing processes

Getting the processes right is the key to successful broadbanding. The design is relatively easy. It is much more difficult to make it work. That is why the processes discussed below have to be planned and tested with great care.

Market pricing

Broadbanded structures tend to be market-driven. Internal equity is still an important consideration but priority is usually given to defining the pay dimensions and fixing reference points or zones on the basis of market comparisons. As an HR manager in a financial services company told us, 'Management believes that internal equity is nice to have, but it is second.'

Tracking market rates by conducting surveys, taking part in a pay club or analysing published material is therefore a vital broadbanding process. It can be time-consuming but it is time well spent. The problem, as always, is that although the concept of a market rate is quite clear, finding out what it is presents much greater problems. As everyone knows who studies market rate data, there may be no clear evidence as to what market rates are, especially in cases where there is a diffuse labour market in which companies will have exercised a range of choices about what they need to pay, and where the jobs being compared can differ considerably, in spite of similar job titles. Even the use of capsule job descriptions and consultants' databanks based on job evaluation does not guarantee that accurate job matching is achieved, and few organisations have the time or inclination to carry out their own job-evaluation-based studies. However, the growth of databases on the Internet has vastly increased the amount of market data, although much of it is of poor quality. The result is that, as so often in reward management, judgement has to be exercised. This may mean producing a 'derived rate' from the source material.

The other problem is that the uniqueness of a job within an organisation may make it impossible to obtain valid comparisons, particularly when roles are highly flexible and personal competence is emphasised. If there is job evaluation data available, the problem can be dealt with by identifying jobs that have been evaluated on both sides of the job in question and for which market data does exist, and then, by reference to the evaluation of the job under review, interpolating a market rate.

Job evaluation

As mentioned in Chapter 5, job evaluation may be used to a much lesser extent than in a conventional narrow-graded structure, if at all. But broad bands can usefully be defined in job evaluation terms, and equal pay considerations are best taken care of if there is a well-conceived job evaluation scheme. The process question is that if there is a job evaluation scheme, should it follow the principal method of defining broad bands and allocating jobs to those bands, or should it have mainly a supporting role? The choices are:

❑ Use a formal analytical job evaluation scheme in the traditional comprehensive way to define bands, place jobs in bands at the design stage, and inform subsequent decisions on placing jobs – eg whenever there has been an increase in responsibilities.

- Use analytical job evaluation in the design stage but subsequently relegate it to a support role, only being deployed exceptionally if an entirely new job has to be slotted into a band or as an audit tool for equal value purposes.
- Do not use analytical job evaluation in the design stage or subsequently: rely instead on market pricing and internal benchmarking (job matching) but hold an evaluation scheme in reserve to deal with equal value issues.
- Do not use analytical job evaluation at all but rely entirely on market pricing and job matching.

Generally, analytical job evaluation is not used comprehensively in broadbanded structures. Instead, many organisations (such as the Children's Society and the Peabody Trust) use it in a support role. It is quite possible to do without an analytical scheme altogether, but if one is available, it is useful as an equal value audit tool. If analytical job evaluation is not used at all, it will be necessary to pay particular attention to equal pay considerations when placing jobs in bands.

Managing pay progression

A decision has to be made on the criteria that should be used to determine pay progression within bands. The choice is between performance, competence or contribution (a combination of performance and competence). The most typical approach in broad bands is to use competence or contribution, as at Glaxo Wellcome, the Children's Society, the Prince's Trust and Volkswagen.

Performance management processes

Whichever criterion for pay progression is used, it is essential to have performance management processes in place which ensure that expectations are agreed and that competence or contribution is jointly assessed against those standards. A decision has also to be made on whether or not to use rating, and the arguments for and against doing so were set out in Chapter 5.

Career development processes

Broadbanding is or should be as much about continuous improvement and career progression as about managing pay.

In fact, it can be argued that the career development aspects of broadbanding – defining lateral and personal development paths and emphasising competence considerations – are the most important reason for adopting it. If competence and continuous development are important concerns, it is necessary to have processes for analysing and defining competence requirements and for including personal development planning as a major feature of performance management.

Implementation

The implementation programme will incorporate the communication and training strategies upon which the success of broadbanding will largely depend. It is also necessary to ensure that performance management processes and the procedures for conducting pay reviews are put into place. Importantly, arrangements have to be made to assimilate employees into the new structure, informing them of their new bands and deciding where they should be placed individually in the structure.

Assimilation

Great care has to be taken over deciding on the policy for assimilation and the procedures for implementing those policies. The damage to morale can be considerable if this is handled badly. However, because of the width of the bands, the process is usually easier than when traditional pay structures are redesigned and more people fall outside the narrower range minima and maxima. There is often more scope to 'manage' the costs of the assimilation process because of the flexible nature of broadbanding.

As in any job evaluation or restructuring exercise, the generally adopted policy when implementing broadbanding is to protect the existing salaries of staff and, if there are zones, 'freeze' the pay of those who are above the pay maxima and bring those who are paid below their zone up to the minimum immediately or on a phased basis over two or three years. Where there are reference points, staff would also have their pay protected if they are above the reference point, and individual decisions would have to be made on what should be done about those paid below that point. Progress towards the point would be determined as part of the normal pay review procedure and would be phased in line with assessments of contribution. These policies must be explained carefully to staff.

Employees can find it difficult to accept that they have lost their old grade, which defined their status, and are now placed in a band which they may share with others who were previously in lower grades. As was noted at Halifax plc when it implemented broadbanding, staff may hark back to the old system. That is why the processes of communicating to staff generally and as individuals the rationale of broadbanding is so important.

Change management

The introduction of broadbanding is an exercise in change management in an area of HR policy and practice which can raise strongly hostile feelings among those affected – who could be everybody. People resist change because it is perceived as a threat to familiar patterns of behaviour as well as to status and financial rewards.

Specifically, the main reasons for resisting change are:

- ❑ *the shock of the new* – People are suspicious of anything which they believe might upset their established routines, methods of working or conditions of employment. They do not want to lose the security of what is familiar to them. They may not trust statements by management that the change is for their benefit as well as that of the organisation – sometimes with good reason. They may feel that management has ulterior motives, and that the louder the protestations of management, the less management is to be believed. All these reactions can and do take place when the introduction of broadbanding is announced.
- ❑ *economic fears* – Loss of money or disappearing expectations of future rewards, including those resulting from promotion or upgrading, is another anxiety.
- ❑ *inconvenience* – The change will make life more difficult because new methods and systems will have to be introduced.

❑ *uncertainty* – Change can be worrying because of the uncertainty about its potential impact.

❑ *symbolic fears* – A change may affect some treasured symbol, such as the grade attached to a job.

❑ *threat to status or skill* – The change may be perceived as reducing the status of individuals or as de-skilling them.

Resistance to change can be difficult to overcome, even when the change is not detrimental to those concerned. But the attempt to overcome the resistance must be made. The first step is to analyse the potential impact of change by considering how it will affect people in their jobs. The analysis should indicate which aspects of the proposed change are likely to be supported generally or by specified individuals, and which aspects may be resisted. So far as possible, the potentially hostile or negative reactions of people should be predicted, taking into account all the possible reasons for resisting change listed above. Those affected can be categorised as 'winners' or 'losers' so that the latters' reactions can be monitored and addressed. It is necessary to try to understand the likely feelings and fears of those affected so that unnecessary worries can be relieved and, as far as possible, ambiguities can be resolved. In making this analysis, the individual who is introducing the change, sometimes called the 'change agent', should recognise that new ideas are likely to be suspect and should make ample provision for the discussion of reactions to proposals to ensure the complete understanding of them.

Involvement in the change process gives people the chance to raise and resolve their concerns and make suggestions about the form of the change and how it might be introduced. The aim is to get 'ownership' – a feeling amongst people that the change is something that they are happy to live with because they have been involved in its planning and introduction – it has become *their* change.

Communications about the proposed change should be carefully prepared and worded so that unnecessary fears are allayed. All the available channels – written communications, briefing groups, the intranet, etc, should be used, although face-to-face communications direct from managers to individuals or through a briefing system are best.

Management should be prepared to answer the following typical questions about broadbanding:

- Why has broadbanding been introduced?
- How will I be affected?
- Does the loss of my old grade mean that my job is considered to be less important?
- Why are people who used to be in lower grades than me now in the same band?
- On what basis were decisions made about the number of bands and their pay ranges?
- How is market data gathered and used?
- How was the position of my job in the band structure determined?
- What happens if my responsibilities increase?
- Doesn't this mean that the scope for promotion and pay progression has decreased?
- On what basis will I be eligible for promotion to a higher band?
- What are the limits, if any, to pay progression in a band?
- On what basis will my pay progress in my present band?
- Why are zones (control points) being used?
- What happens to me if my present rate of pay is either higher or lower than the rate for my job within the structure?
- How does pay progress within zones or between segments?
- Will I be able to appeal against any banding decision for my job?

Case studies

The different ways in which broadbanding may be introduced to an organisation are illustrated by the following five case studies:

- *An international oil company* – This case illustrates how an international company handled the transition to a broadbanded structure.

❑ *The Ministry of Defence* – How the Ministry of Defence introduced a new harmonised and broader banded pay structure.

❑ *A global communications company* – Following a major change to business strategy and an acquisition, a new reward strategy was developed, building on an established broadbanded structure. This involved melding of the two cultures and reward systems.

❑ *Southern Focus Group* – This organisation pioneered an approach which concentrated on getting the processes of competence analysis, job evaluation and performance management right first before developing a broadbanded structure.

❑ *Zurich Financial Services UK Life* – This organisation adopted an approach designed to develop a uniform but flexible broadbanded structure following a merger.

Case study

NORMALISING THE MOVE INTO BROAD BANDS AT AN INTERNATIONAL OIL COMPANY

Background
This case describes the pay management changes currently under way in an international oil exploration and production company. The company has its headquarters in the UK and has approximately 500 staff, with offices in the UK, continental Europe and the USA. Its former traditional evaluation-based hierarchical grading structure had essentially broken down in practice, and the situation was resolved by a move into a broadbanded pay structure.

Previous pay management and the need to change
For at least 10 years, this company – a spin-off from a much larger energy company – had managed the pay of individuals' pay in the UK with a structure of 21 grades. In theory, jobs were evaluated using the Hay system into these grades, but in practice jobs were essentially slotted in on the basis of market pay. The company employs a large number of professional and technical staff such as geologists and geophysicists, and detailed market survey data for these roles in the oil sector is readily available.

Pay ranges for these grades were relatively wide, at around 50 per cent, and the overlaps between grades was very high. The same pay level could be located in any one of five grades. Individual pay increases and movement within these ranges was determined on the basis of market worth and individual performance.

A number of factors led to a review being undertaken of this structure, ranging from a general sense of disquiet with it, to the chief executive's statement that an entrepreneurial organisation should be able to manage with 'five or six levels'. In addition, some grades had very few staff in them following a major series of reorganisations: there were fewer than five employees in three of the grades.

A working party was formed with representatives from all the major functions, and discussions were held with all the international locations. One European office, it turned out, only used 16 of the grades; another used only 11; while the newest office in the USA had set up its own structure of six broad pay bands. Detailed external analysis of market trends in pay management and levels of pay competitiveness was also undertaken.

The group found pay levels to be generally competitive and there seemed to be little disquiet at existing internal relativities. 'Promotions' up the grades, often with little or no associated pay increase, were relatively frequent and popular. However, major downsides of the existing approach included:

❏ the gap between the policy of detailed job evaluation and grading, and the practice of flexible job slotting

❏ the inability to explain or justify grades to staff, or list what additional skills and accountabilities staff needed to take on to obtain a promotion into the next grade; this fuelled perceptions that technical skills were undervalued and that only taking on management responsibilities could lead to promotion into the highest grades

❏ a very low level of staff understanding of how pay decisions were made, reducing the motivational impact of increases

❏ grade drift, with a preponderance of staff in the higher grades, and a strong relationship between grade and length of service; as one manager put it 'Nobody understands the basis for a promotion decision: they just expect one'

❏ perceived inequities in grading between locations, and difficulty in managing pay for the increasing number of staff moving between locations.

In summary, a key vehicle for communicating business priorities, corporate values and required skills and competencies was being ignored, and the stated pay policy flouted. Poor organisation performance meant that no pay increases had been made in the previous year, but now, with the exploration business and labour market rapidly picking up, pay management was threatening to become a major issue.

The changes

The objectives in reforming the internal pay structure were therefore:

❑ to support a stronger focus in pay management on individual contribution, growth in competence and the market, rather than hierarchical level and promotion

❑ to create an international read-across in job size and level

❑ to improve staff understanding of the rationale for pay decisions

❑ to reinforce other HR initiatives; a well-established competency framework was already being used for development and performance management purposes, and it seemed highly logical to link this in some way to pay.

The changes to which the board agreed in 1999 involved two components:

❑ the introduction of a simpler and tailored job evaluation system to compare jobs across the organisation

❑ moving all staff into a flatter pay structure of seven bands.

Using a sample of 40 benchmark jobs, the project group developed and tested the new evaluation system. The scheme uses eight factors – including technical knowledge, creativity and innovation, communications and leadership – which were heavily informed by the existing competency definitions. Benchmark jobs were scored on each factor and then grouped together into seven job bands. Summary descriptions of each band were then drafted and the remaining jobs were slotted into the description that best matched their role. Simpler, briefer role profiles were produced for each job, focusing on core job requirements and competencies.

The band structure is applied worldwide to aid mobility, although the pay ranges reflect local market rates. In the UK the ranges vary from a width of 90 per cent at the top to 60 per cent at the bottom, with overlaps reduced to approximately 30 per cent. The scope for development and pay progression in the current role, and the requirement for a genuine growth in responsibility and skills demanded to move into a higher level, are now much clearer. The introduction of the new arrangements has been carried out following the annual April pay review in 2000.

Learning points

It is too early to judge the success of these pay changes, but this case demonstrates many of the factors that have been encouraging the general introduction of broadbanding. A strong emphasis on the external market and on individual competence development in a professional workforce had led to the existing policy of detailed job definitions and evaluation in 21 grades becoming redundant in practice. Jobs were simply slotted into where they made best sense, and promotions were used to solve most perceived 'pay' problems. But the downside of this was the difficulty in valuing certain specialist jobs and an inability to justify pay decisions, providing plenty of scope for arbitrary and unfair decisions, or at least the perception of them.

Now the company has a scheme which links practice with policy, reflecting a flat organisation structure, considerable scope for personal development, and a market- and performance-oriented culture. A simple evaluation system plays a support role and provides a defence against unfair decisions, while the new broadbanded structure provides a loose common framework for market- and contribution-driven pay, and a global read-across in pay management in this international organisation.

The implementation has not been without its problems. In some areas the loss of promotion ladders was initially viewed negatively, and the collapsing of grades raised some contentious issues over eligibility for benefits such as share schemes. Nevertheless, the company feels it now has a system to support its future business direction rather than its distant history.

Case study

INTRODUCING A HARMONISED PAY AND GRADING STRUCTURE AT THE MINISTRY OF DEFENCE

Background

In common with many other government departments, taking on delegated pay responsibilities (as the former central Civil Service pay structures have been dismantled) and implementing government pay policy in areas such as performance pay have presented the Ministry of Defence with some major challenges in reward management. Introducing a new harmonised and broader-banded pay structure in 2000 has been an important component of the policies designed to address these challenges.

Pay initiatives

Four initiatives were planned in the department:

❑   introducing a common system of performance pay

❑   moving to a common pay review date

❑   introducing single-table bargaining

❑   introducing a uniform and broader-banded pay structure, under-pinned by a common job evaluation system.

The department introduced the first three of these during 1997. Staff moved to a common pay review date on 1 August, and an equity share system of performance pay was established to replace national incremental pay spines. Interestingly, these were implemented prior to the move into broader pay bands.

Job evaluation

Job evaluation was then carried out using the JEG's system developed by the Treasury, and applied to around 1,100 jobs across the department. It largely confirmed the relativities within the existing grading systems. In addition, the Department also used its competency framework, developed in 1996, to align the new pay structure. This defines core competencies for four job families covering all jobs in the Department; support jobs, junior management, middle management and senior management. There are also separate functional competencies – for example, for accountants.

The new pay structure

The new seven-band structure (see Table 18 overleaf) reflects the job-size ranges which underpinned the previous Civil Service grades. The seven old Civil Service grades can therefore be read across into the new structure. The new pay ranges reflect the pay band minima for the former administrative grades and the maxima from the London pay ranges for the old specialist grades. This means that most of the staff moving into the new structure, particularly those in administrative jobs and those outside London, now have a higher pay range maximum in their new band than formerly.

Equal value was an obvious concern in this situation. Historically, specialist staff have generally been paid more than administrative staff at an equivalent level, often reflecting market demand, but the job evaluation exercise confirmed their comparatively similar internal job size.

Administrative staff will for the most part therefore be paid less than specialists on moving into the new structure, and even high performers benefiting from the use of performance-related pay reviews could take many years to catch up with equivalent specialist roles in their band.

As part of the transition into the new structure, therefore, guarantees were negotiated so that administrative staff in Band E2 will be guaranteed to reach the old administrative assistant London scale maximum (£12,230) in no more than five years, and staff in E1 to reach the 1998 administration officer maximum in the same period.

The restructuring also saw the simplification of pay, with the removal of London pay and a range of other skill supplements and additional payments. Terms and conditions were additionally harmonised between staff brought together in the same group. For example, overtime at 1-rate was extended to specialist staff in Band D when it had been available previously only to executive officers in the administrative grades.

Negotiations on the new structure started in October 1998 and agreement was reached in May the following year. The new grade structure became effective from February 2000. The 1999 pay review cost 4.7 per cent of the payroll (adding 2.7 per cent to the paybill); 4.5 per cent was distributed in relation to individual performance through equity shares, 0.7 per cent was included in recognition of the move into the new structure.

Table 18
THE NEW PAY STRUCTURE AT THE MINISTRY OF DEFENCE
FROM 1 FEBRUARY 2000

	Civil Service grades assimilated to the new structure	Minimum £ p a	Maximum £ p a
E2	Administrative assistant, civilian security officer 5, communications officer 4, graphics technical grade 2, mapping and charting technical grade 2, museum support grade 5, photographic technical grade 2, port control assistant, support grade band 2, technical grade 2, typist	8,256	16,581
E1	Accommodation services accountant, administrative officer, assistant scientific officer, assistant telecommunications technical officer, civilian security officer 4, communications officer 3, conservation grade G, curatorial grade G, estate warden, graphics technical grade 1, housing officer 2, mapping and charting technical grade 1, museum support grades 3 and 4, personal secretary, photographic technical grade 1, station warden, support grade band 1, technical grade 1	9,798	20,202
D	Administration and legal assistant, air operations officer, assistant librarian, chaplain's assistant, civilian accommodation services officer, civilian security officer 3, communications officer 3, community relations adviser, conservation grade F, curatorial grade F, executive officer, families officer, graphics officer, instructional officers 1 and 2, intelligence officer, mapping and charting officer, museum officer grades 1 and 2, museum technicians 3 and 4, photographic officer, professional and technology officer, radio officer, scientific officer, stores officer grades C and D, support managers 2 and 3, telecommunications technical officer, typing manager	12,523	22,727
C2	Chief typing manager, civilian security officer 2, communications officer 1, conservation grade E, curatorial grade E, higher executive officer, higher graphics officer, higher instructional officer, higher intelligence officer, higher linguist officer, higher mapping and charting officer, higher photographic officer, higher professional and technology officer, higher psychologist, higher research analyst, higher scientific officer, higher telecommunications technical officer, librarian, museum technician 1, stores officer grade B, supervising radio officer, support manager 1	16,658	26,586
C1	Civilian security 1, community officer, conservation grade D, curatorial grade D, senior executive officer, senior graphics officer, senior instructional officer, senior intelligence officer, senior librarian, senior linguist officer, senior mapping and charting officer, senior personal secretary, senior photographic officer, senior professional and technology officer, senior psychologist, senior research analyst, senior research officer, senior scientific officer, senior telecommunications technical officer, shore galley design and equipment adviser, stores officer grade A	20,834	32,348
B2	Unified grade 7	28,247	44,815
B1	Unified grade 6	32,232	54,747

Greater flexibility

Pay increases in the new structure are performance-related, such that the top performers in 1999 received seven shares and the lowest two performance categories received no shares (see Table 19). In addition, to help address concerns over the time taken to progress staff within the new wider pay bands (a common issue raised by trade unions across Whitehall), those in the lower half of the new pay ranges received an enhancement of 30 per cent to their equity share award.

The system of promotions has also changed within the new structure. Under the previous structures, any proposed move to a higher grade involved a formal process before a promotion board. Now, this applies only to moves from one job group family to the next. A move from a lower to a higher pay band in the same group, involving growth in the same core competencies, is now handled locally. The minimum increase awarded for promotion has also been increased from 5 per cent to 8 per cent. More flexibility is also evident in pay levels for new recruits, involving an ability to pay up to £3,000 above the band minimum in areas of particular recruitment difficulty such as accountancy.

Although particularly the specialist staff and their IPMS trade union had some concerns about the move into this harmonised structure – such as a possible loss of identity and of specialist career paths – more than two-thirds of IPMS members together with the over-

Table 19
EQUITY SHARE INCREASES PAID UNDER THE 1999 REVIEW

| Pay band | Above reference point | | | Reference point | Box 3 | Box 2 | Box 1 |
	Box 1 £	Box 2 £	Box 3 £	£ p a	£	£	£
E2	428	375	375	12,419	398	477	557
E1	536	459	450	15,000	498	597	697
D	822	704	587	17,625	763	916	1,068
C2	1,070	917	764	21,622	993	1,192	1,391
C1	1,363	1,168	974	26,591	1,266	1,519	1,772
B2	1,673	1,434	1,195	36,531	1,553	1,864	2,175
B1	2,105	1,804	1,503	43,490	1,954	2,345	2,736

NB: Box 1 is the highest rating of the five-fold rating categories in the appraisal process.

whelming majority of administrative staff voted in favour of the new structure in a ballot.

A final effect of the new structure is that previous grade titles now cease to exist, and many parts of the department are already using more flexible, generic role-based titles such as 'senior engineer'.

Case study

PAY RESTRUCTURING IN A MERGER SITUATION

Background

The case concerns a long-established global communications equipment company which has been operating for over a century, and has over 50,000 employees worldwide. Historically, it has placed a strong strategic emphasis on manufacturing and a 'grow-your-own' approach to the development of its staff. In the UK it is one of the top 10 largest recruiters of graduates, and the average length of employee service in the company is more than 10 years.

The company was also one of the earliest well-publicised examples of those that adopted a global broadbanding structure in the early 1990s (see Table 20 on page 157). The structure is supported by the company's global competency framework and is designed to provide a consistent structure for pay management and international development throughout the organisation.

Pay ranges and benefits are tied to the global bands but reflect each country's own market practices.

The operation of this structure has reflected the company's historic strategy of long-term career development. Although it was broadbanded, there still has been a strong emphasis on band and position in the hierarchy, with open communication of band levels and obvious associated benefits. Stock options and incentives were restricted to management, and defined benefit pension plans operated in most countries. Pay increases through the ranges in each band were based on a combination of performance and personal development, but all aspects of 'total rewards', including development, have been emphasised in the past by the company.

A major change in the company's business strategy and the resulting acquisition of a networks company in late 1998 has led to the development of a new reward strategy and changes to the pay management practices.

The acquisition

The acquisition of the networks company represented part of what the company's new chief executive called a 'right-angled turn' in its business strategy. This involved focusing the company much more on the development and delivery of data, voice and video networks, innovating and changing much more rapidly, and supplying a full range of customers, together with a progressive selling off of its manufacturing capability. A key feature of this unified networks strategy was strengthening the company's datacoms capability, hence the acquisition.

The American datacoms organisation was in many senses the antithesis of its acquirer's. It was less than 20 years old, had grown rapidly to 10,000 employees, but with the bulk of these in North America. It very much retained the archetypal Silicon Valley culture, and importing this type of dynamism and entrepreneurism was also a key rationale for the acquisition. The culture was supported by a totally different reward approach compared with the buyer's. This focused strongly on individual financial rewards, in the light of the fact that the company's rapid growth had been based largely on external recruitment in a skills-scarce market.

Pay levels in the networks company were set relative to other small datacoms and software start-ups, with no common job evaluation system or pay structure and little open communication about pay policy. Pay levels varied greatly and individual pay increases were based wholly on personal performance. Stock options were used extensively and represented the primary wealth accumulation vehicle for staff, with a low emphasis on benefits, and defined contribution pension plans. Just about the only consistent aspect of reward policy between the two organisations was the use of a global stock purchase plan.

The new rewards strategy

The company's chief executive regarded the introduction of a new rewards strategy as one of the most important aspects of the merger, and a team was set up immediately to develop it. The strategy was designed to provide guiding principles to help with the rapid integration of programme designs locally. It represents a melding of the two cultures and reward systems, trying to go forward by combining the strengths of both different approaches.

Key principles of the new strategy include:

❏ being driven strongly by market competitiveness rather than by internal equity, but on the basis of total financial rewards rather than on just a pay basis; long and valued service is still recognised, but there is more emphasis now on a greater diversity of recruitment sources and career paths

❏ allowing flexibility in financial rewards, so that pay levels can vary depending on business needs and in response to organisation changes, and by providing as much employee choice as possible in determining their mix of rewards

❏ de-emphasising the role of benefits and status, but providing a basic safety net of benefits and assistance to employees to financially secure their future

❏ continuing to balance local market practice with a common global rewards framework

❏ maintaining overall reward costs at current levels

❏ continuing to drive business success through a policy of encouraging employee stock ownership.

The detailed policies in each region and country for putting this strategy into practice are still being worked out, but some clear implications are already emerging.

A stronger emphasis on financial rewards and greater variety and differentiation between individuals and functions, more akin to the approach of the networks company, is already evident. In particular functions, much higher salaries at a given organisation level are already being paid, and historically higher than in the acquiring company. However, whereas support functions such as personnel had also seen their salaries benefit from the generally dynamic networks labour market, there will now be a greater focus on paying high market salaries only where they are required. The market policy line in future is at the median against a mixed group of telecom, datacom, hardware and software companies.

Stock option eligibility will be much wider in the future than has historically been the case in the acquiring company. But whereas virtually everyone in the networks company was given options on joining, now it will be more selective, focusing on key technical specialists. Incentives will be operated for managers and specialists, with a global stock purchase plan for all employees.

In respect of the global broadbanding structure, the chief executive was initially an advocate of its total removal. However, it is being retained to help provide a global underpin and 'glue' for rewards in the organisation, as well as to provide practical assistance in areas such as external market matching and international career development. The company will retain its 'grow-your-own' approach in development, but combine this with more external recruitment at all levels.

Table 20
THE COMPANY'S BROADBANDING STRUCTURE

Band and staff category			Competency matrix example	
Band	Managerial	Individual contributor	Business awareness	Organisational sensitivity
9	Director	Consultant	Has a broad knowledge of business processes across the business	Understands current company affairs and developments in business environment
8	Senior manager	Senior adviser	Has a broad knowledge of all processes in area of responsibility	Understands internal company affairs and major issues in the business environment
7	Manager	Adviser	Has a broad knowledge of all processes in area of responsibility	Understands major issues in the business environment such as market trends
6	Supervisor	Senior specialist	Has a working knowledge of all processes in own team and is sensitive to the impact of each area on customers	Understands major issues in the business environment such as market trends; understands and sees importance of company goals and values
5	Team leader	Specialist	Understands own job and basics of colleague's jobs; understands how the team's output as a whole relates to satisfying customers' needs	Understands and sees importance of company goals and values
4	–	Associate specialist		
3		Assistant/support	Understands own job and how it relates to satisfying customers' needs	Has a broad knowledge of company goals and values
2		Assistant/support		
1		Assistant/support		

However, in future guideline salaries rather than fixed pay ranges will be operated at each level to provide greater pay flexibility, and variations according to different job families will be overlaid onto the broadbanding structure. Benefits and status trappings such as office size and job title will increasingly be de-linked from band level, and incorporate flexible benefits and defined contribution pension plans where possible.

Learning outcomes

In summary, therefore, the changes resulting from the integration of these two very different reward approaches in the company are being implemented in a careful, considered and sensitive manner. Even a broadbanded structure did not provide the level of flexibility required to reward successfully in a networks environment. Yet the key message from this evolving example is that the pay structure and pay management needs to be integrated with all aspects of reward management, career development and HRM if it is to effectively reinforce the business direction in an increasingly volatile environment.

The broadbanded structure and examples of competency requirements are shown in Table 20.

Case study

DEVELOPING AN INTEGRATED APPROACH TO JOB VALUATION, PERFORMANCE MANAGEMENT, EMPLOYEE DEVELOPMENT AND REWARD AT SOUTHERN FOCUS TRUST

Background

The Southern Focus Trust (previously the Portsmouth Housing Association) is a housing association providing direct access hostels, supported housing, care and repair, women's refuges, a housing advice centre and supported employment. As Portsmouth Housing Association it was part of a larger group. Costs were too high – primarily because of the effect of an incremental pay structure with 14 grades – staff turnover was low and a major proportion of staff were at the top of the scale. There was also a problem in delivering care to the standard required by clients, mainly local authorities. Levels of skill were low in some areas of work and more focus had to be placed on quality. The supervision process (of casework as

practised in social service local authority departments and in voluntary organisations delivering care) needed more structure.

Under a newly appointed and dynamic director, a transformation
programme was launched, and it was decided that a reward strategy
should be developed which would underpin the regeneration and the
necessary culture change, but would also ensure that rewards were
aligned to competence and contribution. It was clearly necessary to
replace the existing pay structure and the rigid job descriptions. The
group job evaluation also needed to be replaced because it was quite
inappropriate for the Association's jobs.

Approach

A project team was set up to plan and manage the development
programme. It consisted of management, staff and trade union
(UNISON) representatives. At an early stage it was decided that the
first priority was to develop a competence framework from which
everything would flow – ie a fully integrated approach. The next
steps would follow, consisting of a competence-based job evaluation
scheme and performance management processes based on agreed
competence levels and a review of achievements against those levels.
At this stage it was also decided that a broadbanded structure with
progression related to competence should be designed which would
cut costs by enabling pay to be managed more flexibly rather than
being governed by the fixed incremental system. But it was noted
that this could not be done until the essential preliminary
programme was completed.

Developing the competence framework

The first step taken by the project team was to define the core
competences of the Association. It then split into sub-groups to
prepare competence profiles for generic roles – for example, project
leader and care worker. The framework included both 'hard' competences concerned with outcomes, and 'soft' behavioural
competences. The distinction between the two was made clear. To
achieve the integration of the core and generic competences, the
same headings were adopted. The generic role profiles were,
however, expressed in the language used by the role-holders and
referred to what they actually did and how they did it – there was
never any question of lifting a competency dictionary down from the
shelf or copying profiles used by other care-delivery organisations.

The final step was to produce role-specific competence profiles which were prepared in consultation with individual role-holders or groups of staff in similar roles.

Job evaluation

The new job evaluations scheme was based on the competence framework which included a number of 'output' competences. The factors were:

- service delivery
- service development
- accountability for decision-making
- accountability for planning
- accountability for results
- support and advice
- leadership and line management
- teamwork and personal skills
- communication skills
- administrative and technical skills
- knowledge.

Performance management

Performance management processes were initially developed for care staff. They were based on an improved supervision process. A partnership approach was adopted. The emphasis is on joint agreement of expectations by reference to the role definition which incorporates key result areas and a role-specific competence profile. This is followed by a continuing dialogue and a joint review which is concerned with future development needs – it does not dwell on the past. Initially it was thought that some form of rating was required, but a pilot scheme revealed that rating was disliked intensely by all concerned (staff *and* managers) and it was dropped. The performance management process thus became entirely developmental, with the aim of raising skill and competence levels.

The pay system

Nicky Youern, who project-managed the initial work, has been appointed director of the Southern Focus Trust following the return of the previous director to the USA. Work is now being carried out under Nicky's direction on the development of a broadbanded pay system.

Case study

INTRODUCING BROAD BANDS IN ZURICH FINANCIAL SERVICES UK LIFE

Background
Zurich Financial Services UK Life was formed from the merger of Allied Dunbar, Eagle Star (both formerly owned by BAT Industries) and Zurich Insurance. This new company forms the life assurance and pensions arm in the UK, employing around 4,000 staff, the majority of whom are in sales and customer service functions.

Rationale for the present pay structure
The present pay structure is largely a product of a need to create a uniform pay system from the arrangements that each of the companies had operated in the past. All used formally structured pay systems, but each had a different emphasis. Eagle Star used a fairly traditional Hay-based grade structure while Allied Dunbar's grading system had evolved away from job evaluation to a number of wide grades reflecting functional specialisms and a general desire for more flexibility. Zurich's arrangements were structured, but with a stronger emphasis on market rate matching rather than job evaluation.

To ease the absorption of these different approaches into one framework it was decided that the flexibility provided by a broadbanded structure was required.

The new structure
The structure that has been adopted consists of eight grades. There are no fixed salary scales or zones for jobs. HR monitors the distribution of pay within each grade by calculating median and upper and lower quartiles. These figures are not formally published but are available to managers who want to understand more about the distribution of pay within the organisation.

Introducing the new structure
Moving staff from their old salary structure to the new grades was a crucial step. Alan Measures, reward strategy manager, commented:

'We wanted something that could be done in weeks, not months, and avoided a wholesale re-evaluation exercise for the whole organisation.' Moving to a common grading platform was the first step in the overall process of harmonising terms and conditions between the three organisations, and although it was recognised that a common analytical job evaluation system was needed, they decided to 'map' people to the new grade structure first. This would then allow Zurich to harmonise other pay and benefits arrangements fairly quickly. 'We wanted the harmonisation process to have plenty of momentum and to be completed quickly. Fairly early on we identified some potential showstoppers, such as common competence sets, the need for a single appraisal system, and a single evaluation system. To avoid these issues from delaying the process and distracting us from achieving harmonised terms, we decided to park them, and come back to them later,' says Measures.

HR developed some simple grade definitions, or templates, which outlined the sort of generic accountabilities, skill sets and experience levels one could expect to see at each of the levels. Managers were given these templates, and were given the freedom to add to them to make them suit their functions better. Managers were then told to map staff from the old grades to the new eight grade templates. 'It didn't take rocket science to see where staff fitted in within the new structure,' observes Measures. 'The eight levels were based on the organisational levels that existed within Zurich from chief executive downwards, so they only needed to map to the first five levels using existing reporting relationships as a guide. However, we also wanted to prevent it from becoming a *fait accompli* for staff, so we asked managers to talk each member of staff through their grade-mapping decision and listen to any concerns or objections individuals had. We also allowed for the possibility of some managers' not being able to agree their mapping decision with an individual, and created an appeals process to deal with such situations.'

There was clearly considerable potential for disagreement in the process, and one director took the unusual step of telling his staff that in the event of a dispute, the employee should be allowed to choose the grade he or she was mapped onto. His point was that the grade was not the central issue – it was the level of contribution that was required that was key, and those choosing to determine their own grades should be confident about producing the required level of performance. Ultimately, the mapping process took place very smoothly; there were no appeals, and it took just a few weeks to complete.

Pay reviews

Pay reviews are conducted by managers within a budget based on a mix of what the market indicates is necessary in conjunction with what the company feels it can afford. Spreadsheets are used, on which managers carry out peer-ranking to differentiate levels of performance, and then decide on the pay increase and overall level of pay to be received. Staff are given performance ratings based on an overall appraisal of their performance, and these – along with corporate performance – determine the amount of the annual bonus.

'A peer-ranking approach is designed to get managers to focus on how they can get the best use out of a finite review budget. Where necessary, HR feed in market data about specific functional groups or roles that may be vulnerable. Overall, the aim is to provide managers with an adequate budget, given the market conditions, and then let them allocate it according to performance,' says Measures.

Lessons learnt

There were those who had been unhappy at the constraints that the old systems had imposed on them and welcomed the new freedom. Inevitably, however, the changes caused discomfort among some members of the management team who had been used to letting the system effectively do the managing for them. The reduction in the number of constraints within the pay system put an end to this abdication, and taking accountability for decisions proved difficult for some.

Alan Measures feels that although it was not difficult to make the intellectual argument for broadbanding, managers still had problems with it at an emotional level. 'In some parts of the company there was a very strong promotion ethos. Regular promotions through a narrow-graded structure had become part of the culture. Staff were accustomed to it, as the promotions created a sense of progression and underlined one's status in the company. It was popular with some managers because promotions lessened the need for other forms of performance and career management. The by-products of this approach were that staff tended to focus on what was needed to 'earn' the next promotion to the exclusion of all other considerations. Ultimately, promotions didn't relate to a change in job content, or signify a step change in the challenge presented to the job-holder. It was much more a thank you for a job well done.'

The move to broad bands was designed to encourage staff to think about progression by acquiring skill and knowledge, and moving cross-functionally within the group. However, as much as this was seen as valid and necessary, most of the management reaction focused on the reduction in promotion opportunity, and the adverse impact this would have on morale and motivation.

At the time of the research (1999) Zurich Life was approaching the second anniversary of having introduced broadbanding, and is now going back to line managers to give them more support. Initial reactions to broadbanding seem to have overestimated the difficulties that would arise, and the focus is now on providing managers with guidelines and practical advice on how to manage and motivate in a broadbanded environment.

PART III

JOB FAMILY PAY STRUCTURES

7   FEATURES OF JOB FAMILY PAY STRUCTURES

Definitions

Job family

A job family consists of a group of jobs or roles in which the type of work and the knowledge and skills required to do them are broadly similar, but the work is carried out, and the knowledge and skills are used, at different levels.

There is no common or consistent method for defining job families. Again, organisations are tailoring their definitions to suit their particular needs and circumstances. In some cases they are organised on the basis of functions in the organisation, such as finance, marketing, sales and operations. In other cases they may reflect occupations which span different functions, such as administrators, service staff and accountants. Other organisations, such as the Royal Bank of Scotland, define them in terms of the business units in the organisation – and others, such as Yorkshire Building Society, apply the description to broad vertical categories of staff. The terminology also varies considerably from job and role groups to professional 'communities' (as at ICL) and 'career ladders'.

Job family pay structure

A job family structure contains separate grade structures for different job families. The job family grade structures are divided into a number of levels and the pay ranges for these levels may vary to reflect market rates for the roles in the various families. The job families may have different levels as shown in Figure 12 (overleaf).

Figure 12
A JOB FAMILY STRUCTURE WITH DIFFERING LEVELS

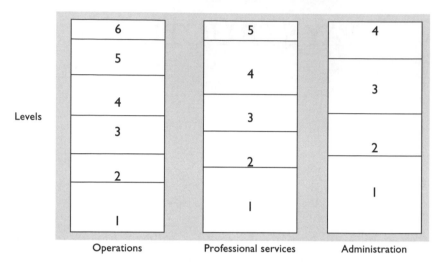

Some organisations, however, have the same number of levels in each job family, which looks like a common grade structure although there may be different pay ranges attached to each level. The job family structure in the Children's Society is illustrated in Figure 13.

Figure 13
JOB FAMILY STRUCTURE, THE CHILDREN'S SOCIETY

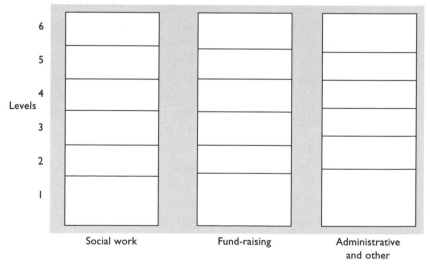

As in the case of broadbanded structures, there are consider-able variations in the ways in which job family structures are designed and managed in terms of the definition of family groups, the existence of common levels across the structure, variations in the numbers of levels between job families, the criteria used for defining job family levels and how job evalua-tion is applied. In some cases, such as the Children's Society and the Prince's Trust, broad bands are incorporated in the job family structure to produce a hybrid model. Within such broadbanded job family levels there may be reference points or zones functioning in the same way as those in a typical broad-banded structure.

Job family structures are not new in the UK. In many types of organisations, specialist types of work with a high market value – such as IT and accounting – have long had separate pay structures. This approach is sometimes called 'market group-ing'. But as the market pressures affecting these traditional areas have spread into other functions, and with the growth in numbers of professional and knowledge workers, so the inci-dence and coverage of job families has extended. It is interesting to note that as broadbanding has extended and the number of horizontal divides in pay structures has diminished, we are now seeing the spread of job families and structures which have more 'vertical' divisions.

Reasons for using job family structures

The objectives of job families as given by respondents to the IPD survey were:

Objectives	percentage of respondents
To map out career paths	29
To achieve more flexibility	25
To identify market groups	24
To provide for rewards to be based on personal contribution and progress	22

This indicates that non-pay objectives are given more promi-nence than those concerned with pay. The scope such structures allow for planning career progression on the basis of increases in skill or competence and the fact that individuals can be made aware of the development opportunities available to them in their job family and between job families is an attractive proposition to management and employees alike. In our experience, it is much easier to convince managers and staff of the benefits of job family structures than it is to explain why broadbanding by itself is desirable. A job family structure which incorporates broad bands can be presented truthfully and with conviction as achieving the best of both worlds, and it gives the *impression* of being more structured, which many people like, as well as recognising their own particular skills.

The achievement of organisational flexibility is also an important job family structure objective. This can be presented as a means of encouraging and facilitating lateral and diagonal career moves and supporting the concepts of continuous development and employability.

Features

The structure

Each of the separate job family structures is aligned to market rates and usually contains a number of grades or bands which reflect the levels of work within the job family, often as defined by job evaluation. Sometimes organisations exclude occupations from job families and these are catered for by a common graded pay structure. This is easier to do within a broadbanded structure which provides a framework for both the job families and the individual roles and is likely to be defined in competence level terms and use competence and contribution as the criteria for progression. The job evaluation process should preferably use a plan which includes aligned competence factors.

Some organisations have conventional graded structures for the majority of their jobs but introduce job families where it is felt that an occupation needs to be dealt with separately, especially one in which job-holders are mainly professional staff or knowledge workers. Separate job families often only cover some roles in the organisation.

Job family structures may also be set up for 'market groups' where the occupations concerned are subject to particular market pressures. The market rates for such jobs are higher than those for other occupations which would be placed in the same grade on the basis of internal relativities alone. However, the creation of market groups means that there may be increased risk of gender discrimination.

Grouping roles into job families

There are a number of different ways of grouping roles into job families. The three basic approaches are:

1 *occupational-based* – grouping by occupations such as scientists, engineers, designers, creative workers, IT specialists, accountants, HR specialists, sales staff, administrators and support staff
2 *work-based* – grouping by the nature of the work carried out, eg administration, data processing, professional services
3 *function-based* – grouping by function, eg production, marketing, finance, HR, regionalised services. In the latter case, a job family may have different levels such as regional, area and branch managers and supporting staff.

In practice, job family structures often contain a mix of these approaches. A typical structure may contain occupational-based families (sales staff and designers), work-based families (data processing), and function-based families (administrators and professional services). For example, the job family structure for the Peabody Trust has three families: administration, customer support services, and professional and technical services.

Number of families

Defining the number of job families is an issue specific to each organisation. At the extremes, Unilever has two families and IBM has more than 40. The key is to create a balance on the one hand between having enough families to reflect skills and market differences and to give clarity and meaning to staff, and on the other to keep the number small enough to operate and administer effectively. The median number of families in the organisations responding to the IPD survey was four, but the number varies considerably – for example:

- the Peabody Trust: three
- the Children's Society: three
- Coventry Building Society: four
- IMS Health: 10
- Nationwide Building Society: 11
- Volkswagen: 24
- Xerox: 34.

The factors affecting the decision on the number of families include:

- the size of the organisation
- the variety of market segments for employees (this is why Xerox has so many families, as described in the case study in Chapter 8)
- the structure and range of functions in the organisation (this was the rationale for the IMS Health structure, as explained in the case study in Chapter 8)
- ease of administration (the explanation for the small number of families in the Peabody Trust and the Children's Society).

Describing job families

Job families can in effect be described by reference to the roles contained within them, but written descriptions may help, as in the following for a retailing organisation:

- *The operational job family* contains all those roles which are concerned with managerial and operational activities in marketing, buying, distribution, selling and providing customer services.
- *The professional services job family* contains all those roles concerned with managing the provision of professional and specialist services and with delivering those services. These services include the following functions: finance, IT, HR, property and facilities management.

❑ *The administration job family* contains all those roles concerned with general management, managing and leading administrative teams and providing administrative, secretarial and support services.

However defined and described, it is important that they have a meaning and significance to the staff who are members of them.

Levels in families

The number of levels also varies. The most typical number is five or six to represent, as in broadbanding, the number of 'value-adding tiers' in the organisation. Examples include:

❑ IMS Health: five to six
❑ the Children's Society: six
❑ Xerox: six to eight
❑ the Peabody Trust: seven
❑ the Prince's Trust: eight.

In some cases, such as the Children's Society, IMS Health and the Peabody Trust, levels are common across all the job families. In others, the number of levels varies in order to enable pay to be flexed in response to market rate pressures.

Defining levels

Definitions of knowledge and skill requirements and key competencies are typically produced for roles in individual job families. These may be generic in a general administration family, or specific in families containing distinct roles – for example, a 'professional services' family, which may contain specialists in finance, IT and HR. In the latter case, it may be necessary to produce separate definitions for each sub-group in the job family. An example of a generic set of level definitions used for an administrative job family in a voluntary organisation is given in Table 21 (overleaf).

Where a common job evaluation system is used across families, common levels may be defined by the range of job evaluation scores. It is usual, however, to describe them in ways which indicate the role requirements at each level in terms of accountabilities and competencies. The levels may be defined generically, and an example of a generic level defined for a voluntary organisation is given below in Table 22.

Table 21
AN EXAMPLE OF JOB FAMILY LEVEL DEFINITIONS

Level definitions: Administration job family		
Level	**Accountabilities**	**Competencies**
1 Support worker/ administrator worker (a)	• Provide basic support/ administrative services in a defined area of activity • Meet service standards • Use and maintain basic equipment and facilities • Meet deadlines and fulfil work programme	• Maintain friendly, helpful and supportive relationships with immediate colleagues and/or customers • Provide services to internal and external customers • Take steps to improve task performance • Improve work methods to achieve higher levels of efficiency • Ensure that quality considerations are given proper attention
2 Support worker/ administrator (b)	• Deliver efficient and effective services in a key area of activity • Meet exacting deadlines • Achieve demanding service standards • Use and maintain a range of fairly complex equipment	• Relate well to internal and external customers and colleagues • Build and maintain good relationships with customers • Develop new procedures and systems for carrying out work • Identify areas for improvement and take action to achieve improvement plans • Give close and continuous attention to the delivery of high-quality services
3 Team leader/ senior administrator	• Lead a small to medium-sized team and ensure that team goals and standards are achieved • Advise client groups on administrative matters and procedures • Assist in the preparation of plans and budgets • Produce accurate and timely reports on administrative or operational matters • Use initiative to respond effectively to enquiries, queries and requests	• Exert influence on day-to-day matters with colleagues • Build effective networks with colleagues and stakeholders • Contribute to the development and maintenance of high standards of customer service • Set targets for improvement • Develop and implement programmes for implementing change • Contribute to the development of quality assurance and control processes and ensure that they are implemented

Level definitions: Administration job family		
Level	Accountabilities	Competencies
4 Manager (a)	• Head an operational or service unit or project or a small department • Formulate plans for the unit/department • Manage, monitor and review the work of the unit/department in order to achieve objectives • Provide leadership, support and learning opportunities to staff • Prepare budgets and control expenditure for the unit/department	• Exert influence on people to take action in ways which will make a positive though short-term impact on the performance of the unit/department • Develop high customer service standards in the unit/department and play an active part in achieving them • Develop and oversee the implementation of quality assurance and control processes • Develop and monitor continuous improvement programmes and stimulate action as required • Contribute to successful outcomes in the management of change
5 Manager (b)	• Head a large department or function • Formulate strategic plans for the department/function • Manage, monitor and review the work of the department/function in order to achieve objectives • Provide leadership, support and learning opportunities to staff • Prepare budgets and control expenditure for the department/function	• Exert influence on people to take action in ways which will make a medium- to long-term impact on the performance of the division/function • Develop high standards of customer service standards in the division/function and play an active part in achieving them • Contribute to the development of a culture which encourages innovation and continuous improvement • Manage major change programmes in area of responsibility
6 Senior manager	• Head a division or principal function • Contribute to formulation of corporate strategies relating to division/function • Achieve agreed objectives by making strategic decisions which have a major impact on the organisation's results • Respond effectively to new organisation-wide opportunities and threats • Provide visionary and inspirational leadership • Monitor the total performance of the division/function and take effective action as required	• Provide visionary and inspirational leadership • Encourage the development of staff at all levels • Exert influence on people to take action in ways which will make a long-term impact on the performance of the organisation • Lead and promote a culture which recognises the importance of meeting the needs of both internal and external customers in key aspects of the Society's operations • Lead the development of a culture which encourages innovation and continuous improvement • Manage major change programmes affecting the organisation as a whole

Some organisations, such as the Woolwich and Coutts, use a two-tiered model, with an overall structure of bands and generic definitions, underpinned by family-specific descriptions of the requirements in a particular family, such as the ATIF qualification in a tax family or a programming language in an IT family.

Table 22
AN EXAMPLE OF A GENERIC JOB FAMILY DEFINITION

Level 2 Definition	
Accountabilities	• Provide fairly complex administrative and support services • The work is largely standardised • Some freedom to decide on methods and priorities.
Knowledge and skills	• Administrative or operational knowledge or skills applied within an area or section.
Manage performance	• Propose targets and standards for role • Plan day-to-day activities • Work under fairly close supervision.
Manage oneself	• Make decisions confidently • Manage own learning • Take pride in achieving results.
Manage others	• Take a leadership role within team when appropriate.
Manage relationships	• Relate well to internal and external customers and colleagues • Take an active part in team meetings.
Manage communications	• Communicate orally or in writing with colleagues or customers in other parts of the organisation or externally on day-to-day matters.
Manage customer service	• Build and maintain good relationships with customers.
Manage continuous improvement	• Identify areas for improvement and take action to achieve improvement plans • Give close and continuous attention to the delivery of high-quality services.
Manage resources	• Use resources efficiently.

Career mapping

Perhaps the most significant feature of job family structures – one which has nothing at all to do with pay – is the fact that they can provide clear definitions of career paths within job families. Sometimes, career paths can be established across job families. This is the case when job family levels are defined in competency terms which are generalised, as in the examples given above (Tables 21 and 22), or spell out the particular knowledge and skills required at each level. The job family levels for finance staff at Volkswagen indicate the qualifications required at each of four levels:

Level 1 – AAT or equivalent
Level 2 – Level 2 CIMA or equivalent
Level 3 – fully qualified accountant
Level 4 – fully qualified accountant with at least two years' post-qualification experience.

Levels can also be defined in NVQ or SVQ terms, or if these are not directly relevant, they can be adapted, as at Advance Housing, where the career ladder is based on the framework provided by the care delivery NVQs.

Examples of the level definitions of the knowledge and skills requirements for professional/technical staff used at BP Amoco tasks are as follows:

Market level J (entry level)
Requires the application of knowledge and experience to routine problems. Incumbent in the job is able to research projects and make evaluations knowing what information to collect and where to find it; needs assistance in interpreting information.

Market level I
Requires the application of knowledge, past practice and experience to non-routine problems. Incumbent in job makes changes to procedures as situation dictates, applies in-depth analysis of routine data to the solution of the problem.

Market level H
Requires the application of knowledge, past practice and experience to relatively complex problems which impact the department. Incumbent in the job offers recommended changes

to procedures as situations dictate; applies in-depth analysis of complex data to the solution of problems.

Level definitions of knowledge and skills requirements can be made even more specific by drawing on job and skills analyses which are used for recruitment, development and training purposes. Indeed, we have found the pressure for links between pay and the skills and competencies required in each family to emanate from the line managers and staff themselves, rather than the HR function. Typically, these requirements have been initially identified for recruitment purposes. They have then driven personal development and career planning processes, and so the logic for extending their use to pay becomes compelling.

In an administration job family, as in the example given in Table 22, the knowledge and skill requirements for the first two levels could be defined as follows:

Level 1   Knowledge of administration procedures in section and the use of basic equipment. Skills required in such areas as basic word-processing and record-keeping, operating a switchboard, responding to telephone enquiries, receiving visitors, relating to customers on straightforward matters, or the operation of printing equipment to carry out simple printing operations.

Level 2   Knowledge of basic departmental procedures and policies and the use of more advanced equipment, facilities or processes (eg software programs for word-processors). Skills required in such areas as advanced word-processing – eg the use of spreadsheets and PowerPoint, keeping complex records requiring some judgement in deciding on what should be entered, preparing reports conveying factual information, taking and preparing minutes, managing a complex appointments diary, dealing with requests for standard information and complaints from customers, using and maintaining complex equipment.

Career mapping could be achieved by specifying these levels in each job family and indicating development routes within and between families as shown in Figure 14, which illustrates a structure with common levels.

Figure 14
CAREER PATHS IN A JOB FAMILY STRUCTURE WITH COMMON LEVELS

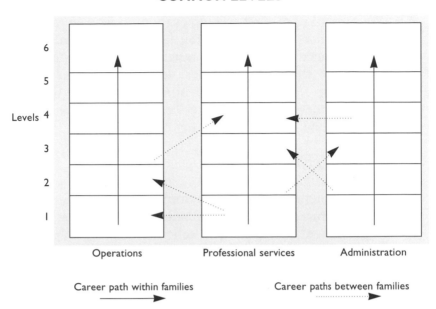

Pay ranges

The pay ranges attached to job family levels are determined by reference to market rate data for roles at each level. These ranges can vary between different market groups as at Xerox (see case study in Chapter 8). However, some organisations such as Nationwide Building Society (see case study in Chapter 8) have standard pay ranges for each level which are intended to cover the market prices of all jobs in each level.

Pay ranges for levels in job families tend to be broadbanded with the characteristics of that approach as described in Chapters 4 and 5. There may or may not be pay limits, and the band may be zoned or segmented as an alternative to having different pay ranges for levels in different job families. This can be described as a 'mixed model', and the conclusions from our research and recent experience is that this will become increasingly common because it can combine the clarification of career paths characteristic of the job family approach together with the ability to flex pay in response to market pressure which typifies broadbanding.

An alternative approach adopted by the Prince's Trust, as described in the case study in Chapter 8, is to have no defined levels or pay ranges for the job families. Instead, a combination of market pricing and job evaluation is used to define zones for separate roles in each job family, each zone having its own reference point and pay range. Thus in the administration job family there are five roles: administration assistant, administrator, administration officer, senior administrator and administration executive. Each of these has individual zones attached to it with a 33 per cent range.

Use of market pricing

As we saw in Chapter 5, market pricing (ie external value considerations) tends to dominate pay decisions in job family structures, just as in broadbanding. The earlier forms of job families were, in fact, called 'market groups' where it was thought that a separate market-driven pay structure was required for occupations such as IT specialists.

Many of the points made in the section on broadbanding apply here, but possibly with ever greater force. Separate market-based structures, using different sources of data, make for excellent market fit in each family. However, the downside can be that each family becomes very isolated from the other families in the organisation. ICL, for example, found that engineers were trying to select the highest-paid family and were unwilling to move into lower-paid areas. The families became very divisive. Glaxo Wellcome abandoned job families for this reason and developed a broadbanded structure.

Pay budgeting can also become a complex issue. In addition, a pattern can develop in which people are nearly all paid at the market rate, with little differentiation according to personal contribution. This is why we are seeing some organisations attracted to the mixed model – job families providing a professional focus for development and close market alignment, and the broadbanded structure underpinned by job evaluation providing a framework for lateral development, and for ensuring that common standards in pay management are applied.

Use of job evaluation

As we also saw in Chapter 5, analytical points-factor job evaluation schemes are used by many of the organisations with job families covered by our research (see Chapter 8 for further details). They determine vertical relativities within job families and, importantly, lateral relativities between job families, as illustrated in Figure 15. Two of the problems associated with job families are the maintenance of internal equity and the provision of lateral career moves between them. This is why lateral comparisons are essential. However, if the emphasis is on development in the family structure, as at Royal Bank of Scotland, and also on close market alignment through the use of good market data, then the organisation may decide that a common banded structure or job evaluation system is not required. Why should someone in, say, the treasury family have their pay influenced by what is happening for branch staff?

As in the case of broadbanding, job evaluation is often relegated to a support role in job family structures after the design

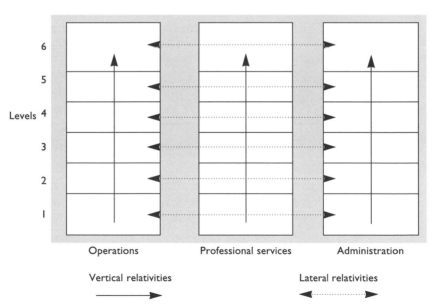

Figure 15
THE USE OF JOB EVALUATION IN FAMILIES

stage. Roles tend to be allocated to levels within families by processes of job matching with level definitions and/or generic role definitions. If these have been carefully prepared, using job evaluation in the traditional sense is unnecessary. But job evaluation may still be necessary to audit pay levels to ensure that equal value considerations are satisfied, and it may be used when an entirely new role is created which does not fit neatly into an existing job family level or does not have a clear match in the external world.

Managing job family structures

When broad bands are incorporated into job family structures, as is frequently the case, reference points, zones or segments may be used as in a broadbanded structure and methods of progression will also be similar.

The allocation of roles into levels in job families should be fairly straightforward if good level definitions and/or generic role definitions exist. Often, the detailed, family-specific definitions make placement in a level relatively easy, as well as gaining high credibility and support from staff in each family. Rather than the often confusing terminology and pseudo-science of traditional point-factor job evaluation, the classification schemes commonly used in job families are highly suited to this approach. As mentioned earlier, analytical job evaluation schemes tend to be kept in reserve rather than being used to grade jobs. Equal value considerations also need to be borne in mind, but as one HR director said to us: 'I refuse to be obsessed by equal value.'

Operating issues

Job family ownership

Generally, we have found that it is helpful to have clearly identified responsibility for pay management and development in each job family. This is reasonably straightforward if the families are functionally defined, but can be more complex if they cut across functions in an organisation. Some of the issues which can emerge if this is not the case include the following:

❑ Market data indicates, say, a high-percentage overall annual increase in a family but a line manager heading up a business refuses to fund the required increase.

❑ A staff member asks to transfer to another department to develop his or her skills and prepare for the next level up in the family, but the business head refuses to allow this because of the immediate inconvenience this would cause him or her.

The HR function can provide the family co-ordination and leadership role, but generally we find it best if the families are 'chaperoned' by members of the senior management team. The job family aspects of their role may include:

❑ reviewing the development, career and succession plan in each family

❑ reviewing market data and agreeing required overall pay budget increases

❑ ensuring a consistency in approach within the family across different departments.

It is also often helpful if training and development in the company is organised in a manner congruent with the job family definition.

All these factors should be taken into consideration when developing a job family structure, but before starting the development programme it is necessary to assess whether or not job families are appropriate and to consider the readiness of the organisation for job families.

Readiness for job families

Organisations are most likely to be ready for the introduction of job families when:

❑ they believe that competitive advantage can be obtained by attracting and retaining high-quality staff through the provision of career development opportunities in addition to rewarding them well

❑ it is recognised that different approaches may be required for developing and rewarding staff in the various functions and occupations

- they are capable of operating the processes required, especially those concerned with role analysis, market pricing, job evaluation, involvement and communications
- it is reasonably easy to identify the different job families (if an organisation has difficulty in doing this, it would suggest that job families are not appropriate)
- the concept has already been used for recruitment and development purposes, making its extension to pay management much more straightforward
- the organisation structure is reasonably clear so that job families naturally 'fall out'
- pay level determination is already strongly driven by market data, and there may already be wide variations in pay levels for jobs at an equal level in the organisation structure.

Disadvantages

In assessing the case for job families, consideration should be given to their advantages as set out earlier in this chapter, particularly those concerned with career mapping. But it is also necessary to consider the following drawbacks:

- Although it can be argued that some occupations are best treated separately because they are different or because of their special market rate position, job family structures can be divisive.
- They can further career development within a family but at the same time inhibit career flexibility (moving between different job families).
- Equity is more difficult to achieve, especially where job families provide rewards which are strongly oriented towards market rates and individual competencies.
- They can be cumbersome to administer, which is why ICL simplified its approach and reduced the number of distinct families.
- The need to track market rates in detail can impose a burden on the HR department. We have come across organisations where market rate analysis in the HR department has become a sort of cottage industry such that several staff are more or less fully employed in collecting and analysing data.

8 JOB FAMILY PAY STRUCTURES IN PRACTICE

Developing job family structures

When the decision is made in principle to consider the development of a job family structure, the steps required are:

1. Conduct analysis and a diagnostic review.
2. Evaluate alternative structures.
3. Define objectives.
4. Develop a project plan.
5. Decide on job families.
6. Establish the number of levels.
7. Define the levels.
8. Decide on pay progression policies.
9. Validate band levels and the allocation of roles to the bands.
10. Decide on pay levels.

1: Conduct analysis and a diagnostic review

The aim of this review is to understand present pay arrangements and to identify issues and problems which might be addressed by introducing a new structure. The approach to such a review is described in Chapter 5.

2: Evaluate alternative structures

In the light of the review at step 1, evaluate the choices along the lines set out in Chapter 2. The evaluation should take into account the advantages and disadvantages of the alternatives and an assessment of the readiness of the organisation for any of them. It is particularly important with job families to look in detail at their career development aspects. In our experience, job families that are introduced purely for pay purposes have little meaning to the staff concerned, and their effectiveness is limited. If the decision is to develop a job family structure, which might incorporate broad bands, proceed to the next steps.

3: Define objectives

Define the objectives of introducing job families and the benefits that will accrue to the organisation and its individual employees.

4: Develop a project plan

Draw up the project plan, including communications, involvement and training strategies.

5: Decide on job families

Examine the organisation structure and the main functions and occupations in the organisation. Consider alternative methods of grouping jobs into job families bearing in mind the different approaches described earlier in this chapter. The aim is to identify groups of roles in which the type of work is similar but the actual work is carried out at different levels. There will always be a choice, and at this stage it is advisable to involve line management in selecting the optimum division of jobs into families. Employees and their representatives should also be consulted. We tend to find that both managers and staff want numerous job families to recognise their own specialities, and there is often a prolonged debate until agreement is reached. Some organisations that have only a few job families, such as the Children's Society and the Peabody Trust, have found that to avoid over-fragmentation because of staff pressures, it is preferable to have only a limited number of families so that no one feels that a particular area, not their own, has been unduly favoured.

One typical area for debate is whether there should be a separate family for administration or whether administrative staff should be placed in the function in which they work. The arguments for a separate administrators' family are that the skills are similar and a well-defined career path in administration can be mapped. The arguments against are that administrators should not be relegated to some form of ghetto – they may well be acquiring specialist experience and expertise in a function and they should be given an indication that there is a career available in that function in some specialist capacity. Some organisations combine vertical and horizontal families with professional families but provide for a common base level in the form of an administration family to allow for upward and lateral development.

Once the family structure is agreed, each job family should be defined as explicitly as possible in terms of the roles within it and their characteristics – the essential nature of the work, common skills, etc.

6: Establish the number of levels

A preliminary analysis of the work carried out in each job family will suggest the likely number of 'value-adding tiers' which will indicate the number of levels required to provide for adequate differentiation between the size of roles likely to be placed in each level. It may be possible to have the same number of levels in each family, but there is no compelling reason why this should always be the case.

7: Define the levels

The factors for differentiating levels are established and defined, and the type of work carried out in the family is analysed. These may be the factors included in an analytical job evaluation scheme, or job-family-specific differentiators may be used. At IMS Health, for example, the four differentiators were knowledge, complexity, accountability and relationships. To provide a further basis for allocating roles to levels it may be useful to prepare generic role definitions against which roles can be matched to establish best fit.

An analytical job evaluation scheme can be used to size jobs in the family, and the ranking of scores produced by job evaluation could be the basis for dividing the jobs into levels and defining the levels in job evaluation score terms. Alternatively, if it is believed that the characteristics of the roles in the family with reference to defined differentiators are well known enough to produce level definitions and to match roles to those definitions, then the time-consuming and expensive process of applying a common analytical job evaluation scheme need not be gone through at this stage (which is what happened at IMS Health).

Levels should be defined in terms of both accountabilities and competence requirements. The latter will provide the basis for mapping career paths. Generally, these level definitions are made available to staff. Since their use in an open vacancy posting system in Yorkshire Building Society, the number of vacancies filled by internal applicants has increased significantly. Level definitions are freely used as aids to development and in building a credible pay system, as distinct from the traditional secretive and controlling use of job evaluation.

8: Decide on pay progression policies

At this stage it is necessary to decide how pay should be progressed within levels, and what criteria should be used. The most typical criteria are competence and contribution, which suit the development emphasis and focus on broad roles and personal contribution in organisations progressing down this path. Generally, the same progression system is used in each family, although there are examples of variations between different areas. For example, the bonus scheme for staff in a sales job family could be quite different from the performance-related pay scheme in a marketing family. Competence pay could be used in a research family and team pay in a customer service family. This could be preferable to applying a common system across all job families which suits nobody particularly well.

9: Validate band levels and the allocation of roles to the bands

It is advisable to validate the band levels and the allocation of roles to bands in some way. This can be a simple review process, preferably involving line managers, or through an independent review as at IMS Health. The review could use analytical job evaluation as the validation mechanism, and/or refer to market data. This will aim to test the degree to which roles have been properly sized within bands and, importantly, establish that internal equity exists laterally between bands. In Xerox, job evaluation was used 'to firm up the matching and cross-check where jobs had been positioned'. Organisations such as IMS Health and Nationwide Building Society also used job evaluation in this way.

10: Decide on pay levels

Job family structures tend to be market-driven. It is therefore necessary before this stage to conduct comprehensive pay surveys. A decision can then be made on the width in pay terms of the levels. The tendency is to have broad bands to provide for flexibility. Each family can have its own broad bands or company-wide bands can provide the framework in which job families operate. Reference should be made to the suggested approach described in Chapters 4 to 6 when defining the bands. Job family bands may have an infrastructure of reference points or zones, or they may be segmented.

Case studies

The IPD research confirmed that there are many varieties of job family structures and a number of approaches to introducing them. The rest of this chapter is therefore devoted to providing case study examples of how organisations have developed such structures in order to illustrate the ways in which it can be done in different circumstances. The case studies are:

❏ *Coventry Building Society* – illustrating a holistic approach which produced a relatively simple structure
❏ *IMS Health* – describing an approach designed to meet special circumstances in which involvement played a major part
❏ *Nationwide Building Society* – showing how a relatively simple approach was developed in a large and complex organisation
❏ *The Prince's Trust* – describing a pay harmonisation project which resulted in the introduction of broadbanded job family pay structure

❑ *The Royal Bank of Scotland* – recounting how a business-focused approach to developing new pay systems was developed which allowed for pay arrangements to be devised in business units to suit their individual needs, on the principle that 'one size does not fit all': it included the introduction of a job family structure for retail managers
❑ *Xerox* – an example of a business-driven and sophisticated approach to using job families.

Case study

COVENTRY BUILDING SOCIETY

Background

Coventry Building Society (CBS) is the sixth largest building society in the UK. It has 50 branches in its network, operating mainly in the Midlands area, and employs just over 1,000 staff. In 1995, Martin Ritchley, the Society's chief executive, master-minded 'Vision 2000' – a strategy setting out where the Society should be in five years' time. There were a number of issues to be addressed in achieving this vision. One of them was the reward/pay system which consisted of a traditional hierarchical grading structure and a profit-related bonus scheme.

Approach

A holistic approach was adopted so that from whatever angle staff looked at the elements of performance, development and reward, they were consistent. The programme was underpinned by a competency framework related to recruitment, training and career development. This was fed into the reward system. A new vocabulary was introduced centred on the concept of a performance, development and reward system.

The pay structure

A 'career stream structure' was developed to replace a traditional graded structure. This consists of what are in effect four job families:

1 customer service and support staff
2 professional and technical staff
3 managers
4 the executive team.

The structure was modelled as follows (note that customer service and support staff are on top):

Customer service and support staff	
Professional and technical staff	Managers
Executive team	

Each role within a career stream is benchmarked to a market median rate. This is paid for effective performance – ie 'performing a role in the way the Society wanted it to be performed with the minimum need for further development'. Initially, the range was from 10 per cent below the rate to the market median. But during the implementation the range was broadened and is now from 25 per cent below market rate to 5 per cent above market rate. This was primarily to take account of staff in the roles who needed more development to reach the market-rate level. The compa-ratio is currently 94.

The development process
The allocation of roles to career streams was carried out by a process of 'role mapping'. The first step was to benchmark each position. Old job descriptions were replaced by role profiles containing a description of the role, and the accountabilities, performance measures and competencies relevant to the role. There were initially 11 competency areas (now 10, following a competency review). Competency is defined as the mix of behaviours, knowledge and skill required to carry out the role. Staff were involved in developing the framework in workshops.

The next step was to look at the role profile and decide where it fitted into the career stream by reference to market-rate data, the role accountabilities and the role competency profile.

Introduction of the new structure
Having benchmarked each role, an analysis of the extent to which pay rates for individuals were below the market median was carried out. Each department was allocated a 'pot' related to the size of the

variance to remedy the situation. It took three pay reviews to achieve rectification. The chief executive acted as the 'project champion'. A group of senior managers – the 'HR stakeholder group' – signed off proposals when they were satisfied that this was 'a business solution rather than an HR solution'. The union (UNIFI) was initially unsure about the new scheme but has come to accept and trust it.

Performance pay

Performance pay is related to ratings on a six-point scale from unacceptable to outstanding. Each rating is underpinned by a description covering achievement of objectives, performance against accountabilities, and development needs. Staff at the top of the range can be paid a non-consolidated bonus. A budget of 0.25 per cent of the payroll is also available for small recognition payments.

Performance management

A 'performance planning and review scheme' was introduced. This is based on reviews of performance against objectives, of performance against accountabilities and of competences. The latter compares the individual competency profile with the role competency profile.

The performance management scheme incorporates a 'performance log' (a record of individual performance), a personal development plan and a performance planning and review form. The latter formally records performance against objectives, accountabilities and competency movement at review meetings, of which there are a minimum of four a year.

Team-based incentive pay

Team-based incentive pay is defined as 'a bonus payment, paid annually based upon the achievement of specific team targets'. The scheme was introduced in appropriate business areas as part of the reward strategy and to replace the profit-related scheme which was inappropriate for a mutual organisation. The idea that team pay would be applied universally was considered but refuted as impractical (it was not possible to develop appropriate team measures of performance in certain parts of the business).

The business areas in which specific performance measures are available have team-based pay related to them. For example, the measures for the branch network are net retail receipts, mortgage advances and insurance sales. Areas where it is inappropriate or diffi-cult to introduce team pay participate in a corporate scheme based on Society growth and cost control.

Annual payments are based on performances related to target in accordance with a scale capped at 15 per cent. For example, the target performance in 1998 was 7 per cent and the branch network teams received a median bonus of 8.47 per cent of the base salary of team members.

The outcomes of team-based incentive pay have been better team-work, especially in the branch network, and increased focus on key measures – eg achieving sales targets.

Outcomes

A fundamental impact was made on the culture of the business. Staff attitude surveys (86 per cent response in 1999) have recorded a continuing increase in favourable reactions – for example:

| | Percentage favourable | | | |
	1996	1997	1998	1999
Society performance	81	84	84	92
Performance				
management	58	70	59	71
Morale	33	39	52	71

The survey results obtained by CBS have been benchmarked against other financial service organisations. CBS was first in eight of the 16 question areas, second in six, and fourth and fifth in the other two. The 'firsts' included responses to questions about job satisfaction, opportunity for development and satisfaction with CBS as an employer. In the same period, staff turnover has fallen from 23 per cent to 12 per cent and the Society has achieved the Investor in People (IIP) award, one of its training and development team being invited to join the Coventry and Warwickshire IIP assessment panel.

Lessons learnt

It is important to involve everyone and communicate thoroughly. It is also necessary to have a formal 'tracking device' to ensure that what is being done is right for the business. Keep it simple! Network with other organisations.

Case study

IMS HEALTH

Background

IMS Health is a company with about 8,000 employees, which provides information to the health care industry, primarily pharmaceutical companies. It operates at a local-country level (90 countries) and at a global level. Local-country information is gathered about which drugs are being patented or are coming out of patent, about sales, about the market effectiveness of drugs, etc – and any information that pharmaceutical companies want to know about each other. This is gathered at local level and the information is then globalised – sold to the headquarters of pharmaceutical companies worldwide to help them with their strategic planning.

Harewood Avenue contains the Global International Commercial Division, half of the European Technology Development Group and the European and Worldwide Corporate Headquarters. There are about 400 staff who are affected by the pay structure.

These different areas of activity were brought together from different sites to Harewood Avenue in 1994, and this prompted the decision to develop a new pay structure. The largest site utilised the Hay system, which was initially rolled out to the other groups. However, it became quickly apparent that Hay was not suitable for the technical group, for which a broadbanded structure was developed instead. The commercial group retained Hay. Because of the changes the company was going through, there was a considerable amount of pressure 'to develop a more flexible approach to the ways in which we evaluated roles and the pay structures that went with them'. The existence of different structures for each part of the business made it difficult to compare rates, and employees were dissatisfied with Hay.

The aim

The aim was 'to evolve a system which could be flexible enough to cope with the ever-changing business environment we were in'.

The reason for going down the job family route was that it would give IMS Health the flexibility needed, bearing in mind the different functions operating in the building. What was wanted was a job family approach to the evaluation of roles coupled with job family pay scales. These would be broadened considerably because the levels would be much wider than those existing under the Hay system. Defining career paths was an important consideration affecting the decision to develop job families, as was the need to focus on establishing appropriate pay levels in each job family that were related to market rates.

Development of the structure

Because there was not a single management team which could make decisions on a new structure, each of the different teams had to be involved in the development programme.

The development programme was carried out in nine stages:

1 the definition of job families and levels within the job families
2 a cross-family comparison exercise to relate levels between families
3 consultation on structure
4 the definition of generic levels
5 the evaluation of roles within families
6 a cross-analysis of the role evaluation levels in jobs
7 analysis of behavioural requirements
8 development of pay scales
9 development of progression policies.

The strategy was to gain the maximum commitment from all concerned by involving managers and staff extensively in the process. The enthusiastic participation of managers was 'driven by their own desire to sort it out'.

1: Defining job families and levels

The initial step to get the process going was taken by HR, who produced a preliminary analysis of job families. Groups of six or so managers from potential job families were then canvassed and asked to discuss and agree whether they were in a definable job family and, broadly, what the function was of people in that family.

They were then asked to identify the jobs within the family and rank them without reference to the job-holders. Four differentiators were used as the basis for ranking:

1 knowledge
2 complexity

3   accountability

4   relationships

Of these, the first three were the most useful.

Benchmark roles were identified in each job family and market rate comparisons were made. This led to the definition of a *reference point* which is the rate for people who are fully carrying out their roles.

The previous system of fixed scales with a mid-point of 100 per cent, an 80-per-cent minimum and a 120-per-cent maximum (ie the standard Hay scale) was dropped. Employees may be engaged at a rate below the reference point and progress towards it, but only in exceptional circumstances will their pay move above the reference point. However, that point may change as market rates change.

The managers then decided how many levels could be distinguished and defined in terms of the differentiators. The number of levels varied between the different families but was typically five or six.

2: Cross-family comparisons
A small consultancy was engaged to make an independent cross-family comparison. The aim was to define a level which would be common to all families so that staff at the same level in different families could see that their jobs were regarded as being broadly comparable. However, it was made clear to them that the pay scales might not be the same so as to take account of differences in market rates.

3: Consultation on structure
Focus groups of employees were set up to review the levels as defined in the initial stages. They were asked to concentrate on the level definitions and not on the jobs themselves, although these would have to be borne in mind. They were also encouraged to consider the flow between job levels – the natural progression from level to level as defined in terms of the differentiators. For example, they would look at knowledge requirements in level 1 and decide whether there was a natural progression to the knowledge requirements in the next level. This exercise invariably results in the elimination of one of the initially identified levels.

As Angela McCorriston, human resources director, remarked, this was regarded as 'the most fundamental process in terms of the buy-in from the whole organisation'.

4: Definition of generic levels

By reference to the earlier results, HR produced generic level definitions (ie definitions applicable to all job families for each level). The aim was to provide a basis for ensuring consistency across the job families.

5: Job evaluation

The teams of managers in each family decided on the allocation of jobs to levels by reference to the simple role definitions they had prepared on a template (one side of one sheet of paper) expressed in terms of the differentiators and the level definitions (so it was a job matching process).

The managers decided what the roles meant in terms of knowledge, accountability and complexity: for example, 'To carry out this marketing role you have to have knowledge of the pharmaceutical industry, you have to have a marketing diploma, etc.' The management would then say 'My marketing manager belongs in level 4' and the group would then discuss that. Following this exercise it was found that most families started at level 3; there were only a few jobs in level 2. One reason for this is that IMS has a relatively small number of support roles.

6: Cross-analysis of evaluations

The cross-analysis between job families to achieve consistency was carried out by getting managers from different functions together (facilitated by HR) to make comparisons – for example, 'The marketing manager has been evaluated at level 5 but that doesn't fit with my data processing manager, who is only level 4.'

7: Behavioural requirements

Work is now being carried out by HR on defining behavioural requirements at each level so that individuals will know how they are expected to behave at higher levels.

8: Development of pay scales

In developing pay scales IMS was 'up front' in saying that the organisation may value a role at a similar level to another one but that the pay scales may be very different because of market considerations.

In other words, the pay levels are market-driven, although the determination of role levels was governed by internal equity considerations and staff will be rewarded if their role grows.

9: Progression policies

The progression policy is that for individuals who are recruited to a role below the reference point, a personal development plan should be prepared so that they reach the level of competence required. A salary development plan would also be prepared for budgeting purposes to bring up the individuals' rate of pay to the reference point.

Progression to the reference point (in effect competence-related pay) is determined by managers within their budgets. Only in special circumstances (eg exceptional performance or the need to retain someone) are staff paid above the reference point if they remain in the same role.

In levels 3 and 4 'roles grow as people grow', so there is a fair amount of flexibility. IMS does not want to recruit people in level 3 who do not have the potential to progress to level 4. The jump to level 5 (senior professionals and junior managers) is, however, a bigger one.

Lessons learnt

The job family structure has delivered the three benefits it was expected to:

1   clarity and consistency
2   transparency and openness
3   getting people at IMS to appreciate that they all work for one company.

The new structure has gone some way towards eliminating the previous status culture. While there is more flexibility, it is still necessary to emphasise to staff that 'ceilings haven't gone away'. They are not going to move to level 5 unless there is a job in level 5.

The most important lesson learnt, however, was the importance of getting managers and staff involved. 'It's the business that has to do it, not HR.' As Angela McCorriston commented:

> By doing it in this way we have created widespread understanding and acceptance of how jobs were evaluated. In addition, because there is

comparability in the levels across the job families (although not necessarily in pay) it is much easier for individuals to identify whether it is
possible to transfer to a position in another area that will provide the
opportunity to develop their skills and competences, and enhance
their career prospects.

Producing a 'home-grown' system was equally important.

Case study

NATIONWIDE BUILDING SOCIETY

Background
Nationwide is the largest UK mutual building society, with 13,500
staff and 750 branches. Following the decision to continue as a
mutual society, the business strategy, as developed in 1995, was to
improve levels of customer service and to streamline services generally. More devolution of decision-making to line managers took place
while simultaneously introducing better controls. One-over-one
reporting relationships were abolished and spans of control for
managers were extended.

A traditional pay structure was in place. This contained 11 grades
and pay progression was related to performance. Job evaluation had
become a 'cottage industry'. There was no facility for managing
market pressures. The result was that staff were recruited near the
top of their scale leaving little room for progression. A new pay
structure was required which would support the implementation of
the business strategy.

Principles of the new pay structure
It was decided that the new pay system should be designed in accordance with the following principles:

❑ Make pay more flexible.
❑ Achieve flexibility and facilitate career planning by establishing job
   families of people involved in similar types of activity but at different levels.
❑ Align pay to the market, but do not lose sight of the principle that
   pay should be related to job size.
❑ Build adequate controls into the system.

The design of the job family structure

The job family structure was developed following a detailed analysis of work.

Role accountabilities

Groups of staff were gathered together to develop sets of role accountabilities – no more than seven or eight per role. Generic role definitions were then produced and published in booklet form. An additional 'information sheet' was given to individuals setting out their accountabilities. As a result of this exercise, many similarities were found between different roles, and the number of separate roles was reduced from 1,600 to 350.

Level definition

Five levels of decision-taking were then identified:

Level 1 – This level contains those roles where the timescale of decision-making extends over a few days or weeks and the work is fairly well patterned and controlled by guidelines.

Level 2 – This is for technical and professional staff who are expected to do things for themselves. For example, staff who are called out at night are expected to make decisions on the spot.

Level 3 – This is the first level of managers who implement action plans and integrate work in the areas for which they are responsible.

Level 4 – This is for senior managers who are concerned with strategic direction – turning corporate strategies into action. They work together as a cohesive group.

Level 5 – This is for directors.

Job family definition

On the basis of the information obtained from the generic role definitions, job families were identified and defined at each level.

Level 1 – four job families: general services, specialist services, support services and customer service

Level 2 – three job families: customer relations (the sales force), leading people (team managers) and specialist advice

Level 3 – two job families: professional development and 'implementation' (the big operational roles)

Level 4 – one family

Level 5 – one family.

Thus there is a total of 11 job families.

Allocation to levels
On the basis of the information from the generic role definitions and the level descriptions, roles were provisionally allocated into levels. The allocation was determined by identifying the largest common denominator – reference was made only to the key aspects of the role. It was validated by a comprehensive job evaluation programme with three panels using the Hay system. This took three months. Everything went reasonably well, although there were some problems in areas such as technology.

Competency framework
A competency framework of six core competencies was also developed for career development planning and potential identification purposes.

Pay
Pay ranges were defined for roles or clusters of roles in each level. The range is 20 per cent above and below the target rate, which was determined by reference to market data. Because of market factors, roles did not necessarily have the same target rates even if they were the same job size.

Pay progression is related to performance ratings on a four-point scale (excellent, good, improvement required, unsatisfactory). As a guideline, it is expected that staff rated excellent will take two years to reach the target rate from the minimum, and three years if rated as good.

Outcomes

As Deborah Rees, at that time senior manager reward at Nationwide commented: the outcome of this process has been a reward system which is flexible, clear, straightforward, transparent and, importantly, supports the business strategy and style.

Case study

THE PRINCE'S TRUST: PAY HARMONISATION THROUGH BROADBANDED JOB FAMILIES

Background

The Prince's Trust was set up by the Prince of Wales in 1976 to help young people to succeed by giving them opportunities which they would otherwise not have. The Trust aims to help young people to improve their lives by creating opportunities and helping youngsters to succeed through training, skill-building, business loans, grants, personal development and study support outside school.

The pay system

There was no overall pay system applying to each of the separate parts of the Trust. To varying degrees, each part went its own way. It was therefore decided that a strategy for harmonising pay should be formulated which would support the overall strategy of establishing more coherence in the direction and management of the Trust. In principle, it was agreed that the pay harmonisation strategy:

- should fit the culture and values of the Trust
- should provide a framework within which a consistent approach to pay would take place
- should provide for a reasonable degree of flexibility in rewarding people for their contribution.

The pay harmonisation project

An advisory project team was set up which was involved in developing a job evaluation scheme. The factors were:

- concern for people
- complexity of decisions and freedom to act
- problem-solving and innovation

- ❑ communication
- ❑ influencing and interpersonal skills
- ❑ the management of resources and process
- ❑ planning
- ❑ flexibility
- ❑ capability.

The scheme was computerised using GAUGE software. A very large proportion of jobs were then evaluated. A market rate survey was also conducted.

To provide for flexibility within a framework it was decided that a job family structure should be designed with 'bands' – ie individual job ranges for roles – in each family. The pay range for each band was fixed at 20 per cent below and 10 per cent above an 'anchor rate'. This rate was determined by reference to both market pay levels and job evaluation scores. Internal equity was regarded as important but it was recognised that the need to be competitive might prevail in certain instances. Progress through a zone would be related to contribution.

The eight job families were:

- ❑ operations delivery
- ❑ administration
- ❑ finance
- ❑ marketing and commercial
- ❑ policy and research
- ❑ human resources
- ❑ management information systems
- ❑ fund-raising.

Each family was defined, and pay band definitions were produced for the generic roles in each family. For example, the operations delivery family was described as including (i) front-line roles where individuals will have contact with clients and responsibility for individuals who have contact with clients, and (ii) roles in which the development of the client base or front-line programmes is key. The pay bands in this family were defined as follows:

Senior manager – responsible to a director or head of department either for managing functional and/or geographic group, including line management responsibility for other managers, and/or for managing and/or developing complex programmes

Manager – responsible either to a senior manager or a director for operations delivery or the development of service delivery; may have line management responsibility for non-managers

Executive – responsible for developing contacts with, delivering programmes to and/or developing programmes for clients; may have supervisory responsibilities; likely to have significant experience of target markets

Junior executive – responsible for developing contacts with, delivering programmes to and/or developing programmes for clients; may have supervisory responsibilities; likely to have less experience and/or less responsibility than operations delivery executives

Assistant – trainee, working alongside an executive or junior executive; likely to have limited experience of programmes or client delivery.

Outcomes
As Vicky Hemming, director of human resources, pointed out, the key components of the system are that it is owned by staff, there is a strong cultural fit and it is transparent. She commented that: 'It's getting it to fit and getting it to develop with the culture that counts. It's relatively easy to design the system: it's getting it to work that matters.'

Case study

BUSINESS-BASED PAY AT THE ROYAL BANK OF SCOTLAND

Background
The Royal Bank of Scotland is a major financial services institution in the UK, with over 700 retail branches and employing some 20,000 staff. The significant changes in its pay management arrangements over the past five years might be summarised as a process of 'managed fragmentation'. The changes have been strongly business-

driven both in terms of supporting a strategy of improved business focus in response to diverse customer demands, and in aligning the differing needs and characteristics of some 40 distinct business units.

The move away from 'one size fits all'

In the early 1990s, in common with other major UK banks, a uniform pay structure of grades supported by Hay job evaluation operated across the Royal Bank. Pay increases for staff were related to a nego-tiated general award. There were 11 managerial grades, with pay progression based on a universal percentage increase for each performance level. Specialists in areas of high demand were paid market supplements, but market pressures had also encouraged considerable grade drift.

Starting in 1992, the bank started to focus its activities on defined customer needs. The UK bank was restructured into three business streams – retail, corporate and institutional, and service and opera-tions – and organisational layers were removed. Over the following years, business units in each of these streams developed new pay arrangements to suit their own particular business and staff charac-teristics. Underneath their different approaches, however, some common themes are evident in all units: greater external market focus and alignment; flatter and more flexible grade structures; stronger relationships between pay, competencies and results; and greater local ownership and accountability for pay decisions.

The first units to move were those most subject to external market pressures, such as the treasury function. They now essen-tially operate individual job salary bands, related to specific external benchmarks. The corporate and commercial banking area also oper-ates a flexible approach, with a single, very wide pay range, broken by a number of market-related anchor points. Roles are assessed against a menu of 13 competencies and, on this basis, managed around one of these points.

The pay structure in service and operations saw a reduction in the number of grades from 15 to seven. Jobs are now slotted into the appropriate pay band, which are 80 to 120 per cent wide, and indi-viduals progress their pay on the basis of competencies and results achieved.

For staff in the retail network, pay management remains more structured, given the greater need to ensure consistency and control costs across a large number of staff in many locations. A total of 25 generic role profiles were evaluated internally, and market-related ranges of varying widths were developed for each, most being from 80 to 110 per cent of the relevant market point. A wide range of market data sources are used to arrive at these points. Pay increases are driven by a matrix related to individual contribution and position in range.

For retail managers a job families approach was introduced, as general branch managers were replaced by functionally specific roles. There are four families: sales, service, processing and credit. Role profiles describe the key competencies required, purpose of the job, major activities and responsibilities, performance 'outputs', and skills and experience required. Also at the time of the restructuring, potential upward and lateral career moves, within and between the families, were identified.

Base salary ranges and bonus levels now relate to the identified external market value of each role. For example, credit managers have a range from 85 per cent to 115 per cent of the market reference point, reflecting on the learning curve and development of competence required in this more technical role. Relationship managers (sales), meanwhile, have a range from 80 per cent to 105 per cent, but a higher sales-linked bonus of up to 30 per cent of pay.

Pay progression within bands depends on a combination of non-financial targets and competencies, while achieving 'hard' financial targets is rewarded by bonus payments. Each year targets are set in the annual appraisal process for key results areas (KRAs), and for the development of competencies to support these KRAs. This reinforces the understanding that competencies are about translating skills into job performance.

This variety is evident in most aspects of reward across the other units of the bank. No 'average' or 'overall' paybill rise is identified by the bank, and even the dates of pay review vary, corporate banking reviewing in January, the retail bank in April, and the treasury unit in October.

The Royal Bank of Scotland recognised early on in the process – according to the reward manager for the UK bank, Alastair Ross – that this process of pay reform was not a 'quick win'. The changes evolved, unit by unit, over five years, and are still continuing.

Partly, the timescale reflects the time necessary to develop sensible and robust business-driven arrangements in each unit. Developing different competency and pay arrangements in each area has taken time, but has ensured this essential 'business fit'. Management at all levels in the bank have consistently supported the changes and required levels of investment to make them work. Staff perceptions did not change overnight, and there is still a tendency for staff to want to compare relativities between units, rather than focusing on their own level of competitiveness and contribution.

However, according to Ross, grade creep and 'chasing of grades' has been eliminated, and the focus is much more clearly now on the market and individual rates. The whole expensive bureaucracy of bank-wide job-description-writing and job evaluation committees has been completely removed. Individual pay increases are now much more flexible and varied, ranging in 1998 from 0 to 22 per cent of pay. The changes have also entailed significant changes in the role of the compensation and benefits staff. That function has taken on more of an advisory than a controlling role, for example providing market data to local line managers and helping to share experiences.

As units have become more comfortable with managing their own pay, more inter-unit co-ordination has been taking place, which helps to avoid an internal market and 'poaching' of staff. There is a common flexible benefits plan across the organisation, giving more scope for individual variation but achieving centralised scale economies in purchasing and administration. This, along with the general reduction in the numbers of grades, has helped to reduce the status-orientation in the traditional culture of the organisation. However, reflecting on the greater variety of new arrangements generally, the reward team has now grown to eight staff to support the new approach.

In summary therefore, Alastair Ross sees the prime benefits of these major changes in reward arrangements as the fact that pay is 'not now primarily driven by internal relativities and status but by value to the business'. In such a large organisation, a common 'averaged' approach across all business units was meeting nobody's needs very well, whereas now the arrangements are 'genuinely business-driven'.

XEROX (GB)

Background

Xerox employs about 6,500 people in the UK, incorporating UK sales and service operations, manufacturing, research and development, and the European headquarters. Aggressive growth targets are driving a major transition in the UK IT market, involving repositioning from being a 'copier' company to a 'document solution' company. This has resulted in significant product changes such as the introduction of digital networked document devices, but has also brought about major changes in the sort of people employed, who are mainly knowledge workers. This has meant significant changes in the approach to their recruitment, retention, development and reward. As James Bray, manager GB total pay, remarked: 'In our industry, advances in digital technology mean a heavy investment in training and development, otherwise skill sets become redundant. Time to market is now 12 months, whereas previously it would have been three to five years – that's what you need to sustain competitiveness now. The way pay is managed has to support this need to keep people "bang up to date" and motivated to learn.'

Philosophy

As explained by James Bray, Xerox is in a very aggressive labour market and pay has to reflect that: 'Going to something relatively simple like linking pay to grades was just not going to fit what we needed at Xerox.' The key principle was that the pay system had to be closely aligned to the marketplace and Xerox therefore bases its pay structures on market-related pay. As James Bray commented: 'We are primarily playing in the knowledge-worker market in the competitive high-tech industry sector which is experiencing key skills shortages – so we need to compete effectively in that market and hang on to the very good people we've got. We need to have our finger on the pulse about what's happening out there.'

This requires a lot of work and careful analysis and decision-making: 'If we over-pitch it, we could seriously affect the bottom line. If we under-pitch, attrition starts to rise which also affects company performance. So we are walking on a tightrope, and good-quality market analysis is the key to maintaining the balance.'

One of the issues that James Bray has to face is that it is a time-consuming and labour-intensive process to obtain, analyse, interpret and process market rate data for all the Xerox employees. In the past there has been a 'black hole' where there was no data available and 'because we didn't have a grade-related pay structure there was no default system for these job communities. So there was a danger that you could end making poor decisions.' What was required was a more systematic structure that would enable Xerox to slot people in when no market data could be found but would equally allow the company to tap into a number of sources of data so that a composite market-related structure could be built up.

As James Bray pointed out: 'We did not want a spot-rate structure. We had to have bands which could cater for the varying levels of skill, competence and performance that people demonstrated.'

The approach adopted by Xerox was to think in terms of the level of growth people can expect along their career path. Limited growth means a narrower band; longer-term career prospects mean a broader hand. The requirement is to 'create bands which fit what the business requirement is for the types of job roles we are creating. There has to be a link between pay policy and what the business is trying to achieve in developing people.' The driver was the extensive re-skilling process that was taking place in Xerox as it developed its role as a 'solutions-selling' company.

The career structure

The pay structure aims to provide 'clarity of focus' with regard to the career paths of the people in the job community in which they work. The main roles have been repositioned and related to one another in terms of those career paths. For example, there are customer service engineers who are out in the field. They previously had no clearly identified career path. Now they are able to understand not only how they can develop their skills and competence within their current role, but also how they can move through their career path to specialist roles. Their pay progression is clearly mapped out to support their career development. Routes are also shown into career paths in other parts of the organisation: 'Thus a clear line of sight is provided on where they can go in their part of the business and at what points they can move to another related role.'

This has led to the development of a structure of career points In each of the main disciplines or areas of activity – ie each job family.

These points are based on descriptions of skills, competence and performance requirements.

A career path indicates not only what people are doing but also the level at which they are doing it. The career points are described by reference to competency definitions. They start from a general profile of the competency requirements and refer specifically to technical expertise, business orientation and interpersonal skills. Thus the career map for a job family consists of a series of these career points.

The development of the career point system enabled 'accreditation models' to be created which could be used to decide whether or not an individual was at, or was ready to move into, a higher career point or a higher point within the pay band.

The pay structure

The pay structure is a market-related job family structure which reflects the many different labour markets existing for Xerox employees. There are 25 job families which recognise the considerable degree to which the labour market is segmented. Each has six to eight typically 40-per-cent pay ranges which are subdivided into three zones of:

❏ the entry/learning zone (10 per cent)
❏ the proficient zone (20 per cent)
❏ the expert/role model zone (10 per cent).

The accreditation models are used to determine whether someone can move into the proficient or expert zones. This is not regarded as purely competency-related pay. As James Bray commented:

> The concept of competency tends to be fraught with interpretative difficulties and jargon. One of the key principles we have drawn upon is that there were other things besides competency we wanted to take into consideration. We wanted a balance of key metrics. We are not getting hung up on whether it is a competency or a skill. They're both relevant and both are part of an accreditation framework. But the outputs in terms of performance are critical too, so we want to use a balance of all three metrics. What we have tried to incorporate in all our accreditation and earnings review processes are common words and common goals. Both accreditations and reviews are based on an employee's contribution to the business and so a better description of the Xerox reward philosophy is 'paying for contribution'.

The pay ranges are built around market median data and at least 95 per cent of the jobs are matched to the marketplace. But market median data is not shown because: 'We don't want managers defaulting to a market median all the time. We want them to think carefully about where they are placing people in a range.'

Grading jobs

Referencing jobs to existing grades was initially carried out by discussions between Total Pay and line managers to get buy-in and as a validation process. As James Bray said: 'The role definitions are less prescriptive than we have been used to. But this supports a cultural shift away from "policing" to business partnership.' The line taken by Total Pay to managers is that: 'If you over-pitch, you will end up paying people more than you need to.' Job evaluation (Hay system) is used to firm up the matching and cross-check where jobs have been positioned.

However, base pay is not linked to grade – only benefits and bonus plans are linked. Hay is a grading validation process, not a pay-fixing process.

Career points are also distinct from grades because Xerox 'did not want automatically to default to pay grades'. But they may be linked together as more is understood about the relationship between them – there is, of course, a strong correlation.

Before the career point structure was developed, managers were giving people new job titles to differentiate them from others. Now they are being told they do not need to do that any more because what a job is called makes no difference to pay. The important factor is the career point at which people are operating.

Pay progression

As people grow in their roles they can move from 'entry' to 'proficient' to 'expert'. Getting a higher-level job is not therefore a prerequisite for increased earnings. The line taken by Xerox is that when people get to the top of the proficient zone and are approaching the expert zone, the majority will probably be looking for a new job. But others will say: 'We don't want to move – we are quite happy to go on progressing in our present job.' This helps to control internal attrition, which was becoming a problem.

Managing pay

Benchmarking to the marketplace is based on total earnings, including all elements of variable pay. The Xerox philosophy is that virtually all employees should have some element of variable pay, typically through a gainsharing scheme. The approach is to work back from the market mid-point of total pay and then take away the variable element to produce the base rate.

The total pay function analyses the distribution of pay to establish how many employees are within their range and what the average pay is, and to calculate a compa-ratio. This is used for planning purposes so that hot-spots can be identified and issues dealt with through market correction adjustments.

Traditionally, the pay review has been carried out at a given point in the year on the basis of a percentage budget. A certain amount of the budget has been allocated for a 'contribution assessment' by the line manager, while other parts have provided separate funding for market adjustments or for continuing skills and competence development programmes.

What is now happening is that there is less emphasis on an annual review and more on an ongoing review. The starting point will be an agreement with the corporation that the paybill can increase by *x* per cent. Managers may, however, ask for a higher budget and Xerox is moving towards the concept of 'productivity-funded pay'. If managers want more, they are asked how they will fund the extra amount. 'We have moved the debate from "What do you pay people?" to "What is the impact on our earnings-to-revenue ratio?" These are going to be the metrics of the future.' This is easily applied to sales staff but there are plenty of other metrics to which pay can be linked – for example, customer service can be measured on how many *effective* calls staff make a day, which is a balance between productivity and quality metrics.

The role of total pay

As James Bray commented:

> Formerly, we had a policing role: 'You can't have this; you can't do that.' Now we surprise line managers by pointing out where they are not spending enough and the resulting risk to performance through attrition. So we focus on what the business requirement is, what is acceptable attrition, what we can do to lock in key employees, what we can do to help develop skills. We are involved in all the debates

about what the business is trying to do. Formerly, pay was a niche specialisation in Xerox; now it is part of the business operation.

Of course there are basic checks and balances – for example, Total Pay signs off increases over 10 per cent. But it exists simply to ensure that there is consistency. As James Bray said: 'We are here to see fair play in terms of equity and consistency. We are not here to say "You can't do this"; instead, we are saying, "Is this right?"'

Learning points

Xerox is naturally concerned with recognising the market worth of individuals in terms of what they do and how they perform that role. As James Bray remarked: 'There is a default for people who are performing steadily in their jobs, but we also want to recognise people who are making an excellent contribution in terms of their performance and improvements in skills and competencies; both these are key metrics.' The key driver for pay is what the business is trying to achieve.

Two further points were made by James Bray. First, he noted that:

> It is important not to underestimate the amount of work involved in the process. Particularly in a job family structure. It's a Forth-Bridge-type job requiring constant maintenance work. If you are in a fast-moving organisation which is constantly creating new jobs and restructuring, you have got to keep up front with the pace of change and feel comfortable with change.

Secondly, he suggested that it is necessary to embed in the organisation the principle that when line managers want to change a job or create a new one, it is necessary for them not only to describe the job but also to find out where it sits in the marketplace and to agree pay ranges and accreditation processes up front. This has got to happen as part of the regular business process.

PART IV

CREATING NEW PAY STRUCTURES

9 DEVELOPING AND INTRODUCING NEW PAY STRUCTURES

Throughout this book, we have been emphasising the vital importance of a contingency approach to base pay structuring and management. Broad bands should not be introduced just because other organisations are using them, and in our opinion it is a high-risk strategy to simply 'borrow' another company's banding methodology. The research and our experience demonstrates that *best fit* needs to replace the concept of best practice, and therefore your arrangements need to be tailored to suit the goals and character of your own organisations.

But how do you do this? How do you assess whether you need to go down a broadbanding route, and how do you tailor the approach to suit your own organisation? What are the characteristics that need to be reflected in your designs, and do you really need to start with a totally blank sheet of paper, or can you benefit from the experiences of all these other organisations we have been documenting in this book?

In this chapter we address such questions and, by describing and illustrating how other organisations have diagnosed, redesigned and implemented new and more effective base pay approaches, we aim to provide a step-by-step guide enabling you to do this in your own company.

Chapters 6 and 8 provide specific guidance and detailed information regarding the practical operation and introduction of broadbanding and job family techniques.

A phased approach

Perhaps the worst thing you can do if you are in a situation where you think your pay structures need to be redesigned is to start with the solution and to rapidly implement it. Yes, in these fast-moving times, the HR function needs to be agile, responsive and results-oriented, as Ulrich tells us. But in respect of such a sensitive and politically- and emotionally-charged issue as base pay management, this is not an area where you want to be acting first and then thinking, or perhaps regretting, later.

A Scottish bank did this, after its HR department responded to the demands of a new chief executive for a less hierarchical and status-based and more results-focused and meritocratic organisation. What better way of symbolising such a change than the removal of the existing hierarchical and multigraded pay structures and their replacement by three broad pay bands, with wholly performance-related pay progression? The implementation of this approach a few months later was disastrous, and staff and union opposition forced the bank to reconsider. Over the following 15 months these concerns and the capability, as well as the needs, of the organisation were examined in more detail. A series of more workable and acceptable approaches was prepared and then progressively introduced.

We generally recommend therefore that a four-phased approach is adopted to work of this nature, consisting of the following:

❑ an initial diagnostic and architecture development phase
❑ then the detailed design of the new or modified approach
❑ thirdly, a period of testing, preparation and implementation
❑ finally, the periodic and ongoing monitoring of the new approach.

The typical components and outputs from each phase are shown in Figure 16.

It is vital that you tailor this process, as much as the resulting new designs and approaches, to suit your organisation. A rapidly expanding dot.com company is probably not going to want you to spend six months on the first phase, although consulting with literally all employees may well be vital in this

Figure 16
TYPICAL PHASES IN A BROADBANDING PROJECT

Typical stages	*Outcomes*

Phase 1: Diagnose current situation, review change options
 • Planning: form project team
 • Investigate business case, senior executive interviews; business drivers, organisation and views on reward
 • Solicit staff and employee views – eg group discussions, surveys
 • Analyse pay, reward and related HR systems – eg distribution in current pay structure, market competitiveness, job definitions, etc
 • Project team workshops
   – briefing/education
   – review key findings
   – options analysis and architecture development
 • Phase report
   – rationale for change/pay goals
   – outline changes
   – requirements and next steps
	and agree pay architecture
	 • Full agreed understanding of current pay situation and change rationale
	 • Selection of optimum approach for our circumstances/goals
	 • Realistic appraisal of the benefits and downsides of change
	 • Views and 'buy-in' of key interest groups developed

Phase 2: Detail and test pay
 • Planning: organise design staffing – eg one or more teams
 • Detail and finalise new arrangements and test on a representative sample of jobs
   – role profiles/job descriptions/job families
   – evaluation and placement method – eg competencies grades
   – pay ranges
   – pay progression
 • Model and cost changes
 • Phase report
 • Possible staff communications
	proposals
	 • Detailed pay and related changes
	 • Team skilled in the new approach
	 • Tested application to a sample of jobs

Phase 3: Prepare and • Possible further pilot test in part of the organisation • Model transition from old to new and agree policies – eg protection • Develop operating and control responsibilities and procedures • Develop administrative support – eg software • Develop and run any necessary training • Possible negotiations with staff representatives • Prepare final communications • Implement • Review after one year against objectives and success criteria	**implement** • Implemented new pay arrangements which can deliver on their objectives

Phase 4: Monitoring and
 • Ongoing monitoring against redesign objectives
 • Periodic testing of bands of a sample of jobs
 • Formal one-year review of effectiveness
   – versus original goals
   – in terms of business needs
   – staff motivation
   – efficiency
	review
	 • Confirmed success in implementation and operation
	 • Modifications to improve operation
	 • Modifications to reflect changes in the organisation

type of organisation. Alternatively, in a large UK telecommunications company that wanted to introduce a new harmonised pay approach across six formerly independent businesses, a major diagnostic study really had to be undertaken. This was necessary to fully understand the nature of all the various existing approaches and to obtain the input into, and support for, change across all the various interest groups involved.

In the following sections we therefore highlight the main components of each phase, and illustrate with examples how specific organisations have tailored their approach to their own circumstances and needs.

Phase 1: diagnosis and architecture design

The process on a major construction project is not to start building straight away and then to worry later about how the roof is going to stay up when the walls are built or when an underground cavern is discovered. Nor is the funding sought from sponsors and owners only after it is built.

No, typically a consortium of sponsors, users, owners and builders is formed. Surveyors are hired to select the best site and to survey the lie of the land. Then architects develop a range of design proposals to best meet the needs of the new owners, and after extensive consultation and redrawing the best is selected. A huge amount of work has been undertaken well before the local dignitary ceremonially digs the first sod or lays the foundation stone.

And so it is with the pay systems in your organisation, the pay structure often being the foundation on which the success of all your reward policies depends.

Diagnostic questions

You need to do a lot of diagnostic work before you can really know whether broadbanding is required in your organisation, and if so, why, and if so, in what form, and if so, how best to develop and implement it.

This is the objective of the first phase of the work which we recommend you undertake. At the end of this phase we hope that you will have answers to some key questions:

❑ What are the objectives of base pay management in our organisation, and how do these fit in with our broader reward strategy? For example, where do we want to position ourselves in the external market? What emphasis do we want to place on the various factors affecting someone's pay? To what extent and on what basis do we want to differentiate between the pay of different jobs, and in the pay of individuals doing the same or similar jobs?

❑ To what extent are these objectives being achieved by our current base pay management methods? What are their strengths and weaknesses, from the perspective of all of those responsible for them and affected by them? In a nutshell, what is wrong with the current approaches, and why (when in most organisations these days there are lots of other changes going on) is it essential that we adopt a new pay management approach?

❑ Why then do we need to change, and what is the extent of the changes required?

❑ What are the alternatives that we have in terms of changes? This may be in respect of our job evaluation system, our pay structure(s) and the number of grades or bands, the width and overlap of pay ranges, general pay movements and the way the pay structure is adjusted, and/or the ways in which people's pay is adjusted and in which they progress through these bands; what are the pros and cons of these various alternatives in terms of achieving our objectives, workability, fit, feasibility and funding?

❑ What changes and/or modifications are we recommending? How do we get people to understand what they involve and to support them?

❑ How are we going to detail, test and finalise the new or modified approaches? Who will be responsible, who will be involved, and how will it be resourced?

❑ What related issues, outside of the original scope of the project but potentially influencing the effectiveness of the project, have been raised?

We recognise that this is a demanding agenda, but from the alternative perspective, could you really see yourself successfully implementing a new and better approach without conducting a thorough analysis and diagnostic review as described below?

Work stages

Typical work stages in this phase include:

- forming a project team to plan and carry out the work and make or recommend the decisions required
- consulting with stakeholders to understand their views on the current systems, and to get any ideas from them in terms of the changes necessary; generally this will include seeing relevant senior managers and talking directly with employees and/or their representatives
- analysing the workings of the current arrangements. What are the stated goals of base pay management at the moment? How many staff are in each grade, and where are they positioned at present? How much differentiation in base pay increases currently occurs? How many job re-evaluations and grade changes have we had in recent years? What is our current voluntary rate of staff turnover, and to what extent is pay a contributor to this?
- reviewing relevant external pay trends and levels. What is our actual pay position in the external market? How do our competitors in both a labour market and business sense manage the base pay of their staff, and what are the pros and cons they experience?
- agreeing the key issues and needs raised by the above stages and then outlining and critiquing possible alternatives to address them
- recommending and agreeing necessary changes. These will typically cover all or some of: the job evaluation methodology and process; the number and structure of pay grades; the width, overlap and market positioning of pay ranges; and the base pay review and adjustment method. You need to demonstrate how each change addresses shortcomings in the existing situation and contributes to the achievement of the relevant reward strategy objectives.

The actual project stages in this first work phase in the telecommunications company we mentioned earlier are listed in Table 23.

Table 23
OUTLINE PROJECT STAGES – PHASE 1: DIAGNOSIS AND ARCHITECTURE DESIGN

1 CHARTERING
- Confirm objectives, scope and coverage
- Plan detailed stages, timing, responsibilities
- Agree governance and work structure – steering group and project team, 'champions', etc
- Detail success criteria
- Agree communications strategy and responsibilities: brief those directly involved, senior managers and possible general employee message
- Agree benchmark job sample
- Begin information-gathering

2 SENIOR MANAGEMENT INTERVIEWS
- Solicit views on
  - value drivers
  - current job/reward issues – eg market hot spots
  - criteria we should value
  - desirable features of new approach

3 STAFF CONSULTATION (eg through team briefing)
- Communicate objectives and process of project
- Solicit views on
  - the general goods and bads of pay and reward
  - criteria to value/reward in future

4 RESEARCH- AND DATA-GATHERING
- Internal: relevant material on
  - benchmark jobs – any descriptions of job information, current pay
  - different job description formats
  - market surveys and market positioning in various areas currently
  - current pay policies and practices
  - existing competencies and any career ladders
  - current HRIS
- External:
  - alternatives, experiences and learning points from broadbanding in relevant companies
  - market competitiveness of pay, particularly for benchmark jobs

5 TWO PROJECT DESIGN GROUP WORKSHOPS
- Agree objectives, process, roles, working style, etc
- Review findings from previous stages in relation to current and desirable situations: key issues to address
- Exercises to analyse 'real' values – eg job ranking of benchmark jobs: draw out learning in terms of system and process
- Review and critique alternative approaches to
  - job descriptions, information-gathering and job families
  - broad bands: definition and numbers, use of competencies, etc
  - base pay management in and between bands
- Agree outline of optimum approach
- Next steps

6 STEERING GROUP MEETING
- Report/presentation:
  - confirming broadbanding approach/objectives
  - outlining key issues
  - recommending new banding structure, job families, measurement criteria and associated pay approach
  - detailed Phase 2 plan and resourcing required

7 GENERAL STAFF COMMUNICATION

Types of analysis

An analysis of the business strategy should identify the direction the organisation intends to go to achieve business goals and the plans for getting there. The implications of these plans for HR strategies, especially those concerned with reward, should also be assessed.

The culture of the organisation – 'the way things are done around here' – should be analysed, possibly in such terms as Handy's classification of cultures into the power, role, task and person categories. The values of the organisation should be assessed with particular reference to beliefs about rewarding and developing people and the need to treat them fairly, and equitably.

A review of the employee relations climate is necessary as the basis for developing communication, consultation and involvement strategies. If one or more trade unions are recognised, their likely views on changes to the existing system should be analysed. So far as possible, a view should be obtained on the degree to which trade unions and employees generally trust management.

An attitude survey is an appropriate method of obtaining views from employees about the pay system. The survey could ask respondents to indicate the extent to which they agree or disagree with such statements as:

- My pay is competitive.
- My benefits package is competitive.
- I feel my pay recognises my contribution.
- Individual performance is adequately rewarded.
- Pay increases are handled fairly.
- I think the pay policy is overdue for review.
- My pay is fair compared with that of people doing similar work in the company.

An attitude survey could be followed up by individual or focus group discussions with senior and line managers, employees and, where appropriate, employee representatives.

The analysis should cover the features and shortcomings, if any, of the present arrangements. It would identify problems and the reasons for those problems. For example, if there are difficulties in attracting or retaining good-quality staff, the analysis would try to establish the extent to which this is a result of uncompetitive pay levels or faults in the ways in which pay is managed.

An analysis of the current pay arrangements should examine the pay structure, methods of progressing pay, performance management processes, pay review policy and practice, the levels of pay compared with market rates, the extent to which the often conflicting goals of internal equity and external competitiveness have been achieved, and the attitudes of managers and other employees to the pay system.

This review of the present arrangements for reward should be carried out by examining written reward policy statements and details of pay structures, pay for performance, competence or skill (contingent pay) schemes, and employee benefit packages. The procedures for tracking market rates, evaluating jobs, measuring and managing performance, flexing benefits (if applicable), managing pay reviews and monitoring the system should be analysed. Any reports and records relating to reward should be studied.

In a conventional grade structure, problems could include:

❑ the structure not reflecting the way work is organised because there are more grades than levels of 'value-adding tiers' in the organisation

❑ an inflexible approach to managing pay because of the rigidities imposed by narrow grades

❑ grade drift (inappropriate upgradings) because of the constant pressure to be regraded as the only real scope for salary progression is upwards through the pay hierarchy

❑ too much bureaucracy in managing the structure because of the overuse of paper-intensive and time-consuming job evaluation

❑ over-rigid control of the pay system because managers are not trained or trusted to make decisions on pay levels

❑ uncompetitive pay levels because insufficient attention is paid to tracking and responding to movements in market rates

❑ the pay system existing as a separate entity without any

link to other HR processes because of a narrow focus on the part of the HR function.

Where there is a pay spine, the same problems may be identified. In addition:

❑ there may be no scope for rewarding people who add value because of a rigid service-related progression system

❑ there may be cost problems because staff automatically progress to the top of the scale and accumulate there if labour turnover is low and promotion prospects are limited

❑ staff may feel aggrieved because there is no further scope for rewards once they reach the top of their scale, except through upgrading.

Checklist

A diagnostic checklist which you may find useful to apply to your current pay systems includes the following seven questions:

1: What are the overall features of the pay structure?

❑ What is the rationale for the current pay/grade structure?

❑ Does it recognise:

- the actual levels of work performed?
- the needs of any specialist/professional groups which are different?
- the need to progress staff spending several years in a grade to reflect contribution and competence?
- union bargaining units if relevant?

❑ Is the structure flexible enough to cater for:

- the current pattern of career development and promotion?
- changes in pay/job market conditions?
- changes in organisational structures and business activities?
- the degree to which roles have to be flexible to respond to changing conditions and demands?

❑ Are there too many people with no further progression or

promotion opportunities who are stuck on the grade maximum and are likely to be demotivated even if well paid?

2: What type of specific pay and grade structure or structures exist in the organisation?

- graded salary scales
- broad bands
- job family
- pay spines
- individual job grades
- spot rates.

3: Is the pay structure relevant to the needs of the organisation as a whole or the part of the organisation in which it operates – ie does it:

- fit the circumstances and culture of the organisation, in that it is flexible in organisations subject to rapid change or is well-defined and rigorously applied where order and predictability are of paramount importance?
- provide a logical framework or system for enabling consistent and defensible decisions to be made on the levels of pay and differentials of all the employees to be covered by the structure?
- make provision for the reasonable and sometimes inevitable fact that external market rate considerations may have to prevail over the requirements of strict internal equity, especially in areas of skills shortage?

4: Is the grade structure designed and maintained properly?

- Are the grades clearly defined? Do they fit the way work is currently organised (eg the number of levels in the organisation)?
- Are the pay ranges wide enough to allow scope for pay progression in accordance with contribution and competence?

❑ Is there an adequate differential (say, 15 to 20 per cent) between grades?

❑ Is there an overlap between grades to provide some flexibility and to recognise the fact that an experienced individual at the top of one grade may be of more value to the organisation than a newcomer in the grade above?

❑ Are consistent methods used to allocate jobs into grades, including decisions on recruitment, promotion and upgrading because of greater responsibility?

❑ Is there any evidence of inequities in the pay structure because of wrongly-graded jobs?

❑ Are pay scales regularly reviewed against external data? If not, what are the factors used to determine annual adjustments to pay scales? Are these factors consistent across grades?

❑ Is there any evidence of salary levels moving ahead of or falling behind market rates?

❑ If so, what are the causes, and are they short-term or long-term in nature?

❑ Is there a consistent and fair basis for allocating benefits?

5: Is the system regularly maintained and updated:

❑ to take account of new jobs?

❑ to take account of the structural change in the organisation?

❑ to allow for movements in market rates?

❑ and if so, how is this controlled?

❑ and if so, are the controls adequate or are inconsistencies emerging?

6: Is the pay structure developed and maintained through systematic processes for benchmarking market rates and job evaluation?

7: Is there scope to reduce the amount of time and trouble taken on job evaluation by introducing a new computerised system and/or using it simply to support pay decisions rather than to drive them?

To summarise, on the basis of answers to the above questions:

- Is the structure appropriate to the characteristics and needs of the organisation and its employees?
- Does it facilitate the management of relativities and the achievement of equity, fairness and consistency in managing employee reward?
- Is it capable of adapting to pressures arising from market rate changes and skills shortages?
- Does it facilitate operational flexibility and continuous development?
- Does it provide scope as required for rewarding performance and increases in skill and competence?
- To what extent does it clarify reward and career opportunities?
- Is it based on systematic processes of market rate analysis and job evaluation?
- Is it constructed logically and clearly so that the basis upon which it operates can readily be communicated to employees?
- Does it enable the organisation to exercise control over the implementation of pay policies within defined budgets?

Example: a UK building society

In a building society which was in the process of converting to become a quoted bank, the diagnostic involved most of the components illustrated in Table 23. However, in keeping with many projects of this nature, the diagnostic components formed part of a broader re-design of the whole HR strategy and process, of which pay management was just a part. A strategy of moving to more business unit-focused and varied HR policies and services had already been adopted. Dissatisfaction with pay management emerged while planning this shift with local business unit heads.

Meanwhile, an organisation and efficiency review had proposed a complete re-design of the branch network, where the bulk of staff were employed. This involved centralising some branch services in regional centres and moving to a much flatter organisation, with fewer multiskilled roles in the branches. This was to be implemented over the next year prior to flotation. In addition, a lot of work on performance management had been undertaken and the outline of a new, looser and local line manager and staff-driven system proposed. This was to replace the existing rigid and uniform points-scoring-type scheme.

The review of base pay management therefore involved bringing together the findings from these various strands of work and drawing out their implications for pay. Currently, there was a structure of 12 pay grades, with a detailed points-factor evaluation system to place jobs in them. Individual progression through the ranges was based on a combination of personal competence and performance. A summary of the project team's analysis of this situation is shown in Table 24.

The direction of change agreed in this case was towards simpler, more flexible and business-driven pay arrangements, but maintaining a common if looser salary structure to aid mobility in the organisation, and to help with benefits determination. The new approach to pay management recommended and agreed by the board had five main components:

❑ a simpler job evaluation scheme
❑ a flatter structure of bands
❑ wider market-related pay ranges
❑ modified pay increase mechanism
❑ modified promotion processes.

The first was to move everyone into a flatter pay structure of five broad levels. Interestingly, it was only towards the end of the second phase that this was decided to be too radical a step – with branch staff and their immediate supervisors in the same band – and so an extra sixth band was created. The objective for this change was to reduce the emphasis on status in the organisation – they still had three categories of car park, for example – and to provide greater flexibility to reward growth in the role, rather than emphasising vertical promotion as in the past.

Roles would be placed into the appropriate band using a simple slotting or classification process, only difficult jobs going through a detailed points-factor analysis. This would

Table 24
ANALYSIS OF THE CURRENT SITUATION IN A UK FINANCIAL SERVICES ORGANISATION

Existing reward systems	Strengths	Weaknesses	Implications for change
Job definition and evaluation	• Jobs defined clearly • System is objective and accepted • Staff/union involved • Defence against equal value complaints	• Reinforces narrow job specification/ demarcations • Traditional criteria emphasise 'inputs' – eg qualifications, numbers of people managed • Excessively detailed, bureaucratic, time-consuming	• Broader roles • Simpler, more flexible system
Grading and pay structure	• Understood/comfortable • Controls costs • Promotion opportunities	• Hierarchical }Conflicts with teamwork/ • Status-driven } performance messages • Excessive emphasis on promotion • Large range overlaps, therefore limited scope to develop	• Fewer grades/more flexibility
Appraisal and pay adjustment	• Assesses results and competence	• Very narrow differentials in increases • Lack of focus on development/improvement • Mechanical points focus • Complex • Competencies don't tie in with development	• Greater focus on improvement • Less mechanical/ more flexible • Integration with other HR processes

simplify and speed up the process, as well as focusing on job competencies and outputs rather than input-driven criteria. The criteria would vary between technical specialists and general managerial and support staff, as would the associated pay ranges on each band. This was designed to clarify career paths as well as to reflect different market values. The retention of specialists – for example, in the treasury function – had historically been a problem.

Pay ranges were to be set using improved market data, to aid recruitment and retention. Finally, promotions would be less common in the future and reflect a significant growth in responsibility, but the associated pay increases were no longer to be constrained by a 10 per cent maximum figure. They were to properly reflect the growth in the role into which the individual was moving.

Figure 17 illustrates how these changes were presented to the board, in conjunction with a range of other changes in reward management and career development. A challenge in these situations is often to get over a lot of detail on the analysis undertaken and the changes recommended in a short time spent with the directors. This type of summary illustration, and a strong focus on the business-related rationale, we often find, helps in such situations.

However, it is important that the decision-makers really understand the nature of the changes being proposed and their implications, and so we often illustrate them with brief additional examples of how the new arrangements might look at the end of Phase 2. This helps to avoid the situation we have seen on a number of occasions, where directors agree to a set of broadbanding changes at this early stage as a 'good thing', and then retreat from them after all the detailed design work has been done, when they finally realise what managing pay in broader bands really means.

Example: an insurance company

The work in an insurance company followed a similar route. Here, the problems caused by the current pay structure had been raised at an annual management conference. The existing structure of nine staff grades and four management grades was seen as hierarchical, restricting the development of high-potential staff, and the recruitment and retention of technical specialists.

A project team with nine members representing HR and all the lines of business and functions was formed to develop a new broadbanding approach. Its terms of reference were to review the need for and, if necessary, propose appropriate broadbanding arrangements. Various conditions were set down at the outset, including the need to focus on staff grades and the stipulation that any changes must be self-financing.

The team carried out a range of detailed analyses, including:

Figure 17
THE PROPOSED REWARD CHANGES AND COMPONENTS IN THE FINANCIAL SERVICES ORGANISATION

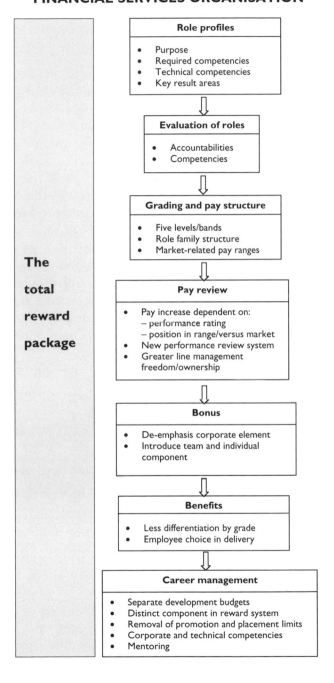

❑ a review of the competitiveness of pay levels in terms of the pay ranges and the actual pay of staff
❑ an analysis of employee turnover
❑ a study of the pay and grade progression of a sample of staff
❑ an analysis of average salary and starting salary by grade.

Staff turnover was found in general to be at the industry average, but much higher in specific geographical areas, such as London. Actual salary levels compared to the external market were found to be below median, and the gap was increasing with seniority, although the pay ranges and mid-points generally were competitive.

The analysis of average salary by grade (see Figure 18), showed that in staff grades, progression was the main issue, in that ranges were already broad by market standards, but actual pay levels low. However, the analysis of starting and actual salary levels demonstrated the pressures to pay competitive rates in grades 8 and 9 (the main specialist grades), and particularly for managers, where large market allowances were being paid, and the current range maxima exceeded, in order to stay competitive. Management ranges were also quite narrow by industry standards, whereas staff scales were already relatively broad.

The group therefore summarised the key issues in the current situation not as too many narrow grades but rather as:

❑ structural problems, in terms of:
  – accommodating senior technicians at market rates in the current scales
  – narrow and uncompetitive management scales
  – a general lack of market alignment of pay
❑ pay management and progression problems:
  – slow progression up scales, and bunching at the lower end of staff grades
  – recruitment low in the staff scales and small promotional and developmental increases.

Simply redesigning the pay scales would therefore not have addressed some of the main problems here, which were to do with a lack of flexibility in pay progression within and between

Figure 18
AVERAGE SALARY BY GRADE: LIFE DIVISION

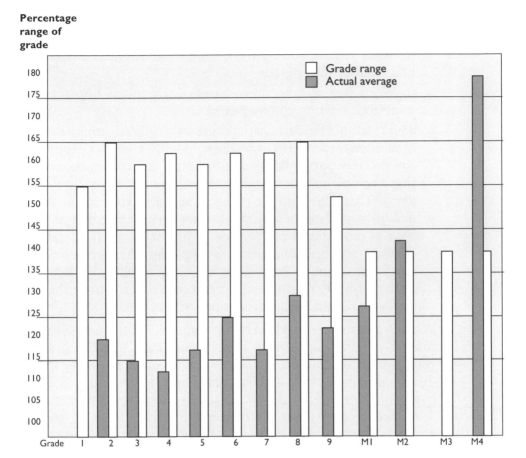

NB: Data includes all current members of staff
    Salaries include market allowances

grades. Interviews confirmed that managers generally tried to contain pay costs and were reluctant to differentiate between staff and to reward high-performers or very able new recruits appropriately.

The project group then reviewed possible changes to address these issues. A job-family-based approach was rejected because of concerns over equal pay and the administration required. An option to broadband management and staff scales, moving to five staff and two management bands, was considered but seen to deliver few practical advantages. It would simply have been broadbanding for its own sake.

The selected option therefore was to:

❑ combine the lowest staff grades 1 and 2, which had few staff in them, and to combine the highest staff grade 9 with the first management grade

❑ move to two management bands with much broader and more market-related pay ranges

❑ adopt more flexible pay progression arrangements with higher pay increases for those low in their existing pay bands; new pay policy guidelines and reward management training was proposed, encouraging managers to differentiate more in the increases they awarded to staff in the same band; in addition, a separate budget was established to fund high potential and rapidly developing staff, with guidelines of 5–20 per cent increases rather than the current 5 per cent; recruitment guidelines were also relaxed, changing from normally recruiting in the lowest 5 per cent of the pay scale, to recruiting anywhere below mid-point.

While separate job family arrangements were rejected, separate market-related pay scales were introduced for IT and for certain staff in London, with a parallel technical ladder introduced alongside the highest staff and lower management bands.

An analysis of the risks of implementing these proposals, and how they were to be addressed, was also presented to the board at this stage, concentrating on such possible issues as:

❑ the potential for pay drift, which might be combated through proper pay budgeting procedures

❑ higher maintenance costs, through the efficient use of market data

❑ the cost of the market uplift, by distributing this in relation to individual performance and current position versus the market, rather than as a general handout.

These proposals were subsequently discussed and agreed by the board.

Phase 2: detailed design

Returning to our construction analogy, this is the phase of the project when all the building work is done, the bricks and the concrete, the wiring and plumbing, the interior fully fitted out and the new structure tested. Having agreed a clear framework of pay changes in Phase 1, then those responsible in Phase 2 can be given a detailed design specification which they can effect with (hopefully) no hidden surprises.

The actual stages in this phase of the work will vary accordingly to the scope of the changes agreed in Phase 1. They may be restricted to a re-design of the grading and pay structure, but they often also include changes to the related job evaluation process, and to the pay adjustment methodology in the organisation.

In the telecommunications company mentioned earlier, for example, as well as the design of a new integrated pay structure, a revised approach to placing jobs in the various pay bands and into specific job families was also required in this phase, both to ensure the market competitiveness of salaries in the new structure and to clarify career paths in the newly integrated organisation. In addition, because this was recognised as a sensitive and important project, an additional work stream focusing on communications and involvement was also established. The outline stages in each work stream are shown in Figure 19 (overleaf).

Work streams

Generally, after the initial planning and organisation of all the work involved in Phase 2, the stages involved in the pay restructuring workstream include:

- selecting a representative sample of jobs across the various families and levels in the organisation
- market pricing these jobs in relevant external markets
- constructing pay ranges of an appropriate width to be linked with each of the new grades/levels, and differentiating between families if necessary, using the market data
- modelling the movement of staff in the sample jobs into the new structure, analysing where they fall in the new scales,

Figure 19
OUTLINE PROJECT STAGES – PHASE 2: DETAILED DESIGN IN A TELECOMMUNICATIONS COMPANY

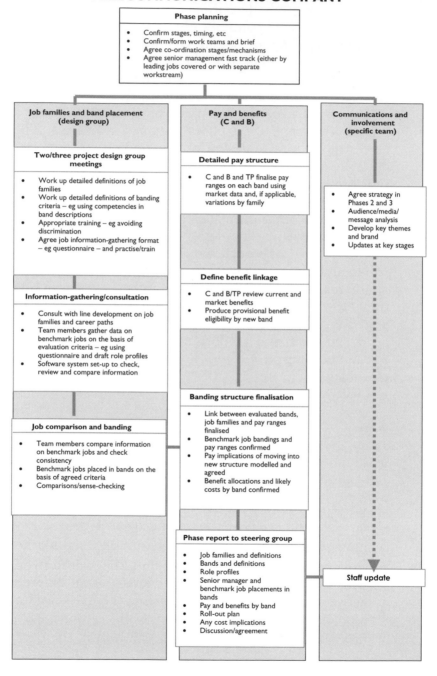

and particularly the costs of any required uplifts in base pay
- determining benefits allocations for the new bands, again typically reflecting market data and also the existing benefit provisions
- recommending the new pay structure for final approval.

Any required changes to the job evaluation approach in this phase generally involves developing and testing the new scheme on the same representative sample of jobs, and typical stages would include:

- detailing the evaluation criteria and factors used to measure and place the jobs in bands
- training the project team in assessing jobs
- gathering information about the sample of jobs, typically these days using a questionnaire
- reviewing and checking the resulting data – for example, using a software system, to ensure its robustness and quality
- placing the sample of jobs in bands and analysing the resultant ordering
- aligning this ranking with the new pay structure and recommending the final band and pay range of all of the sample jobs.

Although these two workstreams are closely related, we generally recommend keeping the job evaluation and pay structure aspects of the work separate in this phase. Otherwise, there is a danger that considerations of current or desired pay corrupt the evaluation work. As soon as pay levels are known, it is easy for the process to be reversed from 'the intended job measurement, *therefore* pay level', to become instead 'this is the pay level I think is needed, *therefore* evaluation required to achieve this pay level'.

There is also a potential workstream in the area of pay adjustment and progression, the work stages in which might involve:

- re-designing the performance appraisal and management scheme
- specifying how the total base pay budget and the new pay ranges will be adjusted in future

❑ detailing how the total pay budget increase will be allocated to individuals, with possible variations according to individual performance and contribution

❑ developing, as in our insurance company example, new policies on pay levels for recruitment and pay increase guidelines for significant development within the job and for movement into new jobs, whether vertical promotions or lateral moves

❑ integrating the proposal with the other pay changes.

The work is by nature more technical in this phase, and the HR function tends to play the leadership role, and carry out a lot of the actual work. However, we would stress the importance of continuing to involve and communicate with line managers and staff, on project teams, in consultation groups, through informal soundings and via regular progress updates. As well as developing technically elegant and robust schemes, process issues such as how trade unions will be involved if the job evaluation system is simplified, or the pay review process devolved in conjunction with broadbanding, must be addressed.

And as illustrated in our building society example, some of the agreed pay architecture may, on detailed reflection, need to be modified, as when it introduced an additional sixth band fairly late on in this phase.

Example: an insurance company (2)

Returning to our insurance company example, the project team's proposals were accepted by the board. In the following two months 'the meat was put on the bones', as the HR director described it.

Market data, which is generally of high quality and readily available in the sector, was reviewed for a sample of jobs in each band, and ranges for each of the 10 new bands constructed. It was decided to do away with the distinction between management and staff grades. Thus the new band 8, for example, went from a minimum of £21,900 to a maximum of £35,700.

Most of the new ranges had a similar width of approximately 60 per cent, with overlaps of around 35 per cent, and increases on the current grade maxima of approximately 15 per cent. A parallel technical ladder was also designed for specialist areas such as IT and accounts.

The performance appraisal system had been re-designed two years previously to include competency criteria and to involve staff more, and so no changes were made to this. The staff job evaluation system was similarly found to be working well, but the management scheme was changed to align with it and produce a less time-consuming and secretive process than in the past.

To address the issue of low positioning in pay scales, a below mid-point 'booster' was designed, with a subsequent move to a matrix arrangement, which would relate pay increases to an individual's position versus the market, as well as their individual contribution. A 2 per cent budget increase to reflect the generally low salary levels against the external market was also included in the proposals. Further costs resulted from establishing benefits provisions for the new management bands, which in the marketplace were generally found to be at the higher grade level of each of the two existing grades which were now being amalgamated into the new management bands. Thus those in the lower management grades qualified for higher levels of benefits in the new bands.

The total cost of the changes was therefore costed at 3.3 per cent of payroll, and this was justified in the final recommendations to the board in terms of improved staff retention and improved allocation of the total pay spend.

Example: a major charity

Phase 2 in a major UK charity involved 11 distinct work streams. This represented a major turnaround from the situation at the start of Phase 1, when a number of the directors were opposed to any further reward analysis or change work. In the previous three years they had introduced a new job evaluation system and moved most of their 900 employees into a harmonised 12-grade structure. This had taken them over two years to complete and created a good deal of internal *angst* and disruption.

In conjunction with the arrival of a new chief executive and reorganisation, however, the charity set up a team to review its current pay structure and progression arrangements. Group discussions, interviews and data analysis highlighted the traditional, automatic and rigid nature of existing pay arrangements in a culture described by one member of staff as 'masculine and militaristic'. Contributors' demands for efficient use of their donations and the pressure of younger staff for more choice in the rewards package and an end to service increments all helped to justify the changes recommended.

These changes included moving all staff into a flatter, eight-grade pay structure and the introduction of pay increases related to individual contribution. Yet the board recognised that this also presented the opportunity to modernise related areas of reward and working conditions, including working hours, overtime and the existing complex variety of grade-related allowances and conditions.

So 11 Phase 2 work streams were set up to produce detailed designs and processes on each issue. Each had a small team working on it, led by a member of the HR function. Team leaders met on a regular basis to review progress and co-ordinate their work. Phase 1 had taken from February to July, and this work was carried out in the August to December period.

The reward strategy team developed a staff communication to explain and justify the new reward principles agreed by the board at the end of Phase 1. The pay banding team worked up both a seven- and an eight-band option, using market data. Testing these on existing job evaluation scores and pay levels, and comparing the cost implications, meant that the eight-grade option was the one that was finally accepted.

The pay progression team meanwhile reviewed different means of relating pay increases to individual contribution. For the higher bands they developed an equity shares approach in which all the pay budget increase was allocated according to an individual's contribution and his or her current range position. For the other grades they proposed continuing with a general cost-of-living award, using equity shares to distribute the remaining merit budget, which would replace service increments. This ensured that lower-graded staff could develop trust in the appraisal process, and also that pay competitiveness was maintained in the local labour market.

The allowances team costed and developed a proposal for a

single disturbance allowance to replace the myriad add-ons, payments and supplements which had grown up over the years. This was to be paid out at three levels, related to the level of disturbance and unsocial hours working, rather than being grade-related as in the past.

And finally, to illustrate the evolving nature of work in this phase, the benefits team came to the conclusion that flexible benefits was a step too far for the organisation to manage and administer, and for staff to understand, at this stage. Intentions were proposed only in outline, therefore, and a detailed review planned for 12 months later.

Phase 3: preparation and implementation

Phase 2 is the most resource-intensive phase of the work in a broadbanding and pay scheme re-design project. Yet virtually all of the researched organisations in our study for this book emphasised the critical importance of adequate preparation prior to implementation. A key learning point for them was to devote more effort to this third work phase, in order to make implementation and operation more effective and easier to achieve. Returning to the construction analogy, this is when the motorway is fully tested and certified by the inspectors – it is when the practices and responsibilities for ongoing operation, maintenance, handling emergencies, and so on, are agreed.

Work stages

Typical work stages in this phase include:

- ❑ determining the overall change/transition strategy and timing
- ❑ modelling the transition into the new structure and developing policies to manage this transition; generally there is a need to model the movement of the staff into the new pay structure, and to determine and cost policies to deal with staff whose pay falls outside of their new bands; this is generally easier with broader bands than with traditional, narrower pay ranges, but nonetheless some staff will often still fall outside of the proposed bands; in addition, an appeals procedure may be required for staff to query their

new banding, either through existing grievance channels or a separate appeals process

- developing detailed operating responsibilities and guidelines for the new banding structure – who, for example, will authorise band changes, how will pay budgets be controlled, and how will future changes in job content be handled? How will overtime payments and benefits be determined and administered in the new flatter structure?

- negotiating the introduction of the new arrangements with staff representatives and trade unions; hopefully they will have been involved throughout the process, but here the detailed nitty-gritty of actual pay levels and costs have to be thrashed out

- designing and running training workshops for managers, and possibly all staff; typically managers have much more freedom and discretion in placing and adjusting the pay of staff in broader bands, but they may well need more than a few guidebooks and pages on the intranet to help them manage this in an appropriate and fair manner; in some cases, for example, a cadre of line managers were trained to coach their colleagues on managing pay levels in broader bands

- producing communications materials; here the benefits of regularly involving and communicating with staff through the earlier phases will now become apparent; the rationale for and outline of the changes should thereby be known already, and so here the focus can be on the detailed designs and their individual impact; we generally prefer using line managers as the focus for this communication, helping them with relevant support (booklets, question and answer sheets, etc) to get the key messages over to their staff, although new technology does offer opportunities to identify and rapidly address specific staff concerns; in one case, for example, the company briefed staff through a sequence of three newsletters, and employee responses to the initial newsletter sent to a website helped to formulate the subsequent newsletters

- running a pilot or simulation exercise, operating the new approach in parts of the organisation, to test its workability and robustness; in the building society example mentioned earlier, for example, the new system was initially introduced in the IT department where the market pressures were greatest; this assisted in estimating the HR support required for full rollout, and also indicated the emphasis required in the staff communication and 'branding' of the changes when full implementation occurred

❑ full implementation and rollout.

The actual stages in the telecommunications company are shown in Figure 20 (overleaf).

Example: a major charity (2)

Many of these work stages were carried out in the major charity referred to in Phase 2 above. The implementation strategy was planned in December, and it was decided to move the introduction of the new pay structure back by a month from the pay review date of the following 1 April. This separated the new scheme from the general 'noise' of an annual pay review, and gave an extra month to develop and test the required changes to the payroll system.

All the managers were briefed on the changes in a full-day seminar by the chief executive and HR director during December. Then in February a two-day workshop was held for them. The first part of this involved developing managers' understanding of the detailed mechanics of the changes. The second day then comprised developing and practising the communication by them of the changes to their staff.

The transition strategy developed in December also included preparing new contracts for all staff, and offering a cash incentive for them to accept.

Example: a large mutual organisation

In a large mutual company, a two-day simulation exercise was held in Phase 3. This involved creating a fictitious department in the company, populated by a variety of 'real' jobs. A team of reviewing managers were then led through a series of exercises simulating the pay management processes in the new banded structure as they would operate in the following year. These exercises included:

Figure 20
OUTLINE PROJECT STAGES – PHASE 3: PREPARATION AND IMPLEMENTATION

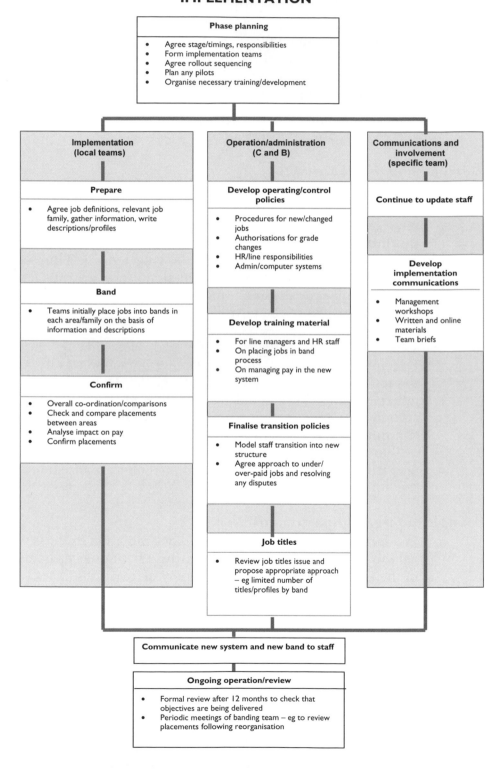

Phase planning

- Agree stage/timings, responsibilities
- Form implementation teams
- Agree rollout sequencing
- Plan any pilots
- Organise necessary training/development

Implementation (local teams)

Prepare

- Agree job definitions, relevant job family, gather information, write descriptions/profiles

Band

- Teams initially place jobs into bands in each area/family on the basis of information and descriptions

Confirm

- Overall co-ordination/comparisons
- Check and compare placements between areas
- Analyse impact on pay
- Confirm placements

Operation/administration (C and B)

Develop operating/control policies

- Procedures for new/changed jobs
- Authorisations for grade changes
- HR/line responsibilities
- Admin/computer systems

Develop training material

- For line managers and HR staff
- On placing jobs in band process
- On managing pay in the new system

Finalise transition policies

- Model staff transition into new structure
- Agree approach to under/ over-paid jobs and resolving any disputes

Job titles

- Review job titles issue and propose appropriate approach – eg limited number of titles/profiles by band

Communications and involvement (specific team)

Continue to update staff

Develop implementation communications

- Management workshops
- Written and online materials
- Team briefs

Communicate new system and new band to staff

Ongoing operation/review

- Formal review after 12 months to check that objectives are being delivered
- Periodic meetings of banding team – eg to review placements following reorganisation

- ❑ using market data to arrive at a market price for a job
- ❑ applying a modelling tool to help allocate a particular pay budget between individuals, with data on current pay and performance supplied
- ❑ determining pay increases in a variety of situations of staff development and promotion
- ❑ role-playing the communication of a pay increase to a member of staff, without the aid of their former detailed grades and compa-ratio methodology.

The simulation was invaluable, particularly in determining the appropriate level of information and support provided by HR to line managers (between the extremes of 'not enough' and 'too much' interference), and for specifying the IT requirements for pay administration, in an organisation with more than 11,000 staff.

Example: an insurance company (3)

In the insurance company mentioned earlier, the work stages in the Phase 3 plan included:

February/March	– announce plans
	– negotiate changes with trade union
	– train managers
	– recruit new compensation and benefits specialist
May	– conduct appraisals for staff and managers
	– communicate details of changes to staff
June	– make market 'booster' award
July	– regular annual pay review.

Phase 4: ongoing monitoring and review

This is the part that everyone forgets. You've done your analysis, developed your architecture, detailed, tested and implemented it successfully. The project team disbands and the new scheme is left to run.

Yet no set of changes will be perfect – minor 'tweaks' and modifications to the new pay designs and processes will generally be required: a loose fitting here, a gap in the floorboards there, a cold draught in that department. In addition, the context in which these new pay schemes will operate is generally not constant. Organisations are changing all the time, and research demonstrates that pay systems need to evolve to reflect this.

Questions and issues you need to address after full implementation therefore include:

❑ How well is the new pay structure working? Is it delivering on the original pay and reward objectives we set out?

❑ What changes in design and/or process will improve its effectiveness? How will we develop and introduce them?

❑ How are we going to assess effectiveness, on an ongoing basis, and perhaps in more detail after a sufficient time has elapsed to witness the full operation of the new arrangements?

❑ How is the organisational and external context for the new pay structure changing and evolving? What pay changes are likely to be required in the future to address this evolution?

The successful companies in our research did not breathe a satisfied sigh of relief after implementing their pay structure changes, and go back to their day jobs. In general, they are following a process of continuing evolution in their reward schemes, in response to the ever-more-rapidly-occurring shifts in their organisation and its markets – a further major change in pay structure here, a shift in communication emphasis there, addressing a problem in a particular division over there, rectifying an administrative bug in the system somewhere else – it's never stopping. This is where the well-known academic Dave Ulrich's demand for HR functions to become much more flexible and adaptable really becomes pointedly appropriate.

Example: a large mutual organisation (2)

In the mutual company referred to earlier, five specific objectives and success criteria for the project were identified during Phase 1. In summary, these were:

❑ having greater flexibility
❑ being more market-driven and aligned
❑ rewarding individual contribution

❑ facilitating career development
❑ removing the overemphasis on grade and status.

Each objective was broken down into sub-components and a range of measures established. Thus the market objective was expressed in terms of a desired market stance in each job family, and measures of success such as actual pay versus market, staff turnover, ratio of recruitment offers to acceptances, etc, were detailed.

Example: a pharmaceutical company

This company introduced a new evaluation scheme and harmonised pay structure for 3,000 staff in its major UK location. The new pay structure had nine bands, to replace more than 30 grades which had existed in the past. They also introduced pay progression related to individual contribution, as well as making various changes to bonus schemes. The changes were phased in over a 12-month period.

Aspects of ongoing review were built into the changes. An evaluation team met quarterly after implementation to review proposals for band changes and to automatically check the bands of a sample of 10 per cent of all jobs. This kept the team familiar with the new system, and also was intended to identify any potential difficulties with its operation proactively.

After 12 months of operation a specific independent review was conducted. Managers were interviewed, staff spoken to, and the pattern of pay changes analysed. The general conclusion was positive, but improvements were proposed in a number of areas, particularly related to the performance criteria on the basis of which pay awards were determined.

A quick but intensive work approach

We recognise that some of the work stages and steps we have proposed may sound excessively detailed and time-consuming, and many companies would not incorporate every step we have listed into their plan. As we said, the process you adopt needs to be tailored, as well as the resulting pay design. Our intention is certainly not to put you off making necessary changes, but to ensure that you take all the steps required to make them a success. Large organisations typically require a more thorough and in-depth approach, but again we would emphasise the need to design the approach to suit your own organisation and needs, and to select only the most relevant components.

Example: a large mutual organisation (3)

The route adopted by a large mutual organisation illustrates this very well. It had introduced pay adjusted in relation to individual contribution in 1996. It looked at moving into broad bands then, but saw this as a step too far. A variety of management and staff consultation exercises raised the issue again in late 1998 and early 1999, and the HR director was thereupon tasked with coming up with a new banding structure.

With an already intensive HR agenda, the route he adopted was to condense Phase 1 and Phase 2 of the work into two four-day workshops. These were attended by a senior line manager and HR manager from each of the major units in the organisation.

The first workshop concentrated on the 'what' – the design of the new structure and associated processes. Key sessions in the workshop included:

❑ critiquing current pay and grading arrangements
❑ reviewing a possible three-level and job-family-based structure proposed by a board member
❑ splitting into three teams to work on
   – job families
   – the pay structure
   – pay and career progression.

In each case, the current approach was critiqued, alternative approaches considered, and an outline of the new approach developed. Sessions also included a focus on team feedback and reviewing the inter-relationship of proposals.

The resulting architecture of changes is summarised in Table 25. It involved:

❑ a move into a number of different job families, each with its own market-related pay structure, and with no common grade structure across the organisation

Table 25
A SUMMARY OF THE PROPOSALS IN A MUTUAL ORGANISATION

The reward package of an employee	**Job profiles**
	• Fewer profiles
	• Common format
	• Main components:
	  – key competencies/outputs
	  – technical competencies
	  – personal competencies
	  – individual contribution
	
	Job families
	• Purpose
	  – to group people/roles together for development purposes
	  – to reflect labour and pay market differences
	• Job families
	• Active job family ownership
	
	Internal job evaluation
	• Move away from the Hay system as the principal means of grading jobs
	• Retain a simplified scheme as a supporting mechanism
	
	Pay structures
	• Generally move to fewer hierarchical bands
	• Introduce separate structures in different job families, without a common read-across
	• Indicative pay levels based on market data
	
	Pay progression
	• Similar to present, but looser process; encourages greater differentiation within overall budget
	  – remove common mid-points and detailed management to compa-ratios
	  – HR provide information/guidance – eg market value range
	  – positioning in band depends on level of contribution
	
	Other reward items
	• Move away from rigid grade-based definition of benefits and conditions, towards market-driven by family with common framework

Supporting processes	*Development:* Encourage moves in families; development in the role; self-reliance; and making it happen in practice *Pay budgeting and planning:* More sophisticated process; more dialogue; more market-driven; improved information and management *Contribution management:* Limited change, but stronger impact on pay and development; improved objective-setting *Roles and responsibilities:* Job family owners with active role across the family to consider pay and development *Training:* General programmes and coaching support *Communications:* Open and honest, phased rationale → specifics, multimedia *IS build:* In-depth involvement on the project

❑ new, briefer, but consistently-formatted role profiles
❑ greater flexibility in individual pay increases and pay range positioning; currently, the vast majority of staff are grouped around the mid-point of their existing pay ranges.

When the proposals were subsequently presented to the board, examples of the new structures were used to illustrate how the approach would work (see Figure 21).

The second four-day workshop concentrated on the 'hows' of managing pay and development within this new job-family-based structure. Some of the work here involved:

❑ developing a detailed implementation plan
❑ brainstorming issues and requirements in making the new designs operational
❑ role-playing pay decision-making, to help to specify the new pay management processes and the information and support required by managers
❑ analysing the current performance management system and proposing modifications to tie in with the new broadbanded structure
❑ integrating existing initiatives under way on staff and career development
❑ listing likely staff concerns with the proposals, and defining actions, communications and support to address them.

Table 25 gives the headlines concerning the new and modified pay and development process. Each pay and development decision within the new structure was mapped out. Thus for recruitment, the future process in a world without a 'recruit at grade minimum' policy would be:

❑ obtain market data
❑ assess fit of individual candidate and role requirements and skills
❑ compare current salary with grade range, and for existing staff doing the same job
❑ indicate and agree new salary level.

In terms of development, lateral development within a family across the organisation would in future be encouraged and

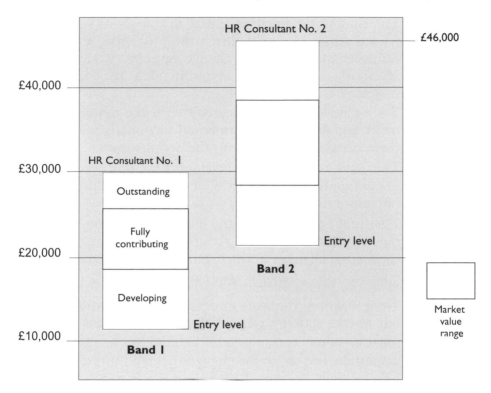

Figure 21
EXAMPLE: HR JOB FAMILY

supported, helping to develop the specialist expertise and business focus required by the organisation's business strategy. But movement across families would be at an individual's own initiative and not specifically encouraged or rewarded.

Through this two-workshop process, in a short if intense period, detailed proposals were developed, and these were then progressively implemented over the course of the following 12 months.

Summary

The process you use to develop and implement new pay structuring and management arrangements, like the design of those arrangements themselves, must be tailored to suit the needs and character of your own organisation.

Generally, we recommend that a four-phased approach to this type of work is adopted:

- ❏ The first phase involves initial diagnosis of your existing reward situation, highlighting the problems, and issues to address; after reviewing change options, it then involves specifying the changes recommended to address these issues.
- ❏ The second phase is concerned with the detailed development and design of the proposed pay changes, and testing them on a sample of jobs in the organisation.
- ❏ The third phase involves developing the processes necessary to operate the new schemes, and then communicating and implementing them.
- ❏ The final phase involves the ongoing operation, review and modification of the new pay approaches, taking account of contextual changes in the organisation and externally.

By adopting this approach, you will be better able to:

- ❏ avoid wasting resources in detailed design work that turns out not to actually address the key reward issues in your organisation
- ❏ guarantee 'buy-in' to the changes from all interested parties
- ❏ progressively develop the capability of your organisation to operate and understand the new arrangements, maximising the chances of success.

REFERENCES

ABOSCH K. S. (1998) 'Confronting six myths of broadbanding'. *ACA Journal*. Autumn. pp28–35.

ABOSCH K. S. *and* HAND J. S. (1998) *Life with Broadbanding*. American Compensation Association.

ABOSCH K. S. *and* HAND J. S. (1994) 'Characteristics and practices of organisations with broadbanding'. *ACA Journal*. Autumn. pp6–17.

ARMSTRONG M. (2000) 'Feel the Width'. *People Management*. 3 February. pp34–8.

ARMSTRONG M. *and* MURLIS H. (1998) *Reward Management*. 4th edn. London, Kogan Page.

BROWN D. (1996) 'Broadbanding: a study of company practices in the United Kingdom'. *Compensation & Benefits Review*. November–December. pp41–9.

BROWN D. *and* ARMSTRONG M. (1999) *Paying for Contribution*. London, Kogan Page.

CBI/HAY MANAGEMENT CONSULTANTS. (1996) *Trends in Pay and Benefits Systems*. London, CBI.

GILBERT D. *and* ABOSCH K. S. (1996) *Improving Organizational Effectiveness through Broadbanding*. Scottsdale, AZ, American Compensation Association.

HAY MANAGEMENT CONSULTANTS. (1996) *Broadbanding: A survey of organisation policy, practice and experience*. London.

HEWITT ASSOCIATES. (1992) *Company Experience with Broadbanding*. Lincolnshire, Illinois.

HOLBECHE L. (1998) *Motivating People in Lean Organisations*. Oxford, Butterworth-Heinemann.

LAWLER E. E. (1986) 'What's wrong with point-factor job evaluation'. *Compensation & Benefits Review*. March–April. pp20–28.

LAWLER E. E. (1990) *Strategic Pay*. San Francisco, CA, Jossey-Bass.

LEBLANC P. V. *and* ELLIS M. E. (1995) 'The many faces of banding'. *ACA Journal*. Winter. pp52–62.

MERCER WILLIAM. (1995) *Broadbanding: Flattening your job and grade structure*. New York.

O'NEALL S. (1994) 'Work and pay in the 21st century'. *ACA News*. May. pp2, 21.

PARUS B. (1998) 'Broadbanding highly effective, survey shows'. *ACA News*. July–August. pp40–41.

RICHTER A. S. (1998) 'Paying the people in black at big blue'. *Compensation & Benefits Review*. May–June. pp51–9.

WATSON WYATT. (1996) *Broadbanding*. London.

INDEX

Abosch, K.S. 55, 57, 95, 97, 118, 133
administration job families 180, 186–7
Advance Housing 177
alignment of business and reward
    strategy 6–9, 16, 44
American Compensation Association
    (ACA) 50, 116, 118
anchor rates *see* market reference
    points
appeals procedures 89, 243–4
Armstrong, M. 11, 12, 97, 99, 127
attitude surveys 224
auditing for equity 43, 108
Automobile Association 67
AXA Insurance 7

band drift 108, 109
bands *see* broadbanded structures
Bass Brewers 7, 46, 64, 65, 90, 101,
    102, 109, 134
BBC 71–2, 73–4
benchmark roles/jobs *see* generic
    role definitions; matching
'best fit' 14–15, 42, 132, 217
best practice 14–15, 42
bonus payments 99, 105
boundary-less organisations 57
BP Amoco 60, 72, 75, 95, 102, 177–8
Bristol Myers Squibb 72, 76–7, 138
British Broadcasting Corporation *see*
    BBC
broad grade structures *see* 'fat-graded'
    structures
broadbanded structures
    ACA survey 50, 116
    advantages and disadvantages of 25,
        120–23
    aims of 20–21
    allocation of roles/jobs to bands 20,
        37–8, 49, 62, 67, 91–4
    band drift 108, 109

BP Amoco case study 72, 75
Bristol Myers Squibb case study 72,
    76–7
and career development 12, 36, 55,
    57, 97–8, 120, 125, 141–2
characteristics of 20, 25, 61–3
communication of 127, 131–2,
    144–5
communications company case
    study 154–8
conditions favourable to 124–6
conditions unfavourable to 126–7
cost control in 108–11
defined 55
definition and description of bands
    66–7
degree of satisfaction with 39, 48
design of 64–71, 132–9
development of processes 139–42
devolution of pay decisions 15, 61,
    62, 101–3, 106–8
employees' questions concerning
    117, 145
external/internal value 96–7
factors influencing effectiveness of
    50, 115–16, 117–18
Halifax plc case study 73, 77–82
implementation of 142–5
integrated nature of 11
involvement of staff 127, 130–31,
    144
IPD survey results 36–40, 45–7
job evaluation and 37–8, 43, 62, 67,
    87–92, 95, 133–4, 140–41
job families within 22, 25, 40, 71
market pricing 49, 95–6, 139–40
market reference points 38, 49,
    68–9, 71, 104, 105
Ministry of Defence case study 146,
    150–54
movement to higher bands 106

number of bands 20, 36–7, 61, 64–5, 133–6
oil company case study 146–9
overlap between bands 66
pay progression 12, 20, 38, 97–106, 141
positioning of roles within bands 95–7
problems encountered 39–40, 48
project planning 129–32
readiness assessment 124, 125
reasons for failure of 48, 50, 116, 123–4
reasons for introduction of 15–16, 39, 46–7, 48, 50, 57–61
resistance to 122, 143–4
RNLI case study 73, 83–6
segmentation 70–71, 105
setting objectives for 128–9
Southern Focus Trust case study 146, 158–61
stages for introducing 119
structure of bands 67–71, 138–9
theory v practice 63
Towers Perrin survey 47–9
training strategy 132
varieties of 55–7
when appropriate 25
width of bands 20, 37, 49, 61, 65–6, 136–8
Yorkshire Building Society case study 111–14
zones 38, 62, 68, 69–70, 98–9, 104–5
Zurich Financial Services case study 146, 161–4
Brown, D. 12, 47, 59, 63, 65, 99, 127
BT 7, 138
budgeting 109–11
'bundling' of HR practices 42
business strategy
analysis of 224
and reward strategy 6–9, 16, 44

career band structures 56–7
career-based structures 36
career development
in broadbanded structures 36, 55, 57, 60, 97–8, 120, 125, 141–2
integration of HR processes 11, 42–3
in job family structures 170

lateral development 12, 57, 97–8
career development pay 12, 20, 104
career mapping 177–9
'central tendency' 107
change management 44–5, 143–5
Chartered Institute of Personnel and Development see (prior to July 2000) Institute of Personnel and Development (IPD)
Children's Society 7, 67, 92, 141, 168, 172, 173, 186
choosing a pay structure 23–6
see also introduction of new structures
Citibank 46, 65, 91, 95
communication with staff 127, 144–5, 244
compa-ratios 20, 56
competence/competencies
broad band definition 67, 93, 94, 95
and growth of broadbanding 58
job family level definition 173–6
underpinning pay structures 11
competence-related job evaluation 89, 90
competence-related pay 12–13, 14, 41, 100
consistency in broadbanded structures 106–8, 109
consultation see involvement and consultation
contingency approach to reward strategy 14, 42, 132, 217
contingent pay see pay progression
contribution-related pay 12–13, 100
IPD survey results 41
at Littlewoods Retail 27–8
cost control 108–11
Coutts & Co. 13, 176
Coventry Building Society 10, 11, 172, 189, 190–93
culture, analysis of 224

delayering see flat organisational structures
designing new structures 237–43
broadbanded structures 132–9
job family structures 186–9
development see career development
devolved responsibility see line managers' role
diagnostic reviews 120, 185, 220–36

case studies 229–36
checklist 226–9
diagnostic questions 23–4, 220–21,
    226–9
types of analysis 224–6
work stages 222–3
differentials
    in broad grade structures 56
    in traditional grade structures 19, 56

Ellis, M.E. 128, 132
employee relations climate 224
    see also involvement and
        consultation
equal pay issues
    market pricing and 96
    possible problems 24, 106, 123
    use of job evaluation 43, 89, 90
    see also internal equity
external/internal value method 96–7

'fat-graded' structures 36, 55–6
'fit' 14–15, 23, 42, 117, 132
flat organisational structures 12, 57,
    122
flexibility 10, 24, 60, 120, 170, 226
flexible benefits, at Littlewood Retail 28
function-based families 171

gender discrimination 22
    see also equal pay issues
generic role definitions 20, 62, 67,
    92–4, 173–4, 187
Gilbert, D. 55, 95, 97, 133
Glaxo Wellcome 46, 65, 66, 67, 90,
    91, 100, 128–9, 141, 180
grade drift 12, 38, 60
graded pay structures 19–20, 25
    distinguished from broadbanding
        with zones 38, 69–70, 98–9
    'fat-graded' structures 36, 55–6
    problems in 12, 225–6

Halifax plc 7–8, 70, 73, 77–82, 90, 92,
    134–6, 138
Hay Management Consultants 60
Hewitt Associates 50
hierarchical organisations 12, 98, 123
Holbeche, L. 12
human resource processes
    bundling of 42
    integration of broadbanding 117

IBM 7, 8, 46, 66, 91, 171
ICL 180, 184
implementation
    of broadbanding 142–5
    of new pay structures 243–7
IMS Health 7, 9, 172, 173, 187, 189,
    194–9
incremental pay systems 22, 100–101
individual job structures 22–3, 24
    Littlewoods Retail case study 26–8
Inland Revenue 46, 65, 66, 99, 136
Institute of Personnel and
    Development (IPD)
    case study research findings 42–5
    research findings on broadbanding
        36–40, 45–7, 57–9, 64, 65, 67–8,
        99
    research findings on contingent pay
        41–2
    research findings on job family
        structures 40–41
    research findings on reward strategy
        6–7
    research methodology 35–6
integration of reward
    with business strategy 6–9, 16, 44
    with other HR processes 10–11, 42–3
internal benchmarking see matching
internal equity
    in broadbanded structures 62, 90,
        95, 106–8, 122
    and external competitiveness 13, 18
    in job family structures 181, 184
    see also equal pay issues
internal value-based model 95
introduction of new structures
    building society example 229–32
    charity example 241–3, 245
    detailed design 237–43
    diagnosis and architecture design
        see diagnostic reviews
    insurance company example 232–6,
        240–41, 247
    intensive approach to 249–53
    large mutual company example 245,
        247, 248–9, 250–53
    monitoring and review 247–9
    phased approach to 218–20
    preparation and implementation
        243–7
    see also broadbanded structures; job
        family structures

involvement and consultation
    of employees 127, 144, 186, 222, 240
    of trade unions 130, 131, 240
    see also attitude surveys

job descriptions, compared with role
    definitions 14
job evaluation
    analytical schemes 88–9, 90
    competence-related analytical
        schemes 89
    development of new schemes 239
    and individual job structures 23
    IPD research results 37–8, 43
    and job family structures 170, 173,
        181–2, 187–8
    non-analytical schemes 90
    reduction in credibility of 12, 87
    role in broadbanding 37–8, 43, 62,
        67, 87–92, 95, 133–4, 140–41
    traditional approaches 10
job family structures
    administration families 186–7
    advantages and disadvantages of 21,
        25, 169–70, 184
    allocation of roles to levels 182
    broad bands within 22, 25, 169,
        170, 179, 180, 189
    career paths in 177–9
    characteristics of 21, 25
    Coventry Building Society case study
        189, 190–93
    defined 167–9
    definition of levels 173–6, 177–8,
        187–8
    description of families 172–3
    development of 185–9
    grouping roles into families 171,
        186–7
    IMS Health case study 189, 194–9
    integrated nature of 11
    IPD survey results 40–41
    job evaluation and 170, 173, 181–2,
        187–8
    market pricing 180
    Nationwide Building Society case
        study 189, 199–202
    number of families 171–2
    number of levels 167–8, 173, 187
    pay progression policies 188
    Prince's Trust case study 189,
        202–4

readiness for 183–4
    reasons for introduction 15–16,
        21–2, 40, 169–70
    responsibility for each family 182–3
    Royal Bank of Scotland case study
        190, 204–7
    validation of levels 188–9
    when appropriate 25
    Xerox case study 190, 208–13
job matching *see* matching
job slotting *see* matching

knowledge requirements, for job family
    levels 177–8

lateral development 12, 57, 97–8
Lawler, E.E. 5, 14
LeBlanc, P.V. 128, 132
line managers' role
    in determining pay 10, 15, 61, 62,
        101–3, 106–8
    at IBM 8
    at Littlewoods Retail 27–8
    in managing change 44–5
    at Thistle Hotels 33–4
Littlewoods Retail 8, 23, 26–8
Lloyds TSB 69

market-driven pay 13–14, 22–3, 43–4
    at Littlewoods Retail 27
    at SLI 31
    at Thistle Hotels 33
market group structures 18, 21–2, 169,
    171, 180
market pricing 49, 95–6, 139–40, 180
market rate data 95–6, 97, 139–40,
    184
market reference points 38, 49, 68–9,
    70, 71, 104, 105
'market stance' 19
market zoning 70, 71
matching
    allocation of roles/jobs to bands 20,
        38, 91, 92–4
    positioning of roles within bands 95,
        96, 97
Mercer, William 60
mergers
    communications company case
        study 154–8
    Zurich Financial Services case study
        161–4

mid-point management 20, 56
Midland Bank 46, 91
Ministry of Defence 146, 150–54
mixed-model structures 22, 25
    broad bands within job family
        structures 169, 170, 179, 180,
        189
    job families within broadbanded
        structures 40, 71
monitoring
    of new pay structures 247–9
    of pay increase proposals 107
multinational organisations 60–61
Murlis, H. 97, 127

Nationwide Building Society 90, 172,
    179, 189, 199–202
non-financial rewards 3–5
Nortel and Bay Networks 9
Nuclear Electric 7

occupational-based families 171
organisational culture 224

parallel structures 18
Parus, B. 124
pay, as component of total reward 4–5
pay-at-risk 99
pay progression
    in broadbanded structures 12, 20,
        38, 97–106, 141
    criteria for 99–101
    IPD survey results 41–2, 99
    in job family structures 188
    pay spines 22
    semi-structured progression 103–5
    unstructured progression 101–3
pay ranges/spans
    in broad grade structures 56
    in broadbanded structures 20, 37,
        49, 55, 61, 65–6, 108, 137–8
    in job family structures 179–80
    in traditional graded structures
        19–20, 55, 56
pay review budgets 109
pay spines 22, 25, 226
pay structures
    broadbanding see broadbanded
        structures
    choice of structure 23–6
    defined 17–18
    'fat-graded' structures 36, 55–6

features of 17–18
graded pay structures 12, 19–20, 25,
    225–6
individual job structures 22–3, 24
job families see job family structures
pay spines 22, 25, 226
reasons for 18–19
types of 19–23
see also introduction of new
    structures
pay systems
    contribution-related 12–13, 14
    flexible 10
    integrated 10–11
payroll costs and budgeting 108–11,
    123
Peabody Trust 23, 171, 172, 173, 186
performance management
    at Halifax plc 80–82
    as integrating process 11
    necessity for 141
performance-related pay 12–13, 41–2,
    99
personal reference points 104
Pfizer Central Research 7
piloting new structures 244–5
Portsmouth Housing Association see
    Southern Focus Trust
PricewaterhouseCoopers 7
Prince's Trust 7, 66, 141, 169, 173,
    180, 189, 202–4
progression see pay progression
project planning 129–32, 186
public sector, pay progression in 22,
    98, 100

qualifications, and job family levels
    177
questions
    diagnostic reviews 23–4, 220–21,
        226–9
    employees', on broadbanding 117,
        145

RAC Motoring Services 46, 65, 66,
    129
ratings, use of 41–2, 99
Reckitt & Colman 47, 65, 66, 91
resistance to change 122, 143–4
reviewing structural changes 247–9
reward strategy
    aim of 3–4

'best fit' concept 14–15
and business strategy 6–9, 16, 44
defined 5
reasons for 6
Richter, A.S. 6
role definitions, compared with job
    descriptions 14
    see also generic role definitions
role flexibility 58
Royal Bank of Scotland 7, 8–9, 167,
    190, 204–7
Royal National Lifeboat Institution
    (RNLI) 73, 83–6

salary administration 9, 10
segmented bands 70–71, 105
service-related pay 100–101
skill requirements, for job family levels
    173, 177–8
Southern Focus Trust 11, 89, 95, 146,
    158–61
spot rates 17, 24
Standard Life Investments 29–32
strategic reward *see* reward strategy

target rates *see* market reference points
team-based pay, at Coventry Building
    Society 192–3
technical ladders 18
Texas Utilities 7
Thistle Hotels 17, 32–4
total payroll budgets 109–11
total reward 3–5
Towers Perrin 47–9, 64, 65, 68

trade unions
    analysis of views of 224
    involvement in broadbanding 130,
        131
    negotiation with 244
training programmes 106–7, 132, 244

Unilever 69, 136, 171

'value-added tiers' 133, 173
variable pay 99
Volkswagen 47, 65, 66, 70, 91, 100,
    105, 141, 172, 177

Watson Wyatt 60, 64
whole job/role comparisons 62, 67, 95,
    96
    see also matching
William Mercer 60
Woolwich plc 176
work-based families 171
works councils 131

Xerox 6, 7, 9, 13, 172, 173, 179, 189,
    190, 208–13

Yorkshire Building Society 7, 62, 64,
    66, 111–14, 167, 188
Yorkshire Water 7, 12, 16

zoning, within broadbanded structures
    38, 62, 68, 69–70, 98–9, 104–5
Zurich Financial Services 62, 65, 66,
    92, 102, 116, 146, 161–4